Trade Specialization
in the Enlarged European Union

Contributions to Economics

www.springer.com/series/1262

Dora Borbély

Trade Specialization in the Enlarged European Union

With 66 Figures and 56 Tables

Physica-Verlag

A Springer Company

Series Editors
Werner A. Müller
Martina Bihn

Author
Dr. Dora Borbély
European Institute for International
Economic Relations (EIIW)
at the University of Wuppertal
Rainer-Gruenter-Straße 21
42119 Wuppertal
Germany

ISBN-10   3-7908-1704-X Physica-Verlag Heidelberg New York

ISBN-13   978-3-7908-1704-1 Physica-Verlag Heidelberg New York

Physica-Verlag is a part of Springer Science+Business Media

springer.com

© Physica-Verlag Heidelberg 2006
Printed in Germany

Typesetting: Camera ready by the author
Cover: Erich Kirchner, Heidelberg
Production: LE-TEX, Jelonek, Schmidt & Vöckler GbR, Leipzig

SPIN 11676621   Printed on acid-free paper – 88/3100 – 5 4 3 2 1 0

Preface

The first steps toward this book were made at the Kiel Institute for World Economics, where I was very pleased to gain greater insight into economic modelling and econometric methods, which proved extremely valuable for the proceedings of this book. The main part of it was written at the European Institute for International Economic Relations (EIIW) at the University of Wuppertal in connection with an EU 5th framework research project on "Changes in Industrial Competitiveness as a Factor of Integration: Identifying Challenges of the Enlarged Single European Market" (HPSE-CT-2002-00148). Financial support by this EU project is greatly appreciated.

I am very thankful to a number of fellow researchers for fruitful discussions and constructive criticism. I wish to mention Dr. Andrea Schertler and Dr. Carten-Patrick Meier from Kiel as well as Prof. Dr. Anna Wziatek-Kubiak from the above-mentioned EU research project. I would also like to thank several of my colleagues from Wuppertal: Ekaterina Markova, PD Dr. Andre Jungmittag, Martin Keim, Michael Vogelsang, Christopher Schumann, Zornitsa Kutlina, and Edeltraut Friese. For his devoted technical and research assistance, I am grateful to Jens Perret. I also wish to thank Michael Agner for his editing of this book. Valuable econometric support by Prof. Dr. Gerhard Arminger is greatly appreciated. Last but not least, while writing this book I received continuous support and encouragement from the president of the EIIW, Prof. Dr. Paul J.J. Welfens, to whom I am deeply grateful.

This book could not have been written without the endless support and understanding of my family, especially my mother Sára, my father Károly, my grandmother Mami and my sister Melinda. Yet who suffered most from me writing this book is my better half Stephan Seilheimer, who has always been there to motivate me with his enormous emotional and technical support.

I would like to dedicate this book to my grandfather Dr. Radnóti István - Szürike - who will, unfortunately, never have a chance to read it.

Wuppertal, May 2006 *Dora Borbély*

Contents

1

Introduction

*"Now, we may say that the most important subjects about which all men
deliberate and deliberative orators harangue, are five in number, to wit:
ways and means, war and peace, the defence of the country,
EXPORTS and IMPORTS, legislation."*
Aristoteles

Since the second half of the 1980s, integration of goods, capital and financial
markets has progressed on a global scale. In particular, international trade
and foreign investment flows have enormously increased worldwide. Globalization and internationalization have been driven by lower trade barriers and
transportation costs, reduced restrictions on foreign direct investment (FDI)
and improvements in communication technologies - facilitating the utilization
of scale economies and a deeper international division of labor.

In Europe, integration in general and EU Eastern enlargement in particular created a wider single market, which stimulates structural adjustment and
economic specialization. These impulses are expected to be part of the driving forces for structural change in the European economies, and for changes
in their competitiveness, which are reflected in changes in the production
structure, trade specialization, and technological upgrading. Western Europe,
in particular, faces a much tougher competitive environment, mainly due to
the opening-up of Eastern European economies, and to some extent to the
emergence of Asian competitors.

One may anticipate accelerated structural change in Central and Eastern
European countries since the beginning of the 1990s as the impulses from system transformation and from anticipated European Union (EU) membership
have stimulated a dynamic adjustment process, including a shift in specializations in particular countries. These impulses included trade liberalization and
rising FDI inflows from EU countries. This process should be accompanied by
shifts in revealed comparative advantages. Moreover, it is widely accepted that
the regional trade orientation of Eastern European countries shifted strongly
towards the EU in the 1990s. It is therefore clear that major changes in sec-

toral specialization in Western Europe will reflect major changes in the new
EU member states.

Against this background the main topics and questions we will deal with
in this book include:

1. How far has economic integration proceeded in the enlarged European
   Union? We will mainly approach this question from a trade point of view
   and analyze the degree of trade integration in the enlarged EU with a
   special focus on the new EU member states.
2. What do trade specialization patterns in the enlarged European Union
   look like? We are especially interested in analyzing which industrial sectors have developed successfully in the new and in the old EU member
   states. To what extent are these specialization patterns in line with the
   predictions of various strands of trade theory? Furthermore, we analyze
   whether these specialization patterns tend to converge or diverge within
   the enlarged EU, which is of special importance in terms of the European
   Monetary Union.
3. How has the competitive picture in the enlarged European Union changed?
   Against which EU countries do the new EU member states particularly
   compete? One might assume that they initially competed against the less
   developed old EU member states, the cohesion countries. However, later
   on, specialization towards higher technology industries is expected.
4. What drives trade specialization in the enlarged EU? What are the main
   determinants of foreign trade patterns? Determining the main influencing
   factors provides opportunities for policy makers to create an attractive
   and sustainable economic environment.
5. Finally, we have to address the issue of how European policy measures
   should look to help in effectively facilitating the goals of the European
   member states and the EU in the 21st century.

Asking these question we will restrict ourselves to the European Union
and will only analyze intra-EU trade flows. For most EU member states, this
covers almost 2/3 of total trade; therefore intra-EU economical specialization
is crucial. At the same time one must not forget that national economies are
interdependent. Large world economies such as the United Statesespecially
have a strong impact on European economic development. Due to the special
focus on European economic agents acting on European markets, however,
these interdependencies will not be the subject of this book.

Within the enlarged EU the main focus will be laid on the new EU member
states, and to some extent on their potential competitors on the EU market:
the cohesion countries. Therefore much of the empirical part will include selected new EU member states - mainly the three largest: Poland, the Czech
Republic and Hungary - and the cohesion countries: Spain, Portugal, Ireland
and Greece. As a matter of course some parts will include all 25 EU countries,
e.g., when dealing with the question of whether trade patterns in the enlarged
EU have been converging or diverging in the last decade.

Moreover, the main focus lies at the secondary sector, the manufacturing industry. Since we analyze trade specialization patterns, we have to cover most tradable goods, which are mainly manufacturing products. Nevertheless, one should be aware of the fact that a major and increasing part of the European economies consists of economic activity in the services sector. Still, we deliberately excluded the services sector, because the two sectors are too different to be directly compared to each other. It makes more sense to concentrate on either of the two, whereas the interaction between industry and services will be dealt with at various points in this book. Moreover, services are largely complementary to the manufacturing sector.

For a better understanding of the main chapters of this book, we start in chapter 2 with an overview of the economic development of European countries, especially with respect to trade development and trade integration within the enlarged EU. The reader can also retrace the link between trade and production within these economies. As the main determinant of the frameworks of EU trade structures, the reader is also given insight into the basics of European trade policy at the end of the chapter.

Since we see theory as the foundation of all proper economic research, chapter 3 presents the three main strands of trade theories and also shows the extent of their applicability to economic data. The Traditional Trade Theory, which emphasizes the role of natural endowments with production factors and the role of comparative advantages, is rather widespread in the economic literature; however, it is unable to explain a great part of real trade flows: Intra-industry trade. The New Trade Theory addresses this issue and the role of innovations and product differentiation. A more spatial view is taken by the New Economic Geography, which assumes that the geographical location as being a peripheral or a central region is crucial for the development of trade. Chapter 3 ends with an assessment of the relevance of these theories for the new EU member states.

Since the theoretical literature does not present a consistent picture of evidence on the outcome of internalization and globalization on specialization patterns, empirical work is needed to shed more light on the answers to the questions stated above. Chapter 4 presents different measures of intra-EU trade, such as the Trade Coverage Index (TCI) which displays the ratio of sectoral exports to imports, the Grubel-Lloyd Index (GLI) which is a measure for the extent of intra-industry trade and therefore also for economic integration in terms of trade, and the modified Revealed Comparative Advantage Index (RCA), which is also called the relative export share index, and reveals sectoral competitiveness in terms of relative exports compared to the EU 15 countries. While the original (sectoral export/import ratio compared to total economy's export/import ratio) and the modified RCA indices are highly correlated, the use of the modified RCA allows much deeper economic analysis of sustainable trade development and competitiveness. We therefore prefer this measure. It is also used to identify the new landscape of competitiveness as suppliers on the EU 15 market, which is done subsequently in chapter 4.

Competitiveness is, however, not only measured by comparative advantages, but also by the ability of industries to upgrade quality, which is proxied by export unit values.

Another interesting question dealt with in chapter 4 concerns convergence or divergence of trade patterns in the enlarged EU. The main idea behind the analysis of convergence in trade patterns is that similarity in production and trade structures among EU 25 countries will ease the integration process. From a macroeconomic point of view, one may state that when integration extends far beyond trade, as is the case in the European Union, convergence in production and trade structures will help in smoothinging the integration process. The more similar countries are in terms of sectoral specialization, the more likely it is that they will face symmetric shocks and an increase in business cycle co-movements. Correlation in business cycles is even more important if countries aim to have a common monetary policy, as is relevant for countries eager to join the Eurozone. Efficient specialization should spur growth and economic catching-up in the new EU countries, which in turn could reinforce convergence of economic specialization. Thus, long term real convergence in production and trade structures within the EU 25 could be achieved. Furthermore, from a theoretical point of view, similar countries integrate more easily, because they are likely to show very similar diversification patterns. Trade in products can, at least to some extent, replace trade in production factors and lead to convergence in factor prices. Thus, incentives to factor mobility, especially migration, will be reduced. This is extremely important in the European context, since there are many concerns about potential migration flows within the EU 25. There is a long tradition of analyzing European structural change in the economic literature, however, most of it has been written about income convergence, whereas the topic of convergence in trade structures has been treated in the empirical literature to a much lesser extent. Moreover, EU Eastern enlargement presents a new challenge for research on structural change and trade to which the analysis presented contributes.

After having analyzed foreign trade specialization patterns, competitiveness of industries, and convergence of trade specialization patterns in the enlarged EU, such an empirical analysis is not complete without having identified the main determinants of these foreign trade specialization patterns. By what factors are they driven? Only if one has identified the crucial factors and their impact on the development of foreign trade specialization, he then can give advice on where, how, and to what extent economic policy makers should intervene. Therefore chapter 4 closes with a dynamic panel analysis, and tests to determine among others if industrial production, imports, export unit values, foreign direct investment, research and development, productivity or wages are factors driving comparative advantages in trade.

Chapter 5 derives policy implications in terms of competition policy, trade policy, industrial policy, as well as structural and cohesion policy. Finally, chapter 6 summarizes the results and draws conclusions.

2

Economic Development and Trade in the Enlarged European Union

The aim of this chapter is to provide solid background knowledge on trade issues in the EU 25 countries since the beginning of the 1990s. As a matter of course trade development is always a result of a general economic development both of the country considered in the analysis and of its main trading partners. From an Eastern European point of view, the EU 15 is the most important trading area, therefore this chapter starts by presenting some stylized facts on the economic development of the enlarged European Union. Trade structures are undeniably correlated with production structures; these interconnections will then be dismantled in this chapter. Finally trade specialization is always to a certain extent the result of a trading regime. Therefore this chapter will close by highlighting the most important aspects of European trade policies.

2.1 Integration Processes and Economic Development within the Enlarged European Union

Since the ratification of the European Coal and Steel Community (ECSC) in 1951 in Paris, European integration has proceeded at a rapid pace. Obviously, the ECSC was meant to foster the coal and steel industries and pool their resources; It was also meant to deal with the issues of policy coordination in order to prevent another European war. The six original members, Germany, France, Belgium, Italy, Luxembourg, and the Netherlands ratified the Treaty of Rome in 1957, which established the European Economic Community (EEC), and the European Atomic Energy Community (Euratom). Euroatom was supposed to pool the non-military nuclear sources of the member states. The main idea behind the European Economic Community was the introduction of a free-trade area based on four freedoms: freedom over the movement of goods, services, capital and people. In 1967, the three institutions (ECSC, EEC and Euroatom) merged. The new institutions established were the European Commission (EC), the Council of Ministers and the European Parliament (European Central Bank, 2005a). The first enlargement of the EEC took place 1973 by the accession of the UK, Denmark and Ireland. In the next phase of enlargement, Greece became a part of the European Economic Community in 1981; Five years later in 1986, Spain and Portugal joined.

The European Union (EU) in its current state came to existence with signing the Treaty of Maastricht in 1992. The cornerstones of the Treaty involved the designing of an economic and the free trade union as well as the implementation of a common economic and defence policy. Through this new inter-governmental cooperation, the Treaty of Maastricht created the European Union. Also the foundations and the conditions for a common European Monetary Union (EMU) were laid down by the Treaty of Maastricht, which entered into force on 1 November 1993. The way for the Eastern European countries to join the EU was paved by the Treaty of Copenhagen in 1993, which defined the criteria and rules for joining the EU. The next round of enlargement came in 1995, when Austria, Finland and Sweden became a part of the EU. In 1997, the Treaty of Amsterdam was signed, which updated the Treaty of Maastricht. In January 1999 eleven EU countries agreed to introduce the Euro as the common currency, by abandoning their own currencies. Greece also joined in January 2001. On 1 January 2002, the Euro notes and coins were introduced in 12 EU countries. On 1 February 2003, the Treaty of Nice entered into force, which geared the workings of the European Institutions up for enlargement. Finally, through the Eastern enlargement on 1 May 2004, ten new countries joined the EU: Poland, the Czech Republic, Hungary, Estonia, Latvia, Lithuania, Slovenia, Slovakia, Malta and the Greek part of Cyprus. In case of a preceded unification of Cyprus, the Turkish part could have joined as well, but this failed. Similarly to Sweden but in contrast to Denmark and the UK, the 10 new EU countries have no opting-out option of the EMU, thus they eventually will have to adopt the Euro as their official currency.

The formal requirements for the Eastern European accession countries to join the EU were the fulfillment of the Copenhagen criteria of 1993, which set political, juristical, institutional and economic conditions upon membership. These are in particular stable institutions, guaranteed democracy, the rule of law, respect for protection of human rights and minorities, a functioning market economy, the capacity to cope with market forces and competitive pressures in the EU, and the ability to take on the obligations of membership (WTO, 2004). The latter also implies the implementation of the Acquis Communautaire, which describes in 31 chapters different fields of interest.[1]

---

[1] The 31 chapters of the Acquis Communautaire are: free movement of goods, free movement of persons, freedom to provide services, free movement of capital, company law, competition policy, agriculture, fisheries, transport policy, taxation, economic and monetary union, statistics, social policy and employment, energy, industrial policy, small and medium-sized enterprizes, science and research, education and training, telecommunication and information technologies, culture and audio-visual policy, regional policy and coordination of structural instruments,

Through the Eastern enlargement of 2004, the geographical area of the EU increased by 23 %, the population by 20 %, but nominal gross domestic product (GDP) only by 5 % (Borbély and Gern, 2003). This highlights the fact that by the time of accession, the stage of economic development between the old and the new member states was still rather heterogenous, although tremendous adjustment processes had already taken place in the Eastern European countries during the 1990s.

Table 2.1. Development of Real GDP in the EU 25 Countries, 1993-2004

	GDP Share	Real GDP (Annual Change in %)											
		1993	1994	1995	1996	1997	1998	1999	2000	2001	2002	2003	2004
GER	21.5	-1.1	2.3	1.7	0.8	1.4	2.0	2.0	2.9	0.8	0.1	-0.1	1.6
UK	16.6	2.3	4.4	2.9	2.8	3.3	3.1	2.9	3.9	2.3	1.8	2.2	3.2
FRA	15.9	-0.9	2.1	1.7	1.1	1.9	3.4	3.2	3.8	2.1	1.2	0.5	2.3
ITA	13.0	-0.9	2.2	2.9	1.1	2.0	1.8	1.7	3.0	1.8	0.4	0.3	1.2
SPA	8.1	-1.0	2.4	2.8	2.4	4.0	4.3	4.2	4.2	2.8	2.0	2.4	3.1
NL	4.7	0.7	2.9	3.0	3.0	3.8	4.3	4.0	3.5	1.4	0.6	-0.9	1.7
BEL	2.7	-1.0	3.2	2.4	1.2	3.5	2.0	3.2	3.8	0.6	0.7	1.1	2.9
SWE	2.7	-2.0	4.2	4.1	1.3	2.4	3.6	4.6	4.3	0.9	2.1	1.6	3.6
AUS	2.3	0.3	2.7	1.9	2.6	1.8	3.6	3.3	3.4	0.7	1.2	0.8	2.4
DEN	1.9	0.0	5.5	2.8	2.5	3.0	2.5	2.6	2.8	1.6	1.0	0.5	2.4
GRE	1.6	-1.6	2.0	2.1	2.4	3.6	3.4	3.4	4.5	4.3	3.6	4.5	4.2
FIN	1.4	-1.2	3.9	3.4	3.9	6.3	5.0	3.4	5.1	1.1	2.3	1.9	3.6
IRE	1.4	2.7	5.8	9.9	8.1	10.8	8.9	11.1	9.9	6.0	6.1	3.7	4.5
POR	1.4	-2.0	1.0	4.3	3.5	4.0	4.6	3.8	3.4	1.6	0.4	-1.2	1.2
LUX	0.2	4.2	3.8	1.4	3.3	8.3	6.9	7.8	9.0	1.5	2.5	2.9	4.5
POL	1.9	3.8	5.2	2.7	6.0	6.8	4.8	4.1	4.0	1.0	1.4	3.8	5.4
CZ	0.8	0.1	2.2	5.9	4.8	-0.8	-1.0	0.5	3.3	2.6	1.5	3.1	4.4
HUN	0.8	-0.6	2.9	1.5	1.3	4.6	4.9	4.2	5.2	3.8	3.5	3.0	4.2
SLA	0.3	7.2	6.2	5.8	6.1	4.6	4.2	1.5	2.0	3.8	4.6	4.0	5.5
SLE	0.3	2.8	5.3	4.1	3.6	4.8	3.6	5.6	3.9	2.7	3.3	2.5	4.6
LIT	0.2	-16.2	-9.8	3.3	4.7	7.0	7.3	-1.7	3.9	6.4	6.8	9.0	7.0
CY	0.1	0.7	5.9	9.9	1.8	2.3	5.0	4.8	5.0	4.0	2.0	2.0	3.7
LAT	0.1	-11.4	2.2	-0.9	3.8	8.3	4.7	3.3	6.9	8.0	6.4	7.5	8.3
EST	0.1	-9.0	-1.6	4.5	4.5	10.5	5.2	-0.1	7.8	6.4	7.2	5.1	7.8
MAL	0.0	na	na	na	na	na	na	4.1	6.4	0.2	0.8	0.2	0.4
EU 25	100	-0.2	2.9	2.7	1.9	2.8	3.0	3.0	3.6	1.8	1.2	1.0	2.4

Source: European Commission (2005), EBRD Transition Report (Various Issues), German Council of Economic Advisors (2005), Kiel Institute for World Economics (2005)

---

environment, consumers and health protection, cooperation in the field of Justice and Home Affairs, customs union, external relations, Common Foreign and Security Policy, financial control, financial and budgetary provisions, institutions, and others.

Table 2.1 provides an overview of the development of real GDP both in the new and the old EU member states since 1993. First, the figures for the EU 15 countries are presented followed by the new EU member states (EU 10). Both country groups are ordered according to their share of EU 25 GDP, starting with the largest.

It is obvious that the new EU member states have experienced much higher GDP growth rates, especially since the middle of the 1990s. This is a clear sign for the catching-up process towards the rest of the EU. However, in the first years of the 1990s, most of the new EU member countries suffered from a transitional recession, experiencing highly negative growth rates. This was due to problems in connection with the immense economic changes which were necessary while moving from a centrally-planned to a market economy structure.[2] However, recovery occurred rather fast after 1993. While in 1993 four countries (Hungary, Lithuania, Latvia, and Estonia) suffered from negative growth rates, in 1994 only two countries (Lithuania, and Estonia) were left, and in 1995 only one (Latvia). In 1996, no new EU member state showed negative growth rates any longer. For the upcoming analysis in this book, we have deliberately chosen 1993 as a starting point, since we are interested in the catching-up process, and not too much in the transition period.

Figure 2.1 provides a comparison in per capita GDP of the member states of the enlarged EU in the year of Eastern enlargement (2004). It is important to take a look at GPD per capita figures, because it displays the economic distance between the countries. Hereby purchasing power standards (PPS) should be used, which allows for direct comparability among countries, because it takes into account the differences in the purchasing power of money in the respective countries. EU 25 is used as a benchmark (EU 25 = 100). Obviously, EU 15 average is higher, showing a value of 109. Both aggregates are marked black in the figure. The new EU countries are marked with a light grey color, whereas the old EU countries are slightly darker. It is obvious that all new EU countries are below the EU 25 (and, of course, the EU 15) average per capita GDP. Considering old EU countries we see that Portugal, Greece and Spain have lower per capita GDPs than the EU 25 average. In addition, Italy's GDP per capita is below the EU 15 average in 2004. All in all, the income gap between new and old EU member states is still rather high, yet it does not seem to be unsurmountable.

According to figure 2.2, the new EU countries (EU 10) and the EU 15 countries show rather similar business cycle movements after the transitional recession.[3] At the same time the new EU countries march on higher growth paths

---

[2] There is a wide range of literature dealing with the issues of system transformation in Central and Eastern European countries, see e.g. Welfens 1995, Chapter F. Various issues of the Transition Report published by the European Bank for Reconstruction and Development provide a comprehensive picture of progress made in system transformation; e.g. EBRD, 2004.

[3] Both aggregates are calculated using 2004 nominal GDP weights in US Dollar taken from the Kiel Institute for World Economics, 2005.

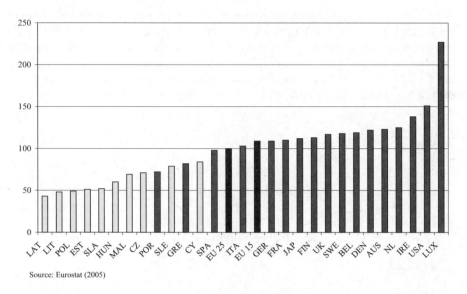

Source: Eurostat (2005)

Fig. 2.1. GDP Per Capita in Purchasing Power Standards (PPS) in the Member States of the Enlarged EU in 2004, EU 25 = 100

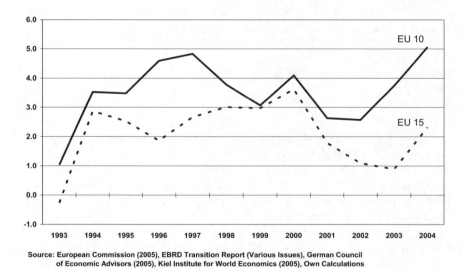

Source: European Commission (2005), EBRD Transition Report (Various Issues), German Council
of Economic Advisors (2005), Kiel Institute for World Economics (2005), Own Calculations

Fig. 2.2. Annual Change of Real Gross Domestic Product in EU 15 and EU 10 Countries, 1993-2004, in %

due to the catching-up process, however, it also seems that especially downwards movements of the business cycle, such as around 1996 and 2002/2003, were more distinctive for the old than for the new EU countries. This might be due to the fact the EU 15 countries' economic development strongly depends on the US business cycle, whereas the EU 10 countries are more dependent on the EU 15 countries, thus just indirectly dependent on the US.

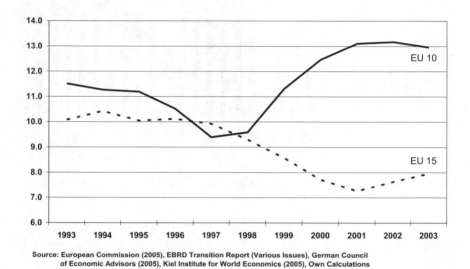

Source: European Commission (2005), EBRD Transition Report (Various Issues), German Council
of Economic Advisors (2005), Kiel Institute for World Economics (2005), Own Calculations

Fig. 2.3. Unemployment Rates in EU 15 and EU 10 Countries, 1993-2004, in % of Labor Force

Figure 2.3 indicates that not only system transformation was a major challenge for Eastern European labor markets. These countries started at the beginning of the 1990s with very high unemployment rates, since unemployment was basically non-existent under the socialist system. However, these countries did well in overcoming that major problem and pushed down aggregated unemployment rates below 10 % by 1997. However, between 1997 and 2002 aggregated unemployment rates began rising. This was mainly due to the sharp and continuous rise of the unemployment rate in Poland. It reflects significant structural deficiencies in the Polish labor market, such as relatively high minimum wage compared to the average salary, strict rules on job termination, and low labor mobility (EBRD, 2004). Also, reforming the Polish agricultural sector is crucial, which still employs 15-20 % of the total labor force, but contributes to GDP only by roughly 3 % (EBRD 2004). The unemployment rate also rose, however, in the Czech Republic, the second largest of the new EU member states, although it never reached two-digit levels. In contrast to the Czech Republic, stubborn two-digit unemployment rates exist (besides Poland) in Slovakia, Lithuania, Latvia, and Estonia.

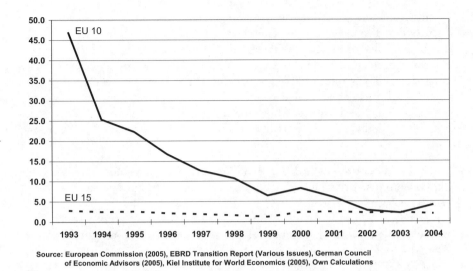

Source: European Commission (2005), EBRD Transition Report (Various Issues), German Council
of Economic Advisors (2005), Kiel Institute for World Economics (2005), Own Calculations

Fig. 2.4. Annual Change of Consumer Prices in EU 15 and EU 10 Countries, 1993-2004, in %

Figure 2.4 displays the annual change of consumer prices, which is commonly called the inflation rate. The rudiments of the change in the economic system with its necessary adjustments of prices is clearly visible. Until 1995/96 most EU 10 countries suffered from two-digit inflation rates. In the largest EU 10 country, Poland, stubbornly high inflation remained at the two-digit level until 2000 (with the exception of 1999), which pushed up the weighted EU 10 average inflation rate until then. However, roughly since 2000/01 we see much more homogenous inflation rates within the EU 25 countries, which seem to be driven mainly by business cycle related factors also in the new EU member states. With the exception of 2003, EU 10 countries tend to have both higher real GDP growth rates and higher inflation rates, which is usually explained in the sense that the motors of business cycles use more oil when running faster. The EU 10 weighted average inflation rate has come down to clearly below 5 % since 2002.

Inflation rates are closely connected to the monetary and exchange rate system of the economy, which at the same time is also crucial for the development of foreign trade. Exchange rate risks need to be taken into account when trading internationally, thus exchange rate fluctuations might hinder foreign trade. As indicated above, the Eastern European EU countries will eventually have to adopt the Euro, which will eliminate exchange rate risks within the EU, therefore exchange rate regimes are crucial. Thus accession to the EU automatically meant accession to the EMU, however, initially only with the status of a member state with a derogation according to Article 122 of the EC contract. Before introducing the Euro, these countries will have to join the European Exchange Rate Mechanism II (ERM II) - while reaching the status of fully-fledged EMU members - which fixes the nominal exchange rate of the respective country to the Euro as a reference. The countries themselves can decide upon the date of accession to the ERM II. Subsequently, if certain economic criteria, the so called Maastricht Convergence Criteria as set out in article 121 of the Treaty of Maastricht, are fulfilled, the new EU countries will adopt the Euro. The Maastricht Criteria entail (European Central Bank, 2005):

- *Normal fluctuation margins within the ERM II:* The nominal exchange rate is supposed to remain within the +/- 15 % fluctuation margins for at least two years.
- *High degree of price stability:* Inflation rate must not exceed that of the three best performing member states in terms of price stability by more than 1.5 percentage points.
- *Sustainability of government financial position:* This is twofold: (1) The ratio of total government debt to GDP at market prices must not exceed 60 %, (2) and current government deficit to GDP at market prices must not exceed 3 %.
- *Durability of convergence measured by the long-term interest rate:* Average nominal long-term interest rate must not exceed that of the three best performing member states in terms of price stability by more than 2 percentage points.

Accordingly, the new EU member states can adopt the Euro two years after joining ERM II at the earliest. The decision upon the date of fixing the reference exchange rate to the Euro within ERM II depends strongly on the exchange rate regime. Countries, which already have fix exchange rate regimes will more easily walk through pegging their currency to the Euro. Countries with a flexible exchange rate regime are expected to face the most difficulties in ERM II. Table 2.2 gives an overview of the exchange rate regimes and the ERM II membership of the 10 new EU member states.

The four largest new EU member states have not joined the ERM II yet, and at the same time all four are pursuing rather flexible exchange rate regimes. However, Slovenia, Lithuania, and Cyprus having a very similar exchange rate regime as Hungary, joined ERM II in June 2004 and May 2005, respectively. As expected, for countries with a currency board - Latvia, Estonia, and Malta - the reference nominal exchange rate to the Euro within

Table 2.2. Exchange Rate Regimes of the New EU Member States

	Exchange Rate Regime	Membership in ERM II
Poland	Free Floating	–
Czech Republic	Managed Floating	–
Hungary	Fix with +/- 15 % fluctuation margins	–
Slovak Republic	Managed Floating	–
Slovenia	Fix with +/- 15 % fluctuation margins	since 28 June, 2004
Lithuania	Fix with +/- 15 % fluctuation margins	since 28 June, 2004
Cyprus	Fix with +/- 15 % fluctuation margins	since 2 May, 2005
Latvia	Currency Board	since 2 May, 2005
Estonia	Currency Board	since 28 June, 2004
Malta	Currency Board	since 2 May, 2005

Source: National Central Banks, DIW (2005)

ERM II has already been set. Accordingly, the first new EU countries can adopt the Euro as their official currency in 2006 at the earliest.[4]

2.2 Trade and Production in the Enlarged European Union

After gaining an insight into the integration processes and the broad economic development of EU countries, we now turn our attention more specifically to the basic facts on the development of foreign trade and production within the enlarged European Union. Firstly, an overview is given on foreign trade figures and foreign trade integration, then the link is established between trade and production.

2.2.1 Facts and Figures on Trade

The European Union is the leading exporter in the world - excluding intra-EU trade - with a share of 20 % in world exports in the year 2002, and it is the second largest importer with 19 % of world imports (EC, 2005). The main trading partner of the EU 15 countries are the United States, of the EU 10 countries these are the EU 15 countries themselves. There is strong empirical evidence in the literature that trade liberalization among countries which trade extensively with each other contributes to income convergence (Ben-David et al., 1999). Therefore economic convergence and economic growth in the EU 25 is expected to rise after the EU-enlargement, partially through more efficient allocation of resources, partially through an increase in productivity as a result of tougher competition on the EU market. A strong increase in trade relations is, however, not expected, because trade liberalization and

---

[4] An extensive analysis of exchange rate related issues in the context of EU Eastern enlargement can be found in Welfens and Wziatek-Kubiak (eds.), 2005.

trade interlacing among the new and the old member states were already
rather intense before EU enlargement in 2004.

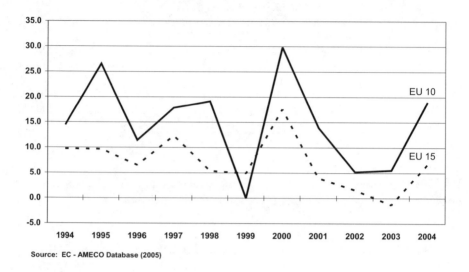

Source: EC - AMECO Database (2005)

Fig. 2.5. Annual Change of Exports of Goods and Services, 1994-2004, in %

Figures 2.5 and 2.6 display the development of exports and imports of
goods and services for the EU 10 and EU 15 aggregates in the time periods
from 1994 to 2004 as described by the annual changes in percent. First of all
it is striking that both export and import volumes increase at a rapid pace
in both regions, whereas annual increase in percent is often at the two digit
level for the EU 10 countries, but only seldom for the EU 15. Furthermore,
comparing the two figures reveals that export and import developments are
rather closely related to each other; both experience upward and downward
movements rather simultaneously. This reflects the interdependence of exports
and imports and points towards a great degree of intra-industry trade. Only
in the year 1996 can one observe a larger deviation of exports and imports for
the EU 10 countries. While export growth slows down to roughly 12 percent,
imports continue to grow strongly with an annual rate of roughly 23 percent.
A connection to GDP growth as shown in figure 2.2 is also obvious, since
especially exports can be a main driver of growth dynamics. At the same
time, one should not oversee that growth in foreign trade volumes is much
more dynamic than growth in GDP. Analyzing growth rates, however, does
not allow us do draw conclusions on the importance of foreign trade for the
economy.

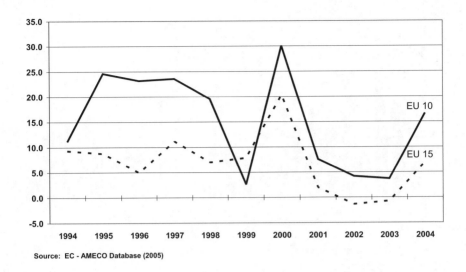

Fig. 2.6. Annual Change of Imports of Goods and Services, 1994-2004, in %

Therefore we now take a look at the average share of exports and imports in GDP, separately for goods and for services. Figure 2.7 shows the extent of trade integration of goods for the EU 25 countries between 1993 and 2004. On the left hand side the figure starts with the new EU countries, followed by the cohesion countries, and the other EU countries to the right of the figure. The figure displays integration of goods as a percentage of GDP, namely the average of imports and exports of goods of the balance of payments divided by GDP. If the index increases over time, the country is becoming more integrated within the international economy. At the same time one has to bear in mind that smaller countries are usually more dependent on foreign trade, because they are not able to produce all goods needed for the economy. Larger countries have a greater ability to produce all goods needed, therefore their trade integration tends to be lower. Accordingly, integration is the highest for some very small EU countries, such as Belgium, Malta or Slovakia, followed by Estonia, Ireland, and the Netherlands. On the contrary, for large countries, such as France, Germany, Italy or the UK, integration of goods is rather low. In general integration is higher in most new EU member states than in EU 15 countries.

More interestingly, figure 2.7 also clearly indicates that integration of goods has increased strongly for most of the new EU countries. This is especially the case for Poland, Hungary, the Czech Republic, as well as for Slovakia and Slovenia. In the baltic states, Estonia, Latvia and Lithuania, the increase of integration has not been continuous. For the years 1998 and 1999 one can see a strong decline in integration patterns, which is probably due to the impact

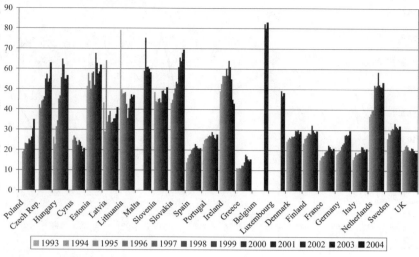

Source: Eurostat (2005)

Fig. 2.7. Trade Integration of Goods

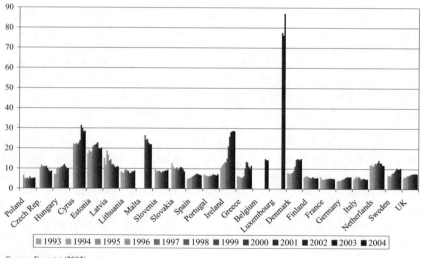

Source: Eurostat (2005)

Fig. 2.8. Trade Integration of Services

of the Russian financial crises. The baltic states' foreign trade in goods is to a great extent interconnected with Russia, therefore it is no surprise that they also suffer from the Russian crises.

For most of the EU 15 countries, including the cohesion countries we see an increase in trade integration for the time period of 1993-2000, however, since 2000 integration has often declined. Against the background of the business cycle development in the European Union a decline in integration is explainable, since growth in the EU 15 countries has been rather slow since then.

Although the detailed analysis of foreign trade patterns coming up in section 4 will focus only on manufacturing industries, for the purpose of completeness we should now take a look at the development of integration of services in the EU 25 countries as shown in figure 2.8. For comparability purposes we use the same scale in both diagrams for goods and services. It is striking that the degree of integration is much lower for services as compared to goods. The only country, where this is not the case is Luxembourg. Here financial services are so dominating that trade integration of services with roughly 80 % is more intense than for goods with roughly 50 %. Otherwise integration of services is rather low at around 10 %. There are only a few countries with slightly higher values; these are Cyprus, Estonia, Malta, and Ireland. In contrast to integration of goods, the development of the integration of services shows hardly any dynamics for most EU countries. Especially for the EU 15 countries we cannot identify an increase in integration over time.

All the foreign trade patterns we have seen so far considered worldwide exports and imports. The main focus of this research will be laid, however, in the next chapters on intra-EU trade specialization patterns. We will identify the changes in specialization as a supplier on the EU 15 market, and see which countries are competitive in what type of manufacturing goods on the EU 15 market. Therefore it is worth taking a look at the share of exports and imports that will be covered when analyzing intra-EU trade.

Figures 2.9 and 2.10 display the share of exports and imports, which is traded with the EU 15, as a percentage of total worldwide exports and imports of EU 10 and EU 15 countries. The use of the same scale for both figures allows direct comparability. Both for the EU 10 and the EU 15 countries, intra-EU trade is very important. Trade with the EU 15 countries amounts to roughly 62-64 % of exports of the EU 15 countries, which has remained rather stable since the beginning of the 1990s. For the EU 10 countries the share of exports which goes to the EU 15 countries has risen from 55 % to 69 % between 1993 and 1999, and declined slightly to 65 % by 2002. The picture is different in terms of imports. For the EU 15 countries the importance of intra-EU 15 imports has declined slightly from 62 % in 1993 to 60 % in 2002. For the EU 10 countries the share of imports from EU 15 had risen from 53 % to 63 % between 1993 and 1998, but then declined almost as sharply to 57 % in 2002. It seems that for all EU 25 countries imports have been increasingly replaced by probably less expensive import goods from other than the EU 15 countries, whereas the EU 15 remains the most important trading partner in terms of exports. These figures point towards changing patterns of traded goods, where intermediate imports probably play an important role. In the next subsection

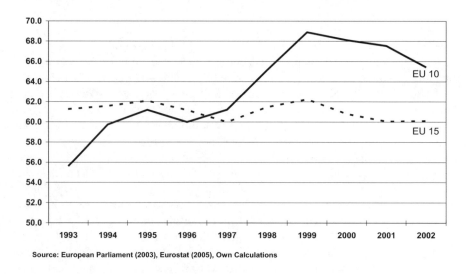

Source: European Parliament (2003), Eurostat (2005), Own Calculations

Fig. 2.9. Share of EU 15 Exports in Total Exports, 1992-2002, in %

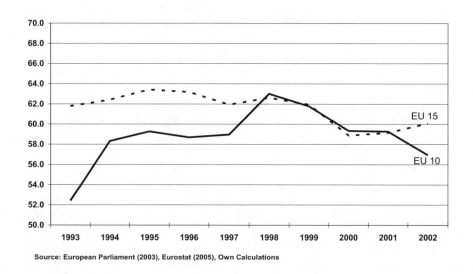

Source: European Parliament (2003), Eurostat (2005), Own Calculations

Fig. 2.10. Share of EU 15 Imports in Total Imports, 1992-2002, in %

we will shed some more light on the interconnection of production, imported intermediates and exports.

2.2.2 The Link Between Trade and Production

It is reasonable to assume that one of the most important parameters influencing export specialization patterns is production of the economy. To shed some light on this link it is useful to take a look at the structure of industrial production as shown in figure 2.11.

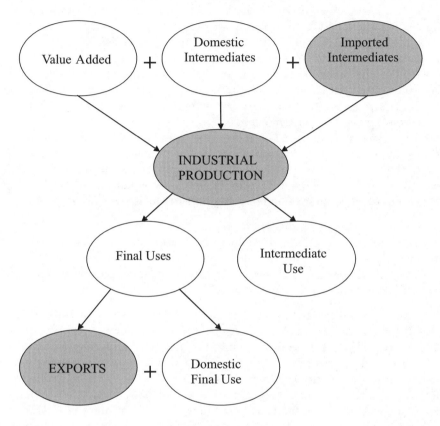

Source: Own Presentation

Fig. 2.11. Simple Connection Between Exports, Imports and Industrial Production

From a sectoral point of view, which we will mainly focus on in the subsequent chapters, industrial production consists of domestic value added and intermediate products. The latter can be produced domestically or abroad. The sum of the three represents industrial production, which can be used as final goods or as intermediates for other products. Final use can be realized on the domestic markets in the form of final consumption expenditures and gross capital formation, or sold to foreign countries in the form of exports. Such a figure as 2.11 could be drawn for each national economy. We will demonstrate the expected cross-country links using the Central and Eastern European countries' (CEEC) exports to the EU 15 and industrial production of the EU 15 as an example. At first sight we expect the CEEC's exports to be positively dependent on the EU 15's industrial production. This is the more extensively the case, the higher the share of intermediates in the imports of CEEC's from the EU 15. Let's suppose that intermediates comprise a great part of imports. Then a rise in the EU 15's industrial production causes the imports of the CEEC's from the EU 15 to rise, which leads to a rise in the CEEC's industrial production and thus in exports. On the contrary, if CEEC's imports from the EU 15 are mainly final products, a rise in the EU 15's industrial production will not raise intermediate imports to a great extent, thus ceteris paribus CEEC's industrial production and exports will not rise respectively. A strong positive correlation is expected as far as intermediates are concerned, which are rather complements of each other. If we mainly deal with final products, however, a more substitutional relationship is expected, thus even a negative correlation might be imaginable.

In the spirit of figure 2.11, let us take a look at the composition of industrial output in selected EU countries for six of the economically - and in export terms - most important manufacturing industries. These contain

- one labor intensive industry: textiles,
- two scale intensive industries: chemicals and motor vehicles,
- one science-based industry: office machinery and computers, and
- two differentiated goods: machinery and equipment as well as radio, TV and telecommunication equipment.

The list of countries - Slovakia, Hungary, Poland, Germany, Italy, Finland, and the Netherlands - is not a complete EU list, however, it covers both Eastern and Western European countries, small and large countries, and less and further developed EU members. It is a rather suitable cross section for our purposes. To justify the industry selection, one should bear in mind that for Hungary these six industries comprise almost 68 % of industry exports in 2003, for Poland 43 %, for Germany almost 62 %, and for the Netherlands roughly 60 %. Figures 2.12 - 2.17 give insight into what share of domestic value added, domestic intermediates and foreign intermediates is contained in sectoral industrial output. Furthermore it shows the change in those shares between two points in time, mostly 1995 and 2000. The choice of years, and also of countries depends to a great extent on data availability, since data is taken from the Eurostat input-output tables (Eurostat, 2005a), which do not offer a complete set of countries and years. The negative or positive sign on the right hand scale indicates a simple tendency of the development of export unit values since the middle of the 1990s. The figures are organized in a way that the share of imported intermediates in the first year of observation declines as moving from the top to the bottom of the figures.

Let us start with the labor intensive industry, textiles. According to figure 2.12 one can see that roughly two thirds of the output is produced do-

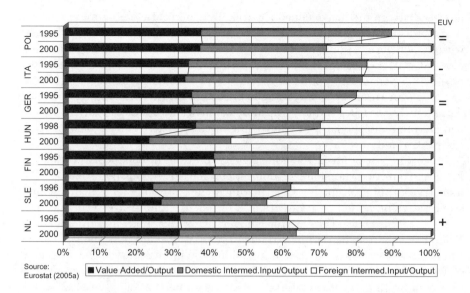

Fig. 2.12. Textiles: Composition of Industrial Production

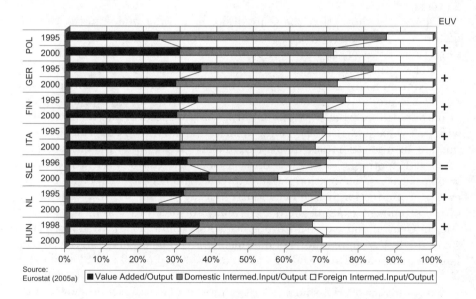

Fig. 2.13. Chemicals: Composition of Industrial Production

mestically, however, this share seems lower for the three Eastern European countries. The Netherlands is the only country in which the share of foreign intermediate inputs has declined (by roughly 2 percentage points); in all other countries this share has increased. The strongest increase occurred in Hungary with 24 percentage points, followed by Poland with 17 percentage points, and Slovenia with roughly 7 percentage points. At the same time, value added rose by 2.5 percentage points in Slovenia and declined by almost 13 percentage points in Hungary. Concerning export unit values it is striking that they decline in the textiles industry in most countries considered. Only in Poland and Germany do the EUVs seem to stagnate, and there is a slight increase in the Netherlands.

According to figure 2.13, homogeneity prevails in chemicals production. In most countries the share of domestic value added makes up 25-35 % of industry output. Except for Italy in which the share has remained constant, domestic value added in production is on the decline in Western European countries. This is also the case for Hungary. However, both in Slovenia and in Poland the share is increasing considerably. At the same time the rise cannot compensate for the loss in the share of domestic intermediates, thus the share of foreign intermediates in output has risen in both countries considerably (Slovenia by 13 percentage points, Poland by 14 percentage points). The only country in which the total domestic share in 2000 exceeded the previous value is Hungary. EUVs show a clear tendency to rise in all countries but one: Slovenia.

Figure 2.14 shows that the share of domestic value added in the German motor vehicles industry fell from 32.5% in 1995 to 21.8% in 2000. At the same time, however, the share of domestic intermediates rose from 51.1% to 60%. The total share of domestic formation of output therefore only slightly declined from 83.6% to 81.8%. This corresponds to relocation to foreign countries in the production of motor vehicles to the extent of 1.8 percentage points of output. However, still 81.8% of output is produced in the home country, either as value added in the motor vehicles industry, or as intermediate production in other domestic industries. This is no support for the so called "Bazaar-Hypothesis" - which is often used in the German literature with a strong negative connotation - that expresses the negative impacts of reallocation of production in the car industry (using the Porsche Cayenne as one of the prominent examples) from Germany to some other lower wage countries in Central and Eastern Europe or in Asia (Sinn, 2005). A similar rather small rise in the share of foreign intermediates can be observed in the Netherlands, Finland and Italy, and to a greater extent in Poland and Slovenia. The Netherlands, Hungary and Slovenia, as small open economies, are expected to have a higher overall share of foreign intermediates, which is shown in the figure. However, the share of foreign intermediates is considerably higher for the small new EU economies than for the Netherlands. The signs at the end of the rows indicate the tendency of EUV since 1993. It seems that a problem might occur if a strong decline of the domestic share of production is accompanied by a declining tendency of EUVs. In the motor vehicles industry, only Finland shows a decline in EUVs, however at the same time its share of domestic production is rather stable.

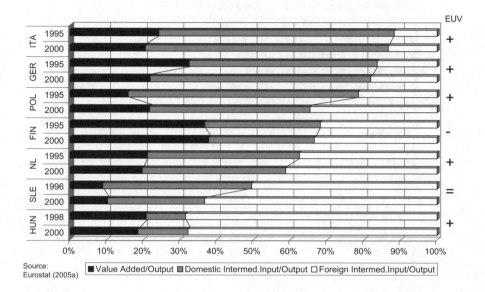

Fig. 2.14. Motor Vehicles: Composition of Industrial Production

Figure 2.15 takes a look at the composition of the industrial production of office machinery. It reveals the most diversified picture of all industries. In general the share of foreign intermediates is highest as compared to the other industries. Starting with 28% in Slovenia in 1995, the average share is roughly 40-60%, with extremely high shares of over 90% again in Hungary. Yet also in Finland and Italy the share of foreign intermediates exceeds 50% of output by far. In Finland, Italy, Germany and Hungary the share of domestic value added decreased strongly. In all these countries the share was already rather low in 1995, but it almost disappeared in the year 2000, mostly in Hungary with 6 % and in Finland with merely 2%. However, we also find countries, where the share of domestic value added increased in the second half of the 1990s. In the Netherlands it rose by 1.5 percentage points, in Poland by roughly 6 percentage points, and in Slovenia by 3 percentage points. In addition the share of domestic intermediates rose in the Netherlands by 4.6 percentage points, which results in an increase in the domestic share of production by almost 6 percentage points. This effect is also visible in Poland with an increase in the domestic share in production by 1.6 %. At the same time EUVs show a clear tendency to rise in Poland, but to fall in the Netherlands. The latter is the case for almost all other countries, too, which indicates that the Bazaar-

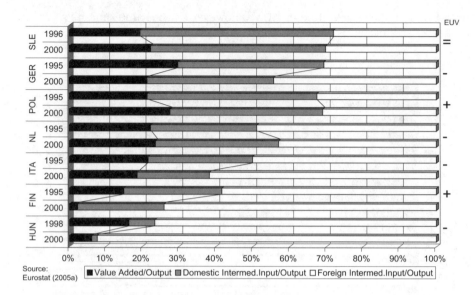

Fig. 2.15. Office Machinery: Composition of Industrial Production

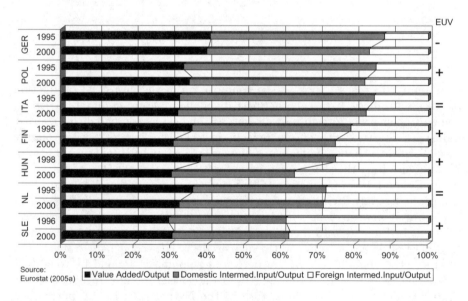

Fig. 2.16. Machinery and Equipment: Composition of Industrial Production

Hypothesis is strongly relevant on the market for office machinery especially in Italy, Germany and Hungary.

According to figure 2.16 most countries display a considerably high share of domestic production in machinery and equipment. The sum of the share of value added and domestic intermediates exceeds 70% in most cases. Only in some new EU member states can one find a higher share of foreign intermediates: Slovenia and Hungary. Except for Slovenia the share of foreign intermediate inputs rose over the time period considered. A relatively strong rise occurred in Hungary with 11 percentage points, followed by Finland and Germany with roughly 4 percentage points. Although there is a negative tendency in the development of the EUVs in Germany, the situation is not alarming, since the share of foreign intermediates is still low (16 %). In most countries the EUVs tend to increase, except for Italy and the Netherlands, where they rather stagnate. All in all, the picture in the machinery industry is rather homogenous with a relative high percentage of domestic activity in production.

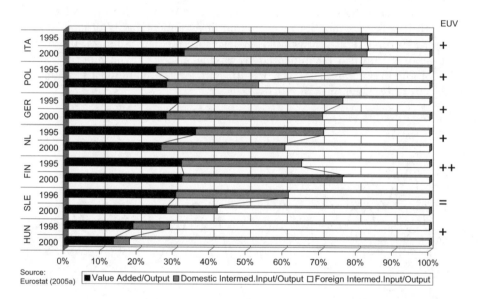

Fig. 2.17. Radio, TV and Telecommunications: Composition of Industrial Production

Finally, figure 2.17 for radio, TV and telecommunication equipment is not too harmonious. The new EU member states stick out through relatively low shares of value added and domestic intermediates. This is valid for Slovenia and Hungary for both years considered and for Poland especially for the year 2000. Furthermore the share of foreign intermediates is extraordinarily high, reaching values exceeding 80 % in Hungary. Also the very strong increase in the foreign intermediates is striking: 27 percentage points in Poland, and 19 percentage points in Slovenia. As mentioned before, small countries are expected to have higher shares of foreign intermediates, since they are more dependent on foreign trade (especially foreign imports) than big open economies, but also compared to other Western European small economies, such as the Netherlands, these ratios are very high. The only country with a relative stable share of foreign intermediates is Italy, and the only country with a decline in the share of foreign intermediates is Finland. The latter is not surprising, and adding the outstanding rise in EUVs in this industry underlines the dominant position of Finland on the telecommunications market. In most other countries, however, one can also observe a rise in EUVs, despite the fast technological development which tends to bring about a fall in the general price level in this sector.

All in all, it is shown that imported intermediate products play an important role in the development of industrial production. It seems that Eastern European EU countries' industrial production (especially Hungary's) contains imported intermediates with a higher share than Western European EU countries. Still this does not harm economic development, as is often feared in Western Europe. This strong link between intermediate imports, production and exports can also be indicated by taking a look at the monthly industrial production indexes for the EU 15 and for the eight CEEC countries' aggregates, as shown in figure 2.18.

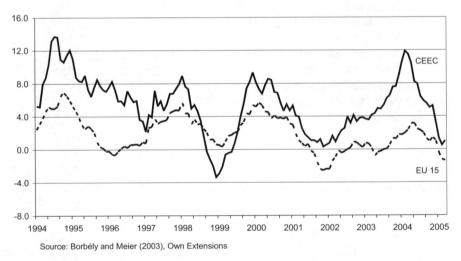

Source: Borbély and Meier (2003), Own Extensions

Fig. 2.18. Year-over-Year Change in Industrial Production - Three Months Moving Average

The EU 15 industrial production is taken from Eurostat, the industrial production for the Eastern European countries come from several sources and are aggregated using GDP weights from the year 2001 provided by the International Monetary Fund.[5] Figure 2.18 shows the three-months moving average of the year-over-year change of aggregated industrial production. Firstly, it is striking that the change in industrial production is generally higher in Eastern than in Western European EU countries. This indicates the catching-up process, in which the new EU member states are involved, and which already has been reflected earlier in this chapter when we took a look at real GDP growth rates. At the same time one can see that the fluctuations in both regions show the same directions. It indicates that the two regions have undergone very similar boom and recession times since the middle of the 1990s. However, it appears that the Eastern European countries' industrial production is less smooth that the EU 15's, which implies that new EU member states react to shocks in a more sensitive way in the short run. This is typical for smaller economies, which are usually less diversified in production than larger economies. Also both the boom and the recession periods are much stronger developed in the new EU member states than in the EU 15. Especially at the lower and upper peaks there is a larger deviation of the two lines, such as in 1999 or 2004. All in all, one can say that the industrial productions move along with rather similar patterns showing distinctive co-movement patterns, indicating that from this point of view there seems to be a rather strong business cycle harmonization. In joint work with Meier (see Borbély and Meier, 2003), we examine the correlation of the industrial production between these two regions (and Germany) using Granger tests on non-causality. We find that the EU 15's industrial production is strongly Granger causal to the industrial production of the new EU member states, but to a much smaller extent is the opposite the case. The first direction of causality is not surprising, at the same time it seems that a roughly 10 % share of EU 15's trade with the new EU member states is sufficiently high to be influenced by the developments in Eastern Europe.

Since some major parts of the upcoming analysis in the empirical chapter will focus on manufacturing industries, it is worth taking a look at the share of agriculture, industry and services in the EU 15 and in the EU 10 countries before moving on to trade policy issues. Even if differences were rather significant at the beginning of the 1990s, for the subsequent one and a half decades structural change has proceeded on such a fast scale in Eastern European countries that differences in terms of the structure of the economy have turned out to be rather small between EU 15 and EU 10. In 2003 agriculture made up 2.0 % of gross value added in EU 15 countries, and 3.5 % in EU 10 countries. Industry accounted for 26.7 % of gross value added in the old EU member states and for 31.3 % in the new member states. Services contributed

---

[5] The Sources for Industrial Production are the following: Estonia - OECD (2005a), Latvia - Central Statistical Bureau of Latvia (2005), Lithuania - IMF (2005), Poland - Polish Statistical Office (2005), Czech Republic - IMF (2005), Slovakia: IMF (2005), Hungary - WIIW (2005a), and Slowenia - Statistical Office of Slovenia (2005).

to gross value added by 71.3 % in EU 15 countries, and to 65.2 % in EU 10 countries (WTO, 2004). In fragments one still can sense the former economic structural of the Eastern European countries, because the share of agriculture and industry is still slightly higher than in the old EU member states. However, one could state that structural adjustment - at least in terms of the so called "Three-Sector-Hypothesis" (Fourastié, 1954) - has almost been completed in the new EU member countries.

As a matter of course economic structures always have to adjust according to the institutional, legal and political frameworks given in an economy. So do foreign trade specialization patterns. The framework that mainly determines foreign trade patterns is trade policy run at the national and supranational levels.

2.3 Trade Policy in the Enlarged European Union

Therefore, we now turn our attention to describing foreign trade policies pursued on the one hand in the European Union, on the other hand at the national level since the beginning of the 1990s. Because most of our analysis deals with the manufacturing industries, we will mostly focus on trade policy concerning trade of goods.

Policy in the European Union is based on the Broad Economic Policy Guidelines (BEPG), where it is emphasized that under the Lisbon Strategy 2000, the European Community is to make the most *"competitive and dynamic knowledge-based economy in the world by 2010"* (WTO, 2004). European Trade Policy is also guided by this slogan. The European Union has a common trade policy, which means that where trade is concerned, the EU acts as a single actor represented by the European Commission. The EC negotiates trade agreements and represents the European interests on behalf of all the 25 current member states internationally, for example with the World Trade Organization. Trade policy in the EC is formulated and implemented through Community acts. These consist of regulations which have direct applicability to all member states and which are binding for all EU countries. The competence for the implementation of the Common Commercial Policy (CCP), which covers trade in all goods and most services, is exclusively given to the EC. The Treaty of Nice furthermore extended the competence of the EC to the negotiations and the conclusions of agreements on trade in services and on commercial aspects of intellectual property (WTO, 2004). Generally, trade policy of the EC is aimed at liberalization of its trade regime, both through multilateral and preferential routes (WTO, 2004). According to Article 131 of the Treaty of Nice, the main objective of the CCP is to *"contribute, in the Common interest, to the harmonious development of world trade, the progressive abolition of restrictions on international trade and the lowering of customs barriers"*.

The principle right of free trade in the European Union is one of the main pillars of the single European Market as laid down in Article 133 of the European Community Treaty ratified in Rome in 1957. According to Article 133, the EC negotiates on behalf of the EU in consultation with the so called "Article 133 Committee", which is composed of representatives of all 25 member states, because since the EU Eastern enlargement, preferential trade relations with the EU 10 countries were consolidated, and the new EU member states adopted the EC's acquis communautaire (European Commission, 2005a). The "Article 133 Committee" meets once a week and discusses the full range of trade policy issues affecting the EU. At the same time the EC presents and secures endorsement of the member states in all trade policy issues in this Committee. The major decisions of the Committee are confirmed by the Council of Ministers.

In accordance with Article 133 of the EC Treaty, joining the EU implies that barriers to the movement of goods are removed. Most products have been subject to Community harmonization, which implies that all tariffs within the Union are abolished, and a common tariff towards third countries is established. This average applied MFN (most favored nations) tariff rate was 6.5 % in 2004; hereby agricultural products experience the highest tariffs with an average rate of 16.5 % (WTO, 2004). It seems that the EC market is rather open to non-agricultural products, but somewhat protective over agricultural goods. For those goods which are not controlled by Community harmonization, Articles 28 to 30 of the EC Treaty forbid the member states to maintain or to impose trade barriers on intra-EU trade of goods (EC, 2005a). Nevertheless, fully free trade has not yet been established in the EU. This is mainly due to nationally different legal regulations. This is most obvious on the basis of the mutual recognition principle, which implies that in all sectors not subject to Community harmonization, EU member states are obliged to accept products in their own territory which are legally produced and marketed by another EU member state. Its aim is to no longer differentiate between national product standards - without abolishing those standards themselves - in order to maintain diversity within the EU. Member states may only deviate from the application of mutual recognition on grounds of public morality, security, protection of human, animal or plant life as well as if protection of national treasures and the environment are concerned. If deviation from this principle is inevitable, any measure taken must comply to the principles of necessity and proportionality (EC, 2005a). Economic reasons, however, such as high unemployment, cannot be used as arguments. Nevertheless, most legal proceedings against breaking the freedom of goods this far have been based on the principal of mutual recognition.

Concerning trade between Eastern and Western Europe before the EU Eastern enlargement, the Europe Agreements signed between the EU 15 and the eight Central and Eastern European former accession countries (Poland 1991, Czech Republic 1993, Hungary, 1991, Estonia 1995, Latvia 1995, Lithuania 1995, Slovak Republic 1993, Slovenia 1996), and the Association Agreements signed between the EU 15 and Malta (1970) and Cyprus (1972), have already introduced free trade in almost all industrial products (EC, 2005b). Therefore, as indicated above, a strong increase in trade relations is not expected after 2004, because trade liberalization mostly took place prior to EU Eastern enlargement. Most opportunities can be seen for trade with agricultural products, because some tariffs and quota restrictions remained despite the Europe Agreements (WTO, 2004). Also trade in services show room for improvement, since service liberalization has taken place under the Europe Agreements to a much lesser extent than trade liberalization in goods. Furthermore, upon EU accession the new EU member states had to renounce their bilateral trade agreements with third countries and comply to all the EC's bilateral and regional agreements. As a result, the geographical coverage of the EC's trade agreements has been extended, increasing market access to EC's preferential partners. At the same time other countries might find it more difficult to gain ground on European markets.

Achieving the goal set by the Lisbon strategy depends to a great extent on the ability of the EU to enhance productivity and competitiveness in its manufacturing industries. Productivity growth in manufacturing has been declining. Furthermore, manufacturing is a major recipient of state aid, second only to transport (46 % in 2001) with 25 % of all state aid, followed by the primary sector (WTO, 2004). The EC is implementing a wide range of measures to make manufacturing industries more productive. Within the framework of the document "Industrial Policy in an Enlarged Europe" (EC, 2005c), the EC addresses the entire business environment to enable enterprizes - independent of their size, legal form or location - to develop in a way which is desirable and compatible with the overall goal of the EC in terms of sustainable development. In particular, the European Community should aim at developing new technologies, and European industries should become more innovative. Entrepreneurial capacity and risk taking should be enhanced, improving market access for goods and services (WTO, 2004). In a dynamic economy one may anticipate structural changes over time and changes in trade specialization.

3

International Trade Theory and Its Empirical Application

Integration of goods, capital, and financial markets has progressed on a global scale since the second half of the 1980s. Especially international trade and foreign investment flows have increased enormously. Globalization and internalization were driven by lower trade barriers and transportation costs, reduced restrictions on FDI, and improvements in communication technologies, which facilitate the utilization of scale economies and a deeper division of labor. These are expected to be the driving forces for a worldwide intensification of trade.

Several strands of the theoretical literature deal with explaining trade specialization patterns. Given that technologies (Ricardo, 1817) or endowments with input factors (Heckscher, 1949; Ohlin, 1933) differ across countries, there should be an increased specialization of regions according to their comparative advantage. However, these so-called *Traditional Trade Theory* models do not explain why intra-industry trade (IIT) takes place. A great part of trade is comprised of the exchange of differentiated goods that fall into the same product category and takes place between industrialized countries with similar factor endowments and production technologies.

New Trade Theory models include scale economies, product differentiation (preference variety) and imperfect competition as the main ingredients for explaining IIT. Increasing returns to scale can hereby apply at the branch level (Markusen and Melvin, 1981; Ethier, 1982) or at the firm level (Dixit and Stiglitz, 1977; Krugman 1979). The major conclusion of the New Trade Theory is that the share of IIT in total trade is in opposition to the share of inter-industry trade and is positively related to the similarities of demand and production characteristics (Love of Variety Approach). More modern theories of trade distinguish further between horizontal and vertical product differentiation (Greenaway et al., 1995).

The literature on *Economic Geography* adds the interaction of increasing returns to scale with transport costs across countries to this (Krugman, 1991). Hereby transportation of differentiated goods often involves the very specific form of iceberg-type transportation costs. The main tool of these models is the use of gravity equations. Later on there is more focus laid on forward and backward linkages associated with large markets (Krugman, 1991a) and intersectoral labor mobility (Puga, 1998). The main question to be answered however remains unsolved: which activities within the increasing returns to scale industries would the core region attract more readily, and which activity would the periphery lose more quickly, if integration of countries induces agglomeration? Only some papers attempt to integrate economic geography models with traditional trade theory based on comparative advantage, thereby investigating the relationship between agglomeration and specialization within the IRS activity. Venables (1998) shows that the resulting division is not unique and is not necessarily in line with comparative advantages. A country which has the most beneficial endowment for fixed costs (skilled labor and much capital) will attract production of new goods. Old goods will be produced, where factor endowment is beneficial for variable costs of production (low skilled labor). The question still remains open as to how trade with intermediate products will develop by means of integration.

The consideration of the existence of multinational companies (MNC) changes the point of view in the literature. Detailed models on FDI and trade (Markusen, 1995, 1998; Markusen and Venables, 1996; Markusen and Venables, 1998) include horizontal investment (MNC has a plant in each country) and vertical investment (MNC has its headquarters in one country and plants in others) and show that MNCs incur significant costs producing abroad relative to domestic firms in those countries. There is no definite conclusion elaborated by the FDI and Trade Models concerning the effects of trade and integration, whether it leads to more or less specialization (e.g. within Europe). On the one hand, lowering transport costs MNCs concentrate activities using lower costs and exploiting economies of scale. This leads to more specialization. On the other hand, integration decreases fixed costs of setting up plants (due to harmonized legislation and reduction of country risk), which intensifies the expansion of horizontal investment. This on the contrary leads to less specialization. It seems to be up to the data to decide whether there is more dispersion or more specialization in the run of international economic integration.

In terms of empirical work there is at first stage the need to decide on the direction in which shares of trade are analyzed. The questions raised are (a) whether the industrial structure of countries become more similar or dissimilar, or (b) whether industries become more concentrated or more dispersed in the geographical dimension. Sectoral specialization and regional concentration are twin issues dealt with by e.g. Dalum et al. (1998). While from the geographical dimension, gravity models suggest that IIT diminishes with distance as an inherent characteristics of such trade, new empirical studies on the geography of trade find that close countries do a lot of IIT, because they have similar economic structures and not just because of the distance (Venables et al., 2003). However, the determinants of the spatial structures of countries' supply and demand characteristics still remain to be identified.

To what extent are they connected to technology and factor endowments? An alternative explanation for IIT is provided by the so-called home market effect, which states that spatial concentration follows from idiosyncratically large demand for the products of a specific industry. Accordingly, specific high demand in a country leads to an export surplus by increasing returns to scale and monopolistic competition, while in a competitive environment with constant returns to scale it leads to an import surplus (Armington assumption). Davis et al. (1998) test this hypothesis for Japan and other OECD countries.

To conclude, there are various open questions to be answered in the context of integration, FDI and trade. There are hardly any studies on whether the process of globalization will drive out labor intensive production to low wages or high wages countries. Does this lead to more intra-European specialization by driving out low wage industries of Europe at different speeds, or does it lead to more dispersion in Europe since all low wage industries decline, making the other parts of manufacturing more similar? There is still no comprehensive empirical investigation on whether higher specialized countries or those with more dispersed structure are better for growth, employment creation and competitiveness. This book addresses the problem of finding a consensus on indicators measuring specialization and concentration of industries and tries to present a consistent picture of evidence on the outcome of internalization on specialization patterns.

Before doing so, we revise the main trade theory models in more detail, based on Feenstra (2004). The aim is to highlight the theoretical basis upon which further analysis can rely.

3.1 Traditional Trade Theory

3.1.1 Overview

The theoretical approach to international trade begins with the *Traditional Trade Theory*, whose main contributors are Ricardo, Heckscher, Ohlin and Viner.

In the classical Ricardian model the economy uses one factor, namely labor, to produce two goods. It deals with two countries - home and foreign - and two industries. Labor is perfectly mobile between the industries in each country, but immobile between countries. Thus each country produces both goods, if wages earned in the two industries are the same. Furthermore it is assumed that tastes are identical and homothetic across countries. One main ingredient of the Ricardian model is to allow for different technologies across the countries. Thus one country has a comparative advantage in producing a certain good if its home autarky relative to the price of the good is lower than that abroad. The outcome of the model is rather straightforward; both countries are better off under free trade than they are under autarky. Trade patterns are determined by comparative advantages, even if one country has not only got a relative, but an absolute advantage or disadvantage in both goods' production. The level of wages across countries is determined by absolute advantages.

While the Ricardian model focuses on differences in technologies, the Heckscher-Ohlin (HO) model emphasizes factors of production, more precisely factor endowments. In its simplest specification, it deals with a single country with two goods and two factors as inputs of production, namely labor and capital. The production function is assumed to be increasing, concave and homogenous of degree one in both inputs. Furthermore we assume constant returns to scale.[1] Both input factors labor and capital are fully mobile between the industries. In contrast to the Ricardian models we assume identical technologies for both countries. The market structure is perfectly competitive and product prices are given exogenously. This is consistent with the assumption of a small open economy, which is very widely used in the economic literature. In equilibrium, the economy is maximizing its gross domestic product (GDP) subject to the constraint within its factor endowments and the zero-profit condition. In equilibrium the economy produces at minimum costs, that is where unit-costs equal both marginal and average costs. To investigate the properties of the HO-equilibrium, there are three key questions to ask.

- Determination of Factor Prices
  What is the solution for the factor prices? The Lemma of *Factor Price Insensitivity* states that factor prices do not depend on factor endowments, if and only if (1) both goods are produced, and (2) there is no factor intensity reversal (FIR). In that case, each good's price vector corresponds to a unique factor price vector.[2] This is important in that in a two-by-two economy with exogenously given fixed product prices, it is possible for the labor force or the capital stock to grow without any impact on factor prices.
- Change in Product Prices
  How do factor prices change if product prices change? The *Stolper-Samuelson Theorem* (Stolper and Samuelson, 1941) gives the answer: An increase in the relative price of a good will increase the return to the factor used intensively in that good, and reduce the return to the other factor. If, for example, industry 1 is labor intensive and the relative price for good 1 increases, wage will increase by more than the price of good 1 (that is more than the increase in the price of good 2), which is again more than the increase in the interest rate, the return to capital. When labor can

---

[1] This assumption is rather restrictive as we will see later on. It has been thought for a long time that increasing returns to scale are the most important explanations for trade between countries, as we will see in the New Trade Theory models.

[2] Factor intensity reversal (FIR) occurs if by given goods prices there is not a unique solution for factor prices, but the unit-cost lines of goods intersect at least twice. Intuitively that means that relative factor intensities change at different factor prices. For a detailed explanation, see Feenstra (2004, Chapter 1).

now buy more of both goods, real wage has increased. The capital owner, however, can afford less of both goods, thus the real return to capital has fallen. This is also called the magnification effect (Jones, 1965). Note that this has the implication that trade has strong distributional consequences.

- Change in Endowments

  How do outputs change, if endowments change? The answer to this question is given by the *Rybczynski Theorem* (Rybczynski, 1955), which states that an increase in a factor endowment will increase the output of the industry using it intensively, and decrease the output of the other industry. If, for example, the labor force increases, increasing labor endowment, output in that labor intensive industry will increase and output in the capital intensive industry will decline. The most prominent example for the Rybczynski theorem is the so called Dutch Disease. When oil was discovered off the coast of the Netherlands in the 1970s, it lead to an increase in energy intensive industries, however other more traditional export industries contracted.

Note that for the solution of all these three questions mentioned above, two assumptions must hold: (1) both goods are produced, and (2) no FIR exists. In the more expanded case when we consider two countries, two goods and two factors, where factors are immobile across countries, we find that we can reach the same world production and equilibrium as if we allowed for mobility of factors across countries. Thus trade in goods replaces trade in factors to satisfy demand in each country. The main outcome of that two-by-two-by-two model is stated by the *Heckscher-Ohlin Theorem*, which states that each country will export the good that uses its abundant factor intensively. Thus the pattern of autarky prices can be used to predict the patterns of trade. A country will export the good whose autarky price is lower than its free-trade price and import the good whose free-trade price is lower than its autarky price. In case both above mentioned assumptions hold, factor prices equalize with free-trade.

Empirically speaking, the Heckscher-Ohlin model preforms poorly, so it seems to be a bad predictor of actual trade patterns, indicating that its assumptions are not realistic. Especially the assumption of identical technologies makes the empirical investigation of the HO model difficult.[3] This can also be seen by the very first empirical results for testing the HO model by Leontief (1953). He developed a set of input-output accounts for the U.S. economy. He measured the amount of capital and labor required for one million US Dollars worth of U.S. exports and the same for imports. Hereby he used the U.S. technology for both the imports and the exports and found that the capital/labor ratio in imports was higher than the capital/labor ratio in exports. Thus according to the HO model, the United States was supposed to be labor abundant in 1947, the year of the investigation. However, this did not seem to match reality. Therefore, this finding has been established in the literature

---

[3] See also Feenstra (2004).

as the *Leontief paradoxon*. There was a wide range of explanation for solving this paradoxon. However, only in 1980 did Leamer provide the most prominent critique on the paradoxon, stating that Leontief simply used the wrong test. Instead of comparing the capital/labor ratios in exports and imports, he should have relied on the factor content version of the HO model, which was developed by Vanek in 1968 and established as the Heckscher-Ohlin-Vanek model.

3.1.2 Heckscher-Ohlin-Vanek Model

The Heckscher-Ohlin-Vanek model (HOV) is an extended version of the HO model, using a multi-goods, multi-factors, and multi-countries framework. For the time being we still stick to the assumption of identical technologies and identical and homothetic tastes across countries and that factor price equalization (FPE) prevails under free trade.

Let us index the countries by $i = 1, ..., C$; the industries by $j = 1, ..., N$; the input factor capital by k, and labor by $l = 1, ..., M$. The (M x N) matrix $A = [a_{jk}]$ denotes the amounts of the factors needed for one unit of production in each industry. The rows of the matrix measure the different factors, and the columns measure the different industries. In the simple case of two factors k, and l, and two industries 1 and 2, the matrix would be represented as follows:

$$\mathbf{A} = \begin{bmatrix} a_{1l} & a_{2l} \\ a_{1k} & a_{2k} \end{bmatrix} \tag{3.1}$$

Let Y^i denote the (N x 1) vector of outputs in each industry for each country, and let D^i denote the (N x 1) vector of demands for each good. Thus we have

$$T^i = Y^i - D^i \tag{3.2}$$

where T^i equals the difference between output Y and demand D in each industry in each country i, and thus stands for the vector of net exports for each country i. The factor content of trade F is then defined as

$$F^i = AT^i \tag{3.3}$$

which is a (M x 1) vector. The main goal of the HOV model is to connect the content of trade AT^i to the underlying endowments of a country V^i. Thus we compute AY^i and AD^i. Former refers to the demand for factors in country i in terms of producing the output and equals the endowments of country i. We can write:

$$AY^i = V^i \tag{3.4}$$

The latter -AD^i- is simplified by using the assumption of identical and homothetic tastes. Since product prices are equalized across countries through free trade, it follows that the consumption (demand) vectors of all countries must be proportional to each other, thus $D^i = s^i D^w$. We obtain:

$$AD^i = s^i AD^w \tag{3.5}$$

where D^w denotes the world consumption vector and s^i stands for the share of country i in world consumption. If in equilibrium world production equals world consumption, we obtain:

$$AD^i = s^i AD^w = s^i AY^w = s^i V^w \tag{3.6}$$

The last part of this equation refers to a world-wide full-employment condition. Based on these equations, we can formulate the statement of the HOV-theorem:

$$F^i \equiv AT^i = V^i - s^i V^w \tag{3.7}$$

We can also relate the statement of the HOV-theorem to individual factors, which can be written as

$$F_k^i = V_k^i - s^i V_k^w \tag{3.8}$$

The interpretation of the HOV-theorem is that a country i is abundant in factor k, if country i's endowment of that factor relative to the world endowment exceeds country i's share of world GDP. Thus country i is abundant in factor k, if $(V_k^i/V_k^w) > s^i$. Accordingly, the HOV-theorem states concerning the Leontief test that if capital is abundant relative to labor in country i, the capital/labor ratio embodied in production for country i exceeds the capital/labor ratio embodied in consumption. Thus the right measure to test the HOV model is to check whether the capital/labor ratio is higher in production or consumption, and not in exports and imports. One should use the factor content of trade to test the HOV model. Leamer's test (Leamer, 1980) is totally robust to unbalanced trade, which was a main problem in Leontief's method that was not robust against unbalanced trade.

We will now turn to the question of how to test the outcome of the HOV-theorem empirically. The starting point is equation 3.7. Hereby we have three sources of data we can use: (1) trade data, (2) data on technology and (3) data on factor endowments. A complete test would require both trade and endowment data for many countries and technology data for at least one country. However, a great body of the empirical literature performs only partial tests of the HOV model using only two rather than three types of data.[4] This is due to the fact that data on technology was not available for a long time. The very first complete test of the HOV-theorem was done by Bowen et al. (1987). Since then, other authors performed complete tests (e.g. Trefler, 1993, 1995) using all three sources of data. Since the partial tests are mostly very limited

---

[4] See e.g. Leontief (1953), Leamer (1980), Baldwin (1971), or Leamer (1984).

in findings or the outcomes are simply wrong, we will only deal with complete
tests.

In general, there are two kind of complete tests when using data on trade
and factor endowments and technology data on only one country:

1. sign test,
2. rank test.

Concerning the sign test we compare the sign patterns on the left and the
right hand side of equation 3.7. With MC number of observations (M factors
and C countries) we are interested in what percentage of these observations
have the same sign on both sides of the equation. A rank test is basically a
pairwise comparison of all factors for each country, so that we have $M(M-1)/2$
pairs for each country. Actually all the above mentioned authors fail to test
the HOV model with sign and rank tests, when they confront it with data.
The main reason lies in the very unrealistic assumption of equal technologies
across countries. However, there are two ways by which different technologies
can be modelled within the HOV-framework. One can (1) either model the
productivity of factors in different countries or (2) model the differences in the
factor requirement matrix A (see equation 3.1). Of course the two approaches
are closely related. If, for example, a factor is 5 percent more productive in
one country than in the other, that means that 5 percent less is needed of this
factor in that country per unit of production.

One analysis using the first approach modelling all factors in every country
to differ in their productivities is done by Trefler (1993). He uses the productivity of the United States as a benchmark, normalizing it to unity. Thus π_k^i
is the productivity of the input factor k in country i, measured relative to the
United States. So the effective endowment of factor k in that country is $\pi_k^i V_k^i$.
The factor content of trade is therefore measured by

$$F_k^i = \pi_k^i V_k^i - s^i \sum_{j=1}^{C} \pi_k^j V_k^j \tag{3.9}$$

where $i = 1, ..., C$ and $k = 1, ..., M$. Equation 3.9 contains MC number of
equations and $M(C\text{-}1)$ productivity parameters. These equations are interdependent in the sense that adding up the factor contents for any factor k across
all countries we will obtain zero on both sides of the equation, because for the
world, exports equal imports, even if we measure it in terms of factor contents.
Therefore we can drop one equation, e.g. for the United States. We then have
$M(C\text{-}1)$ equations with $M(C\text{-}1)$ parameters. Since the productivity parameters enter linearly in equation 3.9, we can find a unique solution for almost
all datasets, where the HOV equation 3.9 holds with equality. This is stated
by the *Trefler Theorem* (Trefler, 1993). That means that in this case HOV is
an identity by the choice of productivity parameters and is not testable any
more.

Trefler (1995) also applied the second method allowing the factor requirement matrix to differ across countries. Thus we have A^i instead of only A as
we had before. In order to receive a testable equation, which allows us to use
an econometric approach, we need to restrict the range of differences in the
A^i matrices, so that the HOV equation does not hold any more with equality,
so it gives less than a perfect fit. We need to choose the parameters of A^i so as
to minimize the sum of squared residuals of the HOV equations. Let's assume
that the matrices A^i differ by a uniform amount across countries relative to
the United States:

$$\delta^i A^i = A^{US} \tag{3.10}$$

Now we derive again the HOV equation, using the full employment assumption $A^i Y^i = V^i$. So we obtain:

$$F^i \equiv A^i T^i = A^i Y^i - A^i D^i = V^i - A^i(s^i D^w) = V^i - A^i\left(s^i \sum_{j=1}^{C} Y^j\right) \tag{3.11}$$

In order to get the factor content of trade for country i by using the U.S.
factor requirement matrix, we multiply both sides of the equation by δ^i.[5]
On the left hand side we then obtain $\delta^i A^i$, which by definition equals A^{US}.
Because A^{US} does not depend on i, we can bring it inside the summation.[6]
The HOV equation for country $j = 1, ..., C$ then is as follows:

$$F^{iUS} \equiv A^{US} T^i = \delta^i V^i - \left(s^i \sum_{j=1}^{C} \delta^j V^j\right) \tag{3.12}$$

Equation 3.12 reflects the HOV model when we allow for uniform technological differences across countries. It can be interpreted in the way that
the factor content of trade as measured with U.S. technology should equal
the relative factor endowments, which are adjusted for each country by the
respective technological parameter. In contrast to equation 3.9, this is not an
identity. Therefore we can introduce an error term and perform a regression
to estimate δ^i by using ordinary least squares (OLS) regression techniques.

How can we compare the three specifications of the HOV model, equations 3.7, 3.9, and 3.12, which we have derived so far? The first specification,
equation 3.7, is based on the very unrealistic assumption of identical technologies across countries. It is therefore not surprising that it clearly fails when
confronted with actual data. If we release this assumption to the extreme and
allow for unlimited differences in productivities of factors across countries as

---

[5] Note that Leontief and the other above-mentioned authors used this same
methodology.

[6] The summation then looks like $s^i \sum_{j=1}^{C} A^{US} Y^j = s^i \sum_{j=1}^{C} \delta^j A^j Y^j = s^i \sum_{j=1}^{C} \delta^j V^j$.

in equation 3.9, the model becomes an identity and is not testable any more. Trefler (1995) shows that the solution between the two extremes as shown in equation 3.12 seems to be on the right track. However, allowing only for uniform technological differences from the United States is not the last word within that model framework. Since data on country-wise technologies has become available recently for some OECD countries, one can go further and generalize the technological differences across countries in the HOV model.[7]

So far we have dealt with the HOV model for many goods and many factors, while we always maintained the assumption that factor price equalization (FPE) holds. Figure 3.1 illustrates FPE graphically for a continuum of goods.

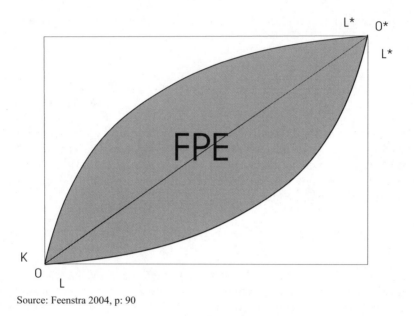

Source: Feenstra 2004, p: 90

Fig. 3.1. Factor Price Equalization

The axes measure the world endowment for labor L and capital K. We sum the endowments of these factors in each country home 0 and foreign 0*. The curves show all the possible combinations of endowments by integrating over worldwide factor demands. All points inside the curves - that means in the shaded region including the border lines - allow for factor price equalization across countries. For endowments outside the shaded area, factor prices would differ across countries.

The question arises, however, as to what happens to the theorems mentioned at the beginning of the chapter if we release the assumption of factor

---

[7] See Davis and Weinstein (2001) for an application to ten OECD countries explained in the next part of this chapter.

price equalization. First we need to differentiate between different cases when we consider many goods and many factors: (1) we can have an even number of goods and factors, (2) we can have more factors than goods, or (3) we can have more goods than factors. As shown by Feenstra (2004), in the even case the factor price equalization naturally holds if we generalize the two-goods-two-factors model to N goods and N factors. Furthermore, both the Stolper-Samuelson and the Rybczynski theorem continue to hold, although not as strong as in the two-by-two case. In the second case having more factors than goods, the factor price equalization theorem does not hold any more; factor prices are rather dependent on the country's factor endowment. A special case of two goods and three factors (labor, capital and land) is known as the Ricardo-Viner model. Also the results of the Stolper-Samuelson and the Rybczynski theorem are valid in a modified way for this special case.[8] Empirically, these first two cases can be tested by using an economy wide production function. However, due to the rather unrealistic assumptions, we will not further proceed here. We rather turn our attention to the third, and in the author's view most realistic, case when the number of produced goods exceeds the number of input factors used in the production. A neat generalization of this type is the use of a continuum of goods, as done by Dornbusch et al. (1980).

Let us denote the range of goods produced $z \epsilon [0,1]$ and $y(z)$ the quantity produced of each of these goods with the input factors L and K:

$$y(z) = f[L(z), K(z)] \qquad (3.13)$$

The production function is assumed to be increasing, concave and linearly homogenous in L and K. Thus the dual unit-cost function c is described by the following equation, where the factor prices of labor and capital are denoted by wages w and rents r:

$$c(w,r,z) \equiv \min_{L(z),K(z) \geq 0} (wL(z) + rK(z)|f[L(z), K(z), z] \geq 1) \qquad (3.14)$$

Furthermore we assume that no factor intensity reversal (FIR) exists. The amount of capital and labor needed to produce one unit of output is described by $a_K(w,r,z)$ and $a_L(w,r,z)$, respectively. We assume that demand under autarky in the home country comes from a Cobb-Douglas utility function:

$$lnU = \int_0^1 \alpha(z)lny(z)dz \qquad (3.15)$$

where $\int_0^1 \alpha(z)dz = 1$. That means that consumers spend a constant share $\alpha(z)$ of their income on each final good $y(z)$. The expenditure on each final good is then $\alpha(z)(wL + rK)$. For the factor endowments L and K, w and r are the

---

[8] For a detailed explanation see Feenstra (2004).

equilibrium factor prices. Dividing this by the equilibrium goods' prices $p(z)$, which equal unit-cost c, we obtain the equilibrium condition, where demand equals supply:

$$y(z) = \alpha(z)(wL + rK)/c(w, r, z) \tag{3.16}$$

In equilibrium we also have equality of factor demand and factor supply. Total demand for labor relative to total demand for capital must equal the relative endowments of labor and capital:

$$\frac{L}{K} = \frac{\int_0^1 a_L(w, r, z)y(z)dz}{\int_0^1 a_K(w, r, z)y(z)dz} \tag{3.17}$$

Thus factor price ratio at home in autarky is (w/r). The foreign country, denoted with an asterisk, faces the same situation in autarky. Assuming that both countries have identical technology and identical tastes, we have factor price equalization, and we cannot determine which country produces which goods. The equilibrium condition in equation 3.16 is modified so that:

$$y(z) + y^*(z) = \alpha(z)(wL + rK) + (wL^* + rK^*)/c(w, r, z) \tag{3.18}$$

There are many combinations of outputs $y(z)$ and $y^*(z)$, which fulfill the condition that in each country, relative demand for factors equals relative endowments. Thus, neither outputs nor the set of goods produced are uniquely determined under factor price equalization.

However, factor prices (w, r) and (w^*, r^*) will differ from each other, giving up factor price equalization, if factor endowments are sufficiently different. To illustrate this, we have a look at the determination of equilibrium prices:

$$p(z) = \min(c(w, r, z), c(w^*, r^*, z)) \tag{3.19}$$

Minimizing costs, goods will be produced in that country with the lowest unit-costs. That indicates that each country will produce and export those goods with lower unit-costs than abroad. We note that unit-costs across countries determine trade patterns. If, for example, in the extreme case of unit costs abroad being lower for all goods, then all goods would be produced abroad and vice versa. Suppose that the foreign country is relatively abundant in labor, having a lower wage/rental ratio than the home country. Accordingly, the foreign country will specialize in labor intensive goods production, because (and as long as) its unit-costs for those goods are lower than at home. To summarize, if factor prices are equalized, there is not a unique solution for the production patterns. When factor prices are not equalized across countries, each country will specialize in a different range of final goods. Thus labor/captial ratios in production and labor/capital ratios in endowments are extremely interdependent in the HOV model framework.

Thus far, we have obtained a rather advanced HOV model and eliminated many of the possible critique points. One main remaining critique, however, concerns the lack of distinction between final and intermediate goods. The theory developed so far considers only trade in final goods, although a great part of actual trade is in intermediate goods, semi-final goods, components or parts. These can cross country borders several times before they get incorporated into a final good. These types of trade flows tend to cancel out if we consider net exports, as in the original HOV model. If we, however, add up gross exports, this can lead to much higher trade volumes due to the trade of intermediate goods. We will, however, deal with the theory of trade with intermediate inputs in the next part, after presenting the econometric applications for the HOV model.

3.1.3 Testing the HOV Model

It is rather challenging to get satisfactory results when facing the traditional trade theory with empirical data. The main obstacle is the very unrealistic assumption of the Heckscher-Ohlin model that technologies are identical across countries. One can, however, incorporate the main Ricardian idea of different technologies into the HO model framework to move away from that unrealistic assumption. Furthermore, one can generalize the HO model for many goods, many factors, and many countries, where we end up in the HOV model. One very nice application of the HOV model for a continuum of goods by Dornbusch et al. (1980) was discussed in the previous chapter. Recent empirical results for this model are available by Davis and Weinstein (2001), to which we will now refer.

When allowing for technological differences, one must avoid the introduction of too many free parameters, so that the HOV equation (see equation 3.9) holds as an equality.[9] The empirical derivation of the HOV model by Dornbusch et al. (1980) is rather straightforward. If factor prices are not equalized, capital/labor ratios of traded goods must be closely related to the country's factor endowments. A country A with a higher capital/labor endowment than country B must have higher captial/labor intensities in all of its traded goods.[10] Thus an empirically testable HOV equation can be written as:

$$\ln a^i_{jk} = \alpha^i + \beta_{jk} + \gamma_k \left(\frac{K^i}{L^i}\right) + \epsilon^i_{jk} \tag{3.20}$$

where a denotes the factor intensities of traded goods, which is the dependent variable, (K/L) the relative factor endowments, $i = 1, ..., C$ denotes countries, $j = 1, ..., N$ traded goods, and $k = 1, ..., M$ denotes factors. HOV equation 3.20 is run over countries, goods and factors. We can interpret the

---

[9] See also Trefler (1993, 1995).

[10] See also Davis and Weinstein (2001), and Feenstra (2004).

right hand side as a prediction for factor requirements. Parameter α^i measures uniform technology differences across countries. Parameter β_{jk} provides country invariant average estimates of the factor requirements across countries. Finally the parameter γ_k measures the impact of actual factor endowments $(\frac{K^i}{L^i})$. By this simple regression we get a parsimonious description of cross-country technological differences.

Davis and Weinstein (2001) estimate equation 3.20 for 20 OECD countries, 34 sectors and two factors, labor and capital, for 1985. They find that simple linear relationships fit the data well. Furthermore, they find that the impact of factor endowments on factor requirements as measured by the parameter γ_k is highly significant. They use several variations of this regression and construct for each country a matrix $\hat{A}^i$, which is the estimated technology matrix using the results of regression 3.20 and its variations. We can then use that matrix to construct the factor contents of trade and test how well the constructed factor contents match the relative endowments of the countries. Thus we do not need to use the technology of one specific country (e.g., the USA as was shown previously), but now we have different technology matrices across countries. According to Feenstra (2004), one should use the technology of the exporting country to construct the factor content of trade, when technology matrices differ across countries. Thus the factor content of exports from country i to country c is:

$$\hat{F}^{ic} \equiv \hat{A}^i X^{ic} \tag{3.21}$$

where X^{ic} denotes the vector of exports of country i to country c. The prediction of the HOV model is that the factor content of trade should be reflected in the country's relative endowments. This can be written as:

$$V^i - s^i \left(\sum_c V^c \right) = \left(\sum_{c \neq i} \hat{F}^{ic} \right) - \left(\sum_{c \neq i} \hat{F}^{ci} \right) \tag{3.22}$$

Depending on how good the specification of equation 3.20 and the constructed factor content matrix A are, we get different results applying the sign test on equation 3.22.[11] Assuming that countries use the same average technology matrix, including only the coefficient β_{ck} in equation 3.20, Davis and Weinstein (2001) find that in only 46% of the cases the two sides of equation 3.22 display the same sign. However, if you just flip a coin, you get a probability of 50% to get same sign on both sides, so this empirical result using the same average technology across countries is not better than a coincidence. However, if Davis and Weinstein estimate equation 3.20 with an additional coefficient α^i, allowing for uniform technology differences, the sign test performs better in 50% of the cases. If they also include the impact of factor endowments measured by the parameter γ_k, then the sign test performs satisfactorily in 86% of the cases. This is significantly higher than the random

---

[11] See also Davis and Weinstein (2001).

50% of the coin. And they go even further. If they model exports not as gross exports as shown before, but as proportional to the purchasing (the importing) country's GDP, the sign test is satisfactory in even 92% of the cases. This simple application of the HOV theory shows the importance of modelling the assumptions to closing the gap between factor contents and endowments.

3.2 The Role of Intermediate Inputs

A great share of trade flows is comprised not of final goods, but parts, components or semi-final goods. In the following we present a model, which makes use of intermediate goods as inputs. This procedure is widely used in the literature as outsourcing or production sharing. A rather recent branch of the literature dealing with it is often referred to as fragmentation or production sharing. A model including trade in intermediate goods is especially feasible for displaying the interactions between input prices and wages. Following the model of outsourcing by Feenstra (2004) shows how trade affects factor demand and wages. To anticipate the main result we will see that trade in intermediate inputs shifts demand for labor within industries but not across industries, thus influencing factor demand and wages within industries.

3.2.1 The Extended Model of Intermediate Inputs

We start right away with an extended model of intermediate inputs, which uses a continuum of inputs (instead of a countable number of inputs) and can be found in Feenstra and Hanson (1996, 1997). Let $z\epsilon[0,1]$ denote all the activities that are needed for the production of the final good. We will list these activities according to their skilled/unskilled labor ratio in an increasing order, that means starting with activities that use unskilled labor intensively such as assembly, and ending with activities that use skilled labor intensively such as R&D. Let $x(z)$ denote the quantity produced of each of these inputs, where $a_H(z)$ denotes skilled labor and $a_L(z)$ denotes unskilled labor that is needed to produce one unit of $x(z)$. For the sake of simplicity we suppose to have two countries. The foreign country is always marked with an asterisk. The dual unit-cost function for producing the intermediate inputs can be written as:

$$c(w,q,r,z) = [wa_L(z) + qa_H(z)]^\theta r^{1-\theta} \tag{3.23}$$

where $c(w,q,r,z)$ denotes the costs of producing one unit of $x(z)$, given the wage for unskilled labor w, the wage for skilled labor q, and the rent on capital r. The parameter θ denotes the share of labor in the costs of producing each input. The production function of the final good is given by:

$$\ln Y = \int_0^1 \alpha(z) \ln x(z) dx \tag{3.24}$$

where $\int_0^1 \alpha(z)dz = 1$. It is important to note that there are no labor costs included into the production function of the final good. It only contains the costs for producing the inputs. Thus the final good is assembled costlessly, so we do not need to keep track of where final assembly takes places, because in this case value added is zero for the final assembly. However, this is a very unrealistic assumption. In addition, one main characteristics of production fragmentation is that the value added is usually highest in the country, in which the final assembly of the product is done. Value added during the production of parts, components or semi-final products is much lower.

For further proceedings we need to use two more assumptions. Firstly, we assume that the home country is relatively skilled labor abundant, thus the relative wage of skilled labor is lower at home than abroad. This is realistic considering countries such as the USA or Germany as home countries. Secondly, we assume that the rent on capital is lower at home than abroad, thus capital wants to relocate from home to abroad if capital mobility is given. This is also a reasonable assumption for a country abundant with capital such as the USA, Germany or the EU 15.

The solution for the resulting production sharing or outsourcing is illustrated by figure 3.2. Remember that $z\epsilon[0, 1]$ is listed in increased order of skilled/unskilled labor ratio.

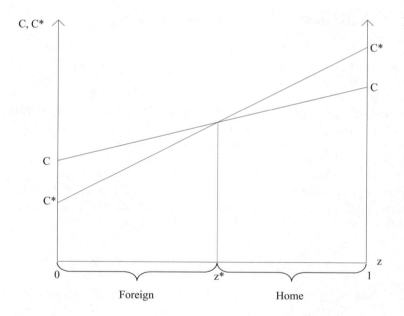

Source: Feenstra 2004, p: 113

Fig. 3.2. Production Sharing with Intermediate Inputs

It reveals the unit costs functions both for the home CC and the foreign C^*C^* country. As indicated before in the assumptions, the home country is relatively abundant with skilled labor, thus its unit costs function is flatter. In case the unit costs functions intercept at least once (as it is the case in figure 3.2), we have no corner solution, rather outsourcing prevails. Thus the foreign country specializes in activities abundant in unskilled labor, that is for all products $[0, z^*)$, where unit costs are lower than in the home country. On the contrary, the home country specializes in all products $(z^*, 1]$ that are relatively skilled labor abundant, and where unit costs are lower than in the foreign country. Based on this we can calculate the relative demand functions for skilled/unskilled labor for each country. Equation 3.25 shows the corresponding demand function for the home country:

$$D(z*) = \frac{\int_{z^*}^1 \frac{\delta c}{\delta q} x(z) dz}{\int_{z^*}^1 \frac{\delta c}{\delta w} x(z) dz} \tag{3.25}$$

The demand function for the foreign country is very similar, except that the integration is done over the range of goods $[0, z^*)$.

In the world equilibrium, when each country produces the range of products minimizing costs as described above, supply should equal demand for both skilled and unskilled labor in each country, and the same should apply for capital. Assuming that the endowments of labor and capital are fixed, the relative wage and the return for capital are determined by the intersection point. Labor costs account for $(wL + qH)$, and the fraction of total costs that makes up for labor is θ. The rental r of capital at home is determined by:

$$\frac{(wL + qH)}{\theta} \frac{(1 - \theta)}{K} = r \tag{3.26}$$

Interpretation of equation 3.26 is easier if you multiply both sides with K. Capital costs on the left hand side equal GDP in each country $(wL + qH)/\theta$ multiplied by the cost share of capital $(1 - \theta)$.

So far we have not allowed capital to move between countries. What happens to fragmentation if we introduce free capital movements? As indicated in the assumptions, the home country is relatively abundant with capital so that $r < r^*$. Accordingly some capital tends to move from home to abroad if we introduce free capital movement. A reduction in K and a rise in K^* results in an increase in r and a fall in r^*. Figure 3.3 illustrates the results graphically.

At unchanged wages, capital movement from home to abroad has the effect of an increase in the equilibrium value of z, moving from z^* to z'. Thus the foreign country now specializes in a wider range of activities $[0, z')$, whereas the home country's range of specialization has contracted to $(z', 1]$. Note that the activities that have been transferred from home to abroad within (z^*, z') are less skill intensive then the activities that remain at home. Therefore relative demand for unskilled labor decreases in the home country, while the relative

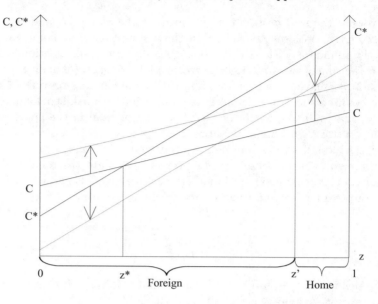

Fig. 3.3. Production Sharing with Free Capital Movement

demand for skilled labor increases. The foreign country gained activities that are more skilled labor intensive than the ones it had before. This has the effect of increasing the relative demand for skilled labor in the foreign country as well.

To get it clear, relative demand for skilled labor rises in both countries, leading to a rise in the relative wage of skilled labor in both countries and a fall in the relative wage of unskilled labor in both countries. Thus unskilled workers are the most disadvantaged if there is outsourcing or production sharing within this model. It is important to stress that this outcome is valid regardless of where increased outsourcing comes from, whether it is due to capital flows as described above, or for example due to a faster growth in the capital endowments abroad than at home, or technological progress abroad exceeding the one at home. Note that this result of movements of the relative wage across countries to the same direction when opening up for trade can hardly be generated from the HOV type of model.

3.2.2 Empirical Evidence on the Role of Intermediate Inputs

According to the model just presented, outsourcing or production sharing has a very similar qualitative effect on the reduction of relative demand for unskilled labor as for example a skilled-biased technological change just like the intensive use of computers or other electronic equipment, which replaces human work with machines, thus reducing the relative demand for unskilled labor. From this point of view determining which of these two factors is more important is the relevant empirical question here. There are two methods for testing the effects of trade versus technological change on wages and employment: (1) One can estimate the demand for skilled and unskilled labor, or to put it differently the relative demand for skilled labor; (2) one can estimate the zero-profit conditions.[12]

The first method uses a short-run cost function similar to equation 3.23, such as $C_j(w, q, K_j, Y_j, z_j)$, which displays the costs for unskilled labor w, for skilled labor q, for a fixed level of capital K and output Y for each industry j. For the question stated above we also need to include any structural variables that shift the production function affecting costs. These are reflected in the parameter z_j. Practically, z_j measures all the expenditure on imported inputs for each industry, such as expenditures on computers and other new types of capital equipment. Using the translog cost function $ln\, C$ is advisable, because its first derivative equals the payments to factor k relative to total costs and also denotes the cost shares of each factor.[13]

With regards to the cost function, there are just two factors that must be chosen optimally, skilled and unskilled labor, because capital and output are treated as fixed in the short run. The equation for the cost shares can be estimated for annual data for a given industry. Alternatively one can estimate the equation using the change between two years by pooling the data across industries. This implicitly assumes that the same cost function applies across industries. This approach is used by Berman et al. (1994). However they find that cross-country variation in wages holds little information, so they dropped it from the equation. We then get a pooled regression, which considers the difference between two years while estimating the wage share of skilled labor s_{jH} in industries $j = 1, ..., N$ with only fixed capital, output, and other structural variables. So we get:

$$\Delta s_{jH} = \phi_0 + \phi_K \Delta \ln K_j + \phi_Y \Delta \ln Y_j + \phi_z \Delta z_j \qquad (3.27)$$

With equation 3.27 we can test how much of an increase in the wage share of skilled labor is due to changes in capital, output and structural variables. This was done by Bartelsman and Gray (1996) for 447 manufacturing industries in the U.S. in the time period from 1979 to 1990. Here nonproduction labor is used as a proxy for skilled labor. The variables in regression 3.27 have been weighted by the industry share of the total manufacturing bill. Based on that, Feenstra and Hanson (1999, 2003) expand that regression by differ-

---

[12] See also Feenstra (2004, Chapter 4).

[13] The first derivative of the translog cost function with respect to w_k is $\delta \ln C / \delta \ln w_k = (\delta C / \delta w_k)(w_k / C)$. Since $(\delta C / \delta w_k)(w_k / C)$ equals the payments to factor k relative to total costs, we get the cost shares.

ent alternatives. They use shipments for each industry as a proxy for for real value-added Y_j, the capital/shipment ratio reflecting the capital input K_j relative to Y_j, and they measure outsourcing by imported intermediate inputs as a share of total intermediate purchases. For the imported intermediate inputs they use different measures. In particular the share of computers and other high-tech capital in the capital stock is calculated in three different ways: (1) using ex-post rental prices to measure capital services, (2) using ex-ante rental prices to measure capital services, and (3) measuring computer expenditures as a share of investment instead of a share of capital stock.

The results show the following. In all regressions both outsourcing and the computer shares have a positive impact on the skilled labor (nonproduction) share of the wage bill. On average outsourcing accounts for 15-24 % of the shift towards skilled labor.[14] The role of the use of computers depends on the specification. Calculating either ex-post or ex-ante rental prices, the contribution of computers to the shift accounts for 8-13 %, which is less than the contribution of outsourcing. This would imply that outsourcing or production sharing plays a more important role in the shift of wage shares than the replacement of labor by technical equipment in the U.S. However, if computers are measured as a share of investment, their contribution increases to 31 %, exceeding the contribution of outsourcing. Thus, both outsourcing and expenditure on computers play an important role; which has a greater influence depends on how the variable, computer, is being measured. Similar empirical evidence for the link between outsourcing and wage shares or relative employment is also available for European countries, for example, Geishecker (2002) for Germany and Görg et al. (2001) for the UK.

An alternative method concerns the estimation of zero-profit conditions. It assumes that skilled as well as unskilled labor and also capital are chosen optimally. In the long-run cost function, we allow factor prices w_j, q_j, r_j to differ across industries j, so it has the form $C_j(w_j, q_j, r_j, Y_j, z_j)$. Hereby the vector z_j denotes structural variables.[15] Due to the presence of these structural variables, changes in product prices reflect more than merely changes in factor prices. Thus we can define total factor productivity as:

$$TPF_j \equiv (\theta_{jL}\Delta \ln w_j + \theta_{jH}\Delta \ln q_j + \theta_{jK}\Delta \ln r_j) - \Delta \ln p_j \qquad (3.28)$$

Hereby the cost-shares of the factors sum up to unity, thus $\theta_{jL} + \theta_{jH} + \theta_{jK} = 1$. The first difference of the variables is denoted by Δ. Reshuffling equation 3.28 and bringing it to an estimable form gives:

$$\Delta \ln p_j = -TFP_j + \theta_{jL}\beta_L + \theta_{jH}\beta_H + +\theta_{jK}\beta_K + \epsilon_j \qquad (3.29)$$

---

[14] See also Feenstra (2004).

[15] The unit cost function is given by $c_j(w_j, q_j, r_j, z_j)$. The zero profit condition in industry j can be written as $p_j = c_j(w_j, q_j, r_j, z_j)$, where p denotes product prices.

where the change in factor prices are estimated as β coefficients, which can be interpreted as the change in factor prices that are given by the change in product prices p, the dependent variable. However, Baldwin and Cain (2000) as well as Slaughter (2000) show for the U.S. manufacturing industries that in reality, the non-production/production wage gap is different from the outcome of the estimation. Furthermore a slight change in the data dramatically changes the results. To filter out the difference between the estimates of the β coefficients and the actual average change in manufacturing wages, we denote the latter with $\overline{\Delta \ln w}$, $\overline{\Delta \ln q}$, and $\overline{\Delta \ln r}$. Replacing the estimated β coefficients in equation 3.29 by the average change of factor prices and incorporating the remaining difference between the real and the estimated change into the error terms gives:

$$\Delta \ln p_j = -TFP_j + \theta_{jL}\overline{\Delta \ln w} + \theta_{jH}\overline{\Delta \ln q} + \theta_{jK}\overline{\Delta \ln r} + \epsilon_j \qquad (3.30)$$

where

$$\epsilon_j = \theta_{jL}(\Delta \ln w_j - \overline{\Delta \ln w}) + \theta_{jH}(\Delta \ln q_j - \overline{\Delta \ln q}) + \theta_{jK}(\Delta \ln r_j - \overline{\Delta \ln r}) \quad (3.31)$$

Basically the error term reflects the wage differentials on an inter-industry level. It gives the difference between the wage paid in each industry and the manufacturing average. However, a serious problem occurs when estimating equation 3.30, namely that the error term is correlated with the independent variables, which is not allowed to be the case for an unbiased estimation. To correct for this one could incorporate the error term as an additional regressor, reflecting the change in interindustry wage differentials. In that case, however, we no longer have an error term for the regression, which means we end up with an identity. Having an identity means, however, that we do not get any new information out of the regression. Therefore Feenstra and Hanson (1999) suggest another solution.

They use a two-step estimation procedure. In the first step the dependent variable is a combination of $\Delta \ln p_j + ETFP_j$, where $ETFP_j = TFP_j - \epsilon_j$. The independent variables of the first step are the structural variables z_j and a constant term. Thus with two structural variables the first step regression has the form:

$$\Delta \ln p_j + ETFP_j = \alpha_0 + \alpha_1 \Delta z_{1j} + \alpha_2 \Delta z_{2j} \qquad (3.32)$$

In the second step they use the estimated coefficients $\hat{\alpha}_1$ and $\hat{\alpha}_2$ to construct the dependent variables of the regressions:

$$\hat{\alpha}_1 \Delta z_{1j} = \theta_{jL}\beta_{1L} + \theta_{jH}\beta_{1H} + \theta_{jK}\beta_{1K} \qquad (3.33)$$

and

$$\hat{\alpha}_2 \Delta z_{2j} = \theta_{nL}\beta_{2L} + \theta_{jH}\beta_{2H} + \theta_{jK}\beta_{2K} \tag{3.34}$$

That means that they use the estimated coefficients of the first step as the dependent variable in the second step of the regression. Thus the estimated β coefficients of the second step can be interpreted as the portion of the total change in factor prices that is explained by each structural variable.[16]

Feenstra and Hanson (1999) estimate this two step procedure for U.S. manufacturing industries from 1979 to 1990, finding a positive significant correlation in the first step regression using two kinds of structural variables: (1) outsourcing, and (2) either the computer share of capital stock or the computer share of investment. In the second step their estimation results indicate that both outsourcing and capital upgrading contribute to a rise in wage inequality in the USA. Which structural factors are more influential depends to a great extent on how these variables are measured. In general, however, they find that outsourcing accounts for 10-25 % of the increase in the relative wage of nonproduction workers.[17]

The same two-stage estimation method is used by Haskel and Slaughter (2001) for U.K. manufacturing industries between 1960 and 1990. Their structural variables include union density (the share of union workers in industry employment), industry concentration (share of sales by the five largest firms), innovations per industry, import prices, and computerization (share of firms in the industry using computers). They find that industry innovation is the structural variable that contributes most to the increase in the skilled-unskilled wage gap.

3.3 New Trade Theory

An important departure from earlier trade models is incorporated into the New Trade Theory by allowing for increasing returns to scale.[18] Through increasing returns to scale firms have the incentive to expand their output. The expansion by some firms will eventually force other firms to exit the market, causing the number of firms in the market to decline. Therefore a monopolistic competition model is the best suited for this analysis.

3.3.1 The Monopolistic Competition Model

In a monopolistic competition market there is a decent number of firms, each producing a variety of differentiated goods, and there is freedom to enter or

---

[16] For further interpretation see also Feenstra (2004).

[17] Within this context one might also deal with the role of non-traded goods and services for inter-industry wage differentials. For some recent works on this, mainly on the USA, see Harrigan and Balaban (1999), Harrigan (2000), or Kumar (2000).

[18] The following description of the New Trade Theory models is based on Feenstra (2004, Chapter 5).

to exit the market. The most widely used model of this type was developed by Lancester (1975, 1979) as well as by Dixit and Stiglitz (1977). In the Lancester model, consumers differ in their ideal variety, in the Dixit and Stiglitz model there is just a single representative consumer who demands a variety of goods. Helpman and Krugman (1985) apply these models to trade, showing that the two types basically deliver the same results. The most prominent New Trade Theory model is the "Love of variety" model by Krugman (1979), which will now be presented.

Let's assume we have different products $j = 1, ...N$, where N is endogenous. The utility function U, which is dependent on consumption c_j of a fixed number of consumers L is described by:

$$U = \sum_{j=1}^{N} v(c_j) \tag{3.35}$$

We assume that the first derivation of the utility function is positive, the second is negative; thus we deal with an increasing and concave function. The budget constraint of each consumer while maximizing utility is given by their labor income w, which restricts their maximum consumption expenditure in a way that:

$$w = \sum_{j=1}^{N} p_j c_j \tag{3.36}$$

where p denotes prices. The first order condition when maximizing utility subject to the budget constraint is:

$$\frac{\partial v}{\partial c_j} = v'(c_j) = \lambda p_j \tag{3.37}$$

where λ denotes the Lagrange multiplier. Total differentiation of the first order condition together with the budget constraint shows the effect of a change in price on consumption. Assuming that the number of goods is large enough, so that the share of each in the budget is very small, one can ignore the impact of one good's price change on the Lagrange multiplier. Thus for a change in price on consumption we get:

$$v''(c_j) = dp_j \lambda \Rightarrow \frac{dc_j}{dp_j} = \frac{\lambda}{v''} < 0 \tag{3.38}$$

Combining the last two equations we can calculate the elasticity of demand for good j, which is given by:

$$\eta_j = -\frac{dc_j}{dp_j} \frac{p_j}{c_j} = -\frac{v'}{c_j v''} > 0 \tag{3.39}$$

Due to the assumption that the utility function is increasing and concave, we know that the price elasticity of demand is positive. However, it is not clear whether it is increasing or decreasing in c_j. Since this will turn out to be important, for the moment we assume that $d\eta_j/dc_j < 0$, which implicates that moving up the demand curve, that is equivalent to falling consumption, elasticity rises.

Turning to the production side, we assume that each firm producing output y_i uses only one input factor, namely labor. In the following equation we define how much labor is needed to produce the output:

$$L_j = \alpha + \beta y_j \tag{3.40}$$

where α denotes the fixed labor input, whereas β the marginal labor input, with equilibrium wage w, average costs AC_j and marginal costs MC_j given by:

$$AC_j = \frac{wL_j}{y_j} = \frac{w\alpha_j}{y_j} + w\beta \tag{3.41}$$

$$MC_j = w\beta \tag{3.42}$$

It is obvious that marginal costs are not dependent on y_j, whereas average costs decline with rising output y_j.

In equilibrium in a monopolistic competition model, firms maximize their profit, which requires that marginal costs be equal to marginal revenue ($MC = MR$). Furthermore there is free entry into the market as long as economic profits exceed zero, therefore we have zero profits in the long-term equilibrium. It thus holds that prices equal average costs in equilibrium ($P = AC$). Assuming that prices and quantities are identical across the varieties j, we can drop this subscript. Thus the equilibrium condition is given by the following two equations:

$$MR = MC \Rightarrow p\left(1 - \frac{1}{\eta}\right) = w\beta \Rightarrow \frac{p}{w} = \beta\left(\frac{\eta}{\eta - 1}\right) \tag{3.43}$$

$$P = AC \Rightarrow p = \left(\frac{w\alpha}{y}\right) + w\beta \Rightarrow \frac{p}{w} = \left(\frac{\alpha}{Lc}\right) + \beta \tag{3.44}$$

where in the last equation supply of goods y is replaced by demand for goods Lc. These two equilibrium equations are used to solve for the two unknown parameters (p/w) and c. The results are demonstrated graphically in figure 3.4.

The first equilibrium equation is represented by the P line. The previously made assumption that the first derivation of the price elasticity of demand function is negative ($d\eta_j/dc_j < 0$) ensures that the P line is upward sloping. The second equilibrium condition is represented in the downward sloping Z line, which is the average cost curve. The intercept of the two determines the equilibrium values $(p/w)_0$ and c_0. Using the equilibrium value of consumption, one can calculate the equilibrium number of goods N, assuming full employment in the economy:

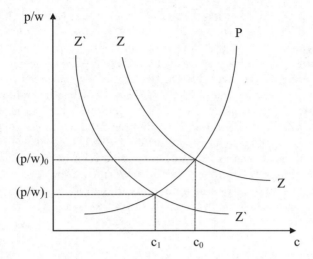

Source: Feenstra 2004, p: 140

Fig. 3.4. Equilibrium in the Monopolistic Competition Model

$$L = \sum_{j=1}^{N} L_j = \sum_{j=1}^{N} (\alpha + \beta y_j) = N(\alpha + \beta y) = N(\alpha + \beta L c) \qquad (3.45)$$

Solving for the N determines the equilibrium number of goods, which is given by:

$$N = \frac{1}{(\alpha/L) + \beta c} \qquad (3.46)$$

Such an equilibrium is valid for a single economy. Yet what happens in the monopolistic model if we introduce more countries, thus introducing trade? Let's suppose we have two countries very similar in terms of size, which move from autarky to foreign trade. According to traditional trade theory models such as the Heckscher-Ohlin model, they do not have an incentive to trade with each other. This is different in the monopolistic competition model, where firms produce differentiated goods and consumers have a love for variety. This is a motivation for mutual trade. The implications for the theoretical model are the following. Having two countries of the identical size doubles labor L. The first equilibrium equation is not affected by that, so that the P curve does not change in figure 3.4. Since L is found in the denominator of the second equilibrium equation, the Z curve shifts down to Z'. This results in a lower equilibrium consumption c_1, and a lower $(p/w)_1$ ratio. The latter can be interpreted a rise in the real wage $(w/p)_0$ to $(w/p)_1$. Equilibrium consumption declines because consumers can spend their income on a higher variety of goods, which raises the elasticity of demand, reducing equilibrium prices and raising real wages. Thus consumers gain from the shift from autarky to free trade. Also a rise in the total number of varieties N brings about additional gain. At the same time, the number of varieties in each country falls when we introduce free trade, as *(p/w)* falls when firms move down their average cost curves causing output y to increase. Any firm that produces both under autarky and free trade will thus produce more under free trade. However, the full employment condition is fixed for each country, so a rise in the output must mean exploitation of economies of scale, and at the same time a reduction in the number of firms in each country. In summary, opening up trade between countries in monopolistic competition models results in a decline in the number of firms on the market, while the remaining firms' output increases, exploiting economies of scale.

3.3.2 Gravity Models

In the monopolistic competition model described above, each country produces and exports a set of differentiated goods. With free trade it is assumed that firms can costlessly change their set of varieties, so that profit maximizing firms will produce different set of varieties. Therefore countries will be specialized on different sets of varieties. Trading these different sets of varieties of differentiated products characterizes intra-industry trade patterns. Trade within industries with differentiated products cannot be explained by traditional models such as the Ricardo or the Heckscher-Ohlin model, because they assume differences to be the main driving force for trade. Trade with different product varieties across countries as described by monopolistic competition models can well be estimated by so-called gravity equations. One of the very first and simplest gravity equations was developed by Tinbergen (1962). He simply related bilateral trade volumes directly to the product of the two countries' GDP. It turns out that larger countries, and countries with a similar size trade more with each other.

For the time being we assume that there are no barriers to trade, demand is identical and that countries are specialized in different varieties of final products. Furthermore we assume that all countries have identical prices. Accordingly, a good produced in any country will be sent to the rest of the world in proportion to the country's GDP which purchases the good. With countries $i, c = 1, ...C$ and goods $j = 1, ...N$, we denote y_j^i the production of good j in country i. With identical prices across countries we can normalize prices to unity, thus y_j^i also measures the value of production. Total GDP of a country is measured by $Y^i = \sum_{j=1}^{N} y_j^i$, and world GDP is the sum of national GDPs measured by $Y^w = \sum_{i=1}^{C} y^i$. We additionally denote the share of country c in world expenditure by s^c. If trade is balanced in each country, this share also denotes the country's share in world GDP, thus $s^c = Y^c/Y^w$. Therefore we can describe the exports E of country i to country c in product j by:

$$X_j^{ic} = s^c y_j^i \tag{3.47}$$

If we consider all products and sum up we get:

$$X^{ic} = \sum_j X_j^{ic} = s^c \sum_j y_j^i = s^c Y^i = \frac{Y^c Y^c}{Y^w} = X^{ci} \tag{3.48}$$

We obtain any bilateral trade volume by summing up X^{ic} and X^{ci}. This equals

$$X^{ic} + X^{ci} = \left(\frac{2}{Y^w}\right) Y^i Y^c \tag{3.49}$$

This is the simplest gravity equation, where bilateral trade volumes are proportional to the product of their GDPs.

3.3.3 Empirical Evidence on Gravity Models

In most empirical estimations of the gravity models, the assumption of cost-less trade is released, because it is not realistic. Costs of trade comprise simply transportation costs, but also different kinds of trade barriers. The most common way to model trade costs is to include the bilateral distance of countries into the regression. There is a very wide range of literature which estimates gravity equations of the following type:

$$ln X^{ic} = \alpha + \beta_1 ln Y^i + \beta_2 ln Y^c + \gamma ln d^{ic} + \epsilon_{ic} \tag{3.50}$$

where d^{ic} denotes the bilateral distance between countries i and c. Usually one takes the distance between the capitals. The expected sign of the two β coefficients is clearly positive, since a rise in the exporting country's GDP increases exports, as does a rise in the importing country's GDP. At the same time the coefficient for the distance parameter γ is expected to show a negative sign indicating that trade is more expensive the further away two countries are situated from each other.

There are several papers in the economic literature which run a gravity equation for explaining trade patterns or trade integration in the enlarged European Union or parts of it (Fidrmuc, 1998; Jakab et al., 2001; Djankov and Hoekman, 1997; Micco et al., 2003; Serlenga and Shin, 2004). However, most of the existing literature runs the analysis on an aggregated level. One of the most recent studies by Marques and Metcalf (2005) uses a sectoral gravity equation in order to explain the determinants of sectoral trade in the enlarged EU. They use a panel of European countries separated into three group of countries: (1) EU-North, a high income group, (2) EU-South, a low income group, and (3) EU-East, also low income countries. The authors estimate bilateral trade flows between these three groups of countries, also taking into account different skilled/unskilled labor ratios and different spatial and non-spatial trade costs in selected manufacturing sectors with different degrees of economies of scale and skill-intensity. The sectors considered are allocated into four groups:

1. High scale economies and high skill intensity: Chemicals, Machinery and Transport Equipment
2. High scale economies and low skill intensity: Metals
3. Low scale economies and low skill intensity: Leather and Footwear, Minerals, Textiles and Clothing
4. Low scale economies and high skill intensity: Wood products

Different locational and endowment advantages are expected to influence the location of sectors with different scale economies and different skill intensities, thus determining the sectoral exports and imports of each country group. The gravity equation is set up to test the two main hypotheses behind the gravity model. Firstly, the volume of trade is positively related to the market size of the trading partners and is negatively related to the physical distance between them. Secondly, the volume of trade is dependent on country wealth, as measured by GDP per capita. The second hypothesis is based on Linder (1961), who highlighted that high-income countries tend to be consumers of high-quality goods, and low-income countries of low-quality goods. The export and import structures of countries should therefore adjust in a way that quality content of foreign trade should increase with rising GDP per capita (GDPPC).

Market size is proxied by population figures (POP). The share of skilled/unskilled labor ratio as an indicator for the human capital endowment of a country is proxied by the share of the country's population with tertiary education (HC). Furthermore, spatial trade barriers include the bilateral distance between trading partners (DIST), and a common border dummy variable (BORDER). Non-spatial trade costs include a time dummy variable for the Eurozone membership (EURO) and the enforcement of the European Agreements (EA) in terms of trade liberalization in Eastern Europe since the beginning of the 1990s. The benchmark gravity equation for trade (TRADE) in sector j between country i and country c is thus as follows:

$$TRADE_j^{ic} = \alpha + \beta_1 POP^i + \beta_2 POP^c + \beta_3 GDPPC^i + \beta_4 GDPPC^c$$
$$+\beta_5 HC^i + \beta_6 HC^c + \beta_7 DIST^{ic} + \beta_8 BORDER^{ic}$$
$$+\beta_9 EA^{ic} + \beta_{10} EURO^{ic} + u_j^{ic} \qquad (3.51)$$

Three alternative specifications of the basic model are estimated by Marques and Metcalf (2005). In the first one, they multiply (1) per capita GDP and (2) the distance variable with the human capital variable and use these product as explanatory variables. The former product crosses demand with supply factors; the latter proxies for knowledge spillover. The reason is that distance is expected to have an impact on the dissemination of information in some sectors, which might cause industrial clustering in some manufacturing branches. At the same time, there is no a priori expectation as to what extent skilled labor would benefit from industrial clustering. In a second modification the GDP per capita and the human capital variables of each country will be replaced by the absolute value of differences between the trading partners. Thus these new variables measure the economic distance on human capital endowment and on trade. One can interpret the latter as a test on intra- versus inter-industry trade. Following the New Trade Theory literature, trade between countries with similar demand structures will mainly be characterized as intra-industry type of trade. Accordingly, if economic distance causes trade to decrease, we are in the world of intra-industry trade. If economic distance causes trade to rise, we face inter-industry trade patterns. The human capital variable can be interpreted as a test on traditional types of trade theories, such as the Heckscher-Ohlin Model, expecting that countries relatively abundant in human capital will be net exporters of skill intensive goods. In a third alternative specification the two variables economic distance and human capital distance are considered interacted as an explanatory variable. The main results of Marques and Metcalf (2005) can be summarized as follows.

- Market size has a positive impact on trade. Home market effects are especially relevant for sectors with high economies of scale.
- Income effects play a role, because richer countries tend to trade higher values of exports and imports. Unit values of traded goods tend to increase with the income of the trading partners. This is especially relevant for high skill intensive sectors, and hardly relevant for low scale economies and low skill intensive sectors.
- Endowment with human capital is important for high skill intensity sectors. Concerning bilateral trade patterns, the authors finds that Eastern European human capital endowments increase imports from Southern European countries, but Southern human capital endowments decrease Southern exports to the North. This implies that South-North trade is based on the absence of human capital endowments in the South, which is not the case for East-North trade.
- The interaction of income levels and endowments is important, while endowments alone do not perform very well. This indicates that low-income countries could face difficulties when trying to turn their potential comparative advantages into effective comparative advantages. At the same time, it seems that Eastern European countries' specialization in low skill intensity sectors seems to have been driven by low income levels and not by endowments. Therefore one can expect the importance of endowments to rise when income starts rising.
- The Europe Agreements have been especially beneficial for high scale economies, hardly affecting East-South trade. Being a member of the Eurozone does not directly affect trade among these countries.

- Some evidence is found for border effects, which states that bordering countries trade more with each other. However, Davis (2000) shows that product differentiation tends to reduce border effects. Thus border effects are the strongest when trade with homogenous goods is involved.
- The distance variables are in general negative, indicating that trade tends to decrease with distance, because distance increases trade costs. These costs play a role especially in South-East trade, which is characterized as trade among peripheries.

As indicated in the theoretical description of gravity models, one expects the sign of the distance parameter - the core gravity parameter - to be significantly negative. However, in an increasingly knowledge based economy, where the distribution of information proceeds more and more electronically, distance might not play such an important role any more.[19] There is a strand of literature, which explains the "death of distance", however, this is sector dependent as shown by Venables (2001). Among other things, the "death of distance" gave rise to other explanations of trade between countries, focusing more on spatial and regional patterns.

3.4 New Economic Geography

Since the beginning of the 1990s, regional economists have increasingly been working on explaining the building of different types of economic agglomeration concentration within a geographical space (Fujita and Krugman, 2004). These type of models have established themselves in the literature as New Economic Geography (NEG). Agglomeration can take place at different geographical levels, such as clustering of small shops, restaurants or enterprises, or clustering of bigger industrial areas. Thus regional activity can be spread across a country rather unevenly. Furthermore you can observe central and peripheral economic structures both on the national and the international level.

3.4.1 The NEG Models

One main focus of NEG is on modelling increasing returns to scale in connection with spatial concentration. One wants to know how and when a change in the returns to scale leads to a change in the geographical distribution of economic activity. More specifically, general equilibrium models have been developed to show the effects of centripetal and centrifugal forces simultaneously. Centripetal forces pull together economic activity to one location, whereas centrifugal forces push them apart. NEG models should explain how

---

[19] For a new interpretation of the distance coefficient in gravity models see Buch et. al, 2004.

a geographic structure of an economic location emerges due to these two opposite forces. The outcome is strongly dependent on fundamental decisions of economic actors on the microeconomic level.

These microeconomic decisions are strongly influenced by returns to scale. Increasing returns to scale and transportation costs are some of the core characteristics of NEG models. Furthermore, imperfect competition is assumed, which is due to other "invisible" forces which do not allow for perfect competition. However, embedding imperfect competition into general equilibrium models is rather challenging.

In their book "The Spatial Economy" (Fujita, Krugman and Venables, 1999), the authors explain the NEG world with the following slogan: "Dixit-Stiglitz, icebergs, evolution and computer". This refers to the main intellectual elements, which researchers have used to overcome the technical problems when dealing with NEG models. More specifically it explains the strategic ways to ease the NEG models. The slogan will be explained below.

"Dixit-Stiglitz" refers to the work of Avinash Dixit and Joseph Stiglitz (1977). They have already emphasized the existence of monopolistic competition within the framework of (product-) innovations. Thus firms have market power, which they use without breaking the simple rules of the supply-demand principle. Firms with monopolistic power act unilaterally, so there are no cartels or secret common price setting. Firms have monopolistic power of either just one product or in just one region; other firms can only offer imperfect substitutes. With these assumptions one can describe an economy with increasing returns to scale.

"Iceberg" refers to the model of Paul Samuelson of (1952) with transportation costs. It is one of the few traditional models considering transportation costs. The idea is rather simple: goods can be shipped for free, however, transportation costs imply that a part of the goods gets lost on the way, similarly to an iceberg being transported, where a part of it simply melts on the road.

"Evolution" refers to the fact that locational decisions are mainly taken on the basis of current conditions (historically emerged). This implies that the geography of an economy evolves in a way that reflects history and coincidence.

"Computer" refers to the tendency of the NEG to use high-technology numerical simulations. Ultimately the status quo of the NEG has been strongly dependent on the development of powerful computers.

Answering the question on the spatial distribution of economic activity, NEG models are based on the model framework developed by Krugman (1991a). Through the interaction of producers and consumers, externalities - centrifugal and centripetal forces - emerge. As a result we observe a core-periphery-equilibrium, where economic activity is symmetrically distributed within the geographical space. Two main research areas have developed within the NEG. One builds directly on the standard model by Krugman (1991a) and assumes existing concentration forces to emerge from consumers' preferences for variety. In addition, labor mobility is assumed. The other area builds on

Krugman and Venables (1995) and assumes that locational dynamics emerge from producers' preferences for variety. In addition, labor immobility is assumed. However, both research areas conclude that there is a symmetric equilibrium for high transportation costs, where economic activity is equally distributed among the regions. For low transportation costs, on the contrary, there is a core-periphery-equilibrium, where economic activity is fully concentrated within one region. For medium high transportation costs, multiple equilibria emerge.

Both models can be encompassed by taking Puga (1999) as the starting point. The basics of the model will subsequently be presented.[20]

Demand

We assume an economy with two sectors, one is a numeraire (H) such as agriculture, the other is manufacturing (M). All consumers have Cobb-Douglas type of preferences for both commodities:

$$U = M^\delta H^{(1-\delta)} \tag{3.52}$$

The parameter δ $(0 < \delta < 1)$ indicates the share in income spent on the manufactured good. M is a CES utility function of the following type:

$$M = \left(\sum_{j=1}^{n} c_j^\rho\right)^{1/\rho} \tag{3.53}$$

where j is the number of goods, c stands for demand, and ρ indicates the elasticity of substitution ε such that $\varepsilon = \frac{1}{1-\rho}$.

We maximize the utility function with respect to the income constraint:

$$c_v = p_v^{-\varepsilon} I^{\varepsilon-1} \delta E \tag{3.54}$$

where the share of income spent on manufacturing goods, δE, multiplied by the prices (where I is the price index for manufactures, $I = [\sum_v (p_v)^{(1-\varepsilon)}]^{1/(1-\varepsilon)}$) gives the demand for each variety v. Furthermore it is assumed that firms also demand varieties of M as intermediate inputs. If the elasticity of substitution is the same for producers and consumers, we can use the same CES function and the same price index I for both consumers and producers. Thus total demand for variety v is given by:

$$c_v = p_v^{-\varepsilon} I^{\varepsilon-1} Y \tag{3.55}$$

where Y is given by $Y = \delta E + \mu X$, and represents the sum of the share of income E of consumers spent on all M varieties, and of the share of intermediates in the production process of the value of all varieties in a region, X.

---

[20] The description of the following model is based on Brakman, Garretsen and Schramm (2004).

Manufacturing Supply

Manufacturing supply for each variety v is produced by the following cost function:

$$C(x_v) = I^\mu W_v^{(1-\mu)}(\alpha + \beta x_v) \qquad (3.56)$$

where I is the already known price index for the intermediate inputs, W corresponds to factor costs for labor (wages), and α and β stand for fixed and marginal input requirements per variety respectively.

Profit maximization results in a mark-up pricing rule given by:

$$p_v\left(1 - \frac{1}{\varepsilon}\right) = I^\mu W^{(1-\mu)}\beta \qquad (3.57)$$

where the marginal input requirement given by β consists of two elements: intermediates and labor. The zero profit condition is given by $p_v x_v = C(x_v)$; combined with the mark-up pricing rule, it provides the break-even supply of any variety v:

$$x_v = \frac{\alpha(\epsilon - 1)}{\beta} \qquad (3.58)$$

Equilibrium

In the following we will derive the equilibrium conditions for a two region model with iceberg type transportation costs, $T_{1,2}$. $T_{1,2} > 1$ meaning that more than one unit of manufactured goods must be shipped away from region 1, if one unit ought to arrive in region 2. These iceberg transportation costs are paid by the consumers and the firms of region 2 as import costs. Therefore total demand for a variety produced in region 1 is given by:

$$x_1 = Y_1 p_1^{-\varepsilon} I_1^{\varepsilon-1} + Y_2 p_1^{-\varepsilon}(T_{1,2})^{-\varepsilon} I_2^{\varepsilon-1} \qquad (3.59)$$

When looking for an equilibrium, total demand should be equal to the break-even supply. However, doing this, demand from region 2 should be multiplied by the transportation costs in order to compensate for the part that melts away during transportation. This gives the following equation:

$$\frac{\alpha(\epsilon - 1)}{\beta} = Y_1 p_1^{-\varepsilon} I_1^{\varepsilon-1} + Y_2 p_1^{-\varepsilon}(T_{1,2})^{1-\varepsilon} I_2^{\varepsilon-1} \qquad (3.60)$$

In order to get the two-region version of the wage equation in the presence of intermediate demand for varieties, which is also known as the *vertical linkages model* of the New Economic Geography, one should insert the mark-up pricing rule in the last equation and solve for the wage rate. It is advisable to solve for the wage rate instead of for prices, because labor migration is determined - among other influences - by wages, and from an empirical point of view it is easier to obtain data for regional wages than for regional prices. The equilibrium wage equation for any region $n = 1, ..., r$ is given by:

$$W_r = CONST(I_r)^{-\mu/(1-\mu)}[\sum_s Y_s I_s^{\varepsilon-1} T_{r,s}^{(1-\varepsilon)}]^{1/\varepsilon(1-\mu)} \qquad (3.61)$$

where $CONST$ is a function of fixed model parameters, and r and s denote regions. W is the wage rate, I is the price index for manufactured goods, μ is the share of intermediate inputs, Y is demand for final consumption plus intermediate inputs, ε is the elasticity of substitution for manufactured goods, and T are iceberg type transportation costs.

Note that equation 3.61 presents the short-run equilibrium wage, because only in the short-run are the spatial distribution of firms and labor fixed. Thus in the short run we have immobility of labor, and the degree of agglomeration is exogenously fixed. Only in the long-run is the spatial distribution of economic activity endogenous, because both footloose firms and labor are mobile.

The sum in equation 3.61 implies that regional wages are higher where there is access to high-wage regions, which means that high-wage regions are close by. According to Redding and Venables (2003), this is called the *nominal market access*. The inclusion of the price index I into the wage equation implies that we are also dealing with *real market access*. A low price index shows that a great variety is produced in the nearby regions, thus a low price index decreases regional wages. This is not the case for the gravity equations of the New Trade Theory, where usually only nominal market access matters. Finally, a third effect can be identified in equation 3.61, namely the *supplier access* - see also Redding and Venables (2003). It is expressed by the term $I^{-\mu/(1-\mu)}$. If the price index is low, agglomeration is strengthened due to the fact that firms supplying intermediate inputs are rather close to the location of production. The better the supplier access, the lower the wages. In addition, the larger the share of intermediate inputs, the larger the supplier access effect.

However, to learn more about the relationship between spatial distribution of economic activity and economic integration, we must also get involved with the long-run perspective, where agglomeration is endogenous. Within the long-run perspective we have to differentiate between two scenarios: (1) interregional labor mobility or (2) no interregional labor mobility.

The Tomahawk: Interregional Labor Mobility

Based on Puga (1999), NEG models with interregional labor mobility predict that economic integration will ultimately lead to a complete agglomeration of footloose agents. Assume we have two regions and two industries as before, agriculture (H) and manufacturing (M). The first industry is characterized by perfect competition producing with constant returns to scale, and its output can freely be traded between the two regions. The other industry is characterized by monopolistic competition producing with increasing returns to scale, and its output can be traded between the two regions facing Iceberg type transportation costs. The allocation of labor in the second industry among the two regions is illustrated by figure 3.5.

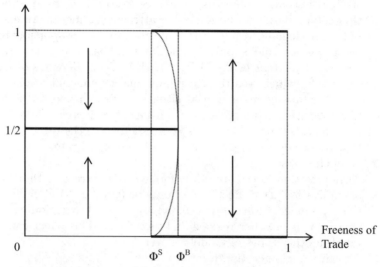

Source: Brakman et al. 2004, p: 9

Fig. 3.5. The Tomahawk Figure

It shows the connection between the degree of agglomeration (y-axis) and the degree of free trade (x-axis), where $\Phi = 0$ indicates autarky and $\Phi = 1$ free trade. The y-axis shows the share of labor distributed to either region. The bold lines display the possible long-run equilibria for the monopolistic competition industries in the two regions. The arrows point towards the long-run equilibria. Accordingly, with very high transportation costs - meaning a low degree of free trade or autarky ($\Phi < \Phi^S$) - we see an equal distribution of labor among the regions, indicated by the horizontal line at 1/2. For much lower transportation costs, meaning a higher degree of free trade ($\Phi > \Phi^B$), agglomeration of labor in either of the two regions turns out to be the equilibrium. For intermediate transportation costs ($\Phi^S < \Phi < \Phi^B$), both dispersion and agglomeration are possible long-run equilibria. Fujita et al. (1999) named two points Φ^S and Φ^B sustain and break point. Starting with high transportation costs and decreasing them gradually, one eventually passes point Φ^S, beyond which agglomeration can be sustained as long-term equilibrium. Decreasing transportation costs even further, one eventually passes point Φ^B, beyond which dispersion is broken as long-term equilibrium.

Figure 3.5 also displays the seven main characteristics of the NEG models as described by Baldwin et al. (2003).

1. Home Market Magnification

   The well known "home market effect" has been identified by Helpman and Krugman (1985). It describes the net effect of a market enlargement by stating that large countries tend to be exporters of goods due to the fact that ceteris paribus a large market attracts producers. An exogenous rise in foreign demand results ceteris paribus in a disproportionate expansion of production and supply in the large domestic country. In the NEG-context the extent of the "home market effect" depends of the degree of free trade, which was termed "home market magnification" by Baldwin (2000). Starting in an initial situation with dispersion, a reduction of transportation costs gives firms an incentive to relocate to regions with large markets, whereas this is contradictory to the often expected result that free trade reduces incentives of firms to migrate.

2. Circular Causality

   Agglomeration forces are self-enforcing. In contrast to the "home market magnification" this effect cannot only be found in NEG models. With spatially bounded externalities the enlargement of a region can lead to the enlargement of other regions and vice versa. This effect can be incorporated in other types of models as well.

3. Concave Agglomeration Rent

   The connection between the degree of free trade and agglomeration rents can be described with a hump-shaped, concave curve. Using agglomeration as a starting point in a region, agglomeration rents for low degrees of freedom ($\Phi < \Phi^S$) are negative. In point Φ^S the rents equal zero. Beyond the sustain point Φ^S, agglomeration rents rise to a certain maximum. Beyond that point, rents start to decline when transportation costs keep on falling, until they reach zero at $\Phi = 1$.

4. Endogenous Asymmetries

   The circular causality effect is crucial for the existence of endogenous asymmetries. Starting with dispersion as the long-run equilibrium and gradually decreasing transportation costs, one ultimately ends up in an asymmetric equilibrium among regions. Beyond point Φ^B, symmetric dispersion is not an equilibrium any more, thus firms will concentrate in either of the regions. This implicates that spatial asymmetries can occur as long-run equilibria, irrespective of the natural conditions in the regions. To put it differently, initially similar regions can develop very diversely.

5. Catastrophic Agglomeration

   The accumulation of economic activity is called in a slightly theatrical manner "catastrophic" agglomeration. This refers to agglomeration as a long-term equilibrium, which occurs when the degree of free trade is relatively high and transportation costs are relatively low. It makes allowance for the fact that the way endogenous asymmetry occurs is highly unstable.

Starting at point $\Phi = 0$ in figure 3.5 and gradually reducing transportation costs, the spatial distribution of economic activity is unaffected as long as point Φ^B is not surpassed. Beyond Φ^B, however, the smallest increase in Φ will yield a "catastrophic" agglomeration as the only long-run equilibrium.

6. Spatial Hysteresis

   Spatial hysteresis is of importance when multiple equilibria are possible; this is valid for example for $\Phi > \Phi^S$. In such cases past events play an important role. Assuming $\Phi > \Phi^B > \Phi^S$, figure 3.5 shows by means of the arrows the direction towards a long-run equilibrium indicating that all firms will settle down in either of the two regions. The crucial factor hereby is that even a temporary shock can trigger agglomeration. When the temporary shock is over, agglomeration will not regress, thus agglomeration remains. Temporary shocks have a permanent impact.

7. Overlap and Self-enforcing Expectations

   This characteristics is relevant in the interval where both dispersion and agglomeration are possible equilibria. This is valid in the overlap interval of $\Phi^S < \Phi < \Phi^B$. A changeover from dispersion to agglomeration can be triggered here by a shock in expectations. Agglomeration rents are self-enforcing, therefore firms might agglomerate in only one of the regions, because this is the general expectation. In the presence of circular causality, the expectations of firms to settle in either of the regions pays off and is therefore self-enforcing.

But how relevant is the Towahawk figure in the case of EU integration? Since labor mobility is restricted for the new member states for the first seven years of EU membership, the other type of model which assumes no interregional labor mobility might be more relevant for Europe at least until the year 2011.

The Bell-Shaped Curve: No Interregional Labor Mobility

The assumption of no interregional labor mobility reflects the fact that labor is more mobile within regions and countries then across borders. The absence of interregional labor mobility still allows agglomeration if one considers intermediate goods. The main idea is that firms prefer to be near to their suppliers, therefore they have an incentive to agglomerate. The labor required for agglomeration comes from the immobile sector H. Firms wishing to agglomerate will offer higher wages for labor in the monopolistically competitive industry M than in industry H with constant returns to scale, and thus pull labor from agriculture into manufacturing. Agglomeration in this second type of model is associated with wage differential between the regions, which was not the case in the tomahawk world. Agglomeration drives up wages in the core region, but this ultimately reduces the incentives of firms in the manufacturing industries to concentrate production for at least two reasons: (1) the importance of agglomeration decreases as transportation costs decrease due to increased economic integration, and (2) the peripheral regions become more attractive due to lower wages. The long-run relationship between agglomeration and free trade in the absence of interregional labor mobility is shown in the Bell-shaped curved in figure 3.6. The name of the figure comes from Head and Mayer (2003).

Degree of Agglomeration

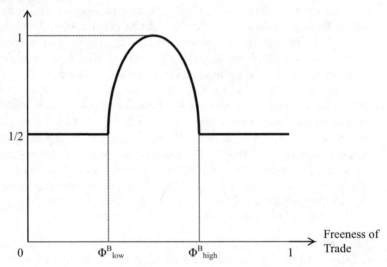

Source: Brakman et al. 2004, p: 12

Fig. 3.6. The Bell-Shaped Curve

The axes are the same as in the tomahawk figure. However, we now have two breaking points, Φ_{low}^{B} and Φ_{high}^{B}. For low degrees of free trade ($\Phi^{B} < \Phi_{low}^{B}$), we find dispersion as the long-term equilibrium. Again, as trade costs gradually decrease and we surpass point Φ_{low}^{B}, agglomeration starts. However, there is a great difference here to the previous results. Here, agglomeration goes along with interregional wage differences. In that sense, if transportation costs keep on falling the second break point Φ_{high}^{B} is reached, beyond which we find re-newed spreading; no agglomeration is left, because interregional wages will now again be equalized. This is due to the fact that both regions will have the same number of manufacturing firms, and the size of the two manufacturing industries will also be the same.

Note that the difference between the two types of NEG models can only be found in the long-run. In the short run the equilibria in the two types of models are the same. In the long-run we have the tomahawk kind of equilibrium with interregional labor mobility, and the bell-shaped kind of equilibrium with no interregional labor mobility.

To summarize, we can say that spatial economic structure as a consequence of economic integration depends in the New Economic Geography world on the parameter constellation of scale economies and especially of trade costs, including both transportation costs and any other trade barriers such as tariffs. If trade costs are very high, spatial structure is stable, and regional production structures are fostered. If trade costs are intermediate, agglomeration through internalization of scale economies is a possible outcome, thus we get a center-periphery type structure. If trade costs are very low, competition is rather intense in the center region, therefore incentives for reallocating production into the periphery are strong, dismantling the center-periphery economic structure.

3.4.2 Empirical Evidence on the New Economic Geography

Since the development of the NEG models is rather new, direct empirical application drawn from NEG models is hard to find in the economic literature. Most analysis use variables connected to the spirit of NEG models rather indirectly, instead of directly estimating equations drawn from them.

Some of the rather direct implications include Midelfart et al. (2003), Head and Mayer (2003), Crozet (2004), and Bruelhart et al. (2004). Brakman, Garretsen and Schramm (2004) make an effort to estimate the short-run equilibrium wage equation 3.61 for NUTS II European regions. However, since sufficient regional price index data is not available, they express the regional price index as an average of the regional wage. At the same time regional wages may differ across Europe for reasons that have nothing to do with the demand and cost linkages from the NEG literature. Therefore they allow for labor productivity to differ across the EU regions, because human capital externalities or technological externalities might give rise to a spatial wage structure. Furthermore they address the issues that physical geography (e.g. access to waterways or climate) as well as the political geography (such as borders or institutions) might also influence regional wages. By estimating an accordingly modified version of the short-run equilibrium wage equation including a parameter for distance as a measure of trade costs, they find that the coefficient for the substitution elasticity is relatively high, indicating relative weak economies of scale. At the same time the estimates for the distance coefficient indicate that transport costs increase less than proportionally with distance.[21]

In a next step, they confront the short-term estimation results with theoretical insights with respect to the relationship between agglomeration and economic integration. This implies adopting a long-run view as expressed by

---

[21] See Brakman, Garretsen and Schramm (2004) for further details on the estimation.

the tomahawk and the bell-shaped figures. In order to get some estimates for the critical values of Φ, the authors need to use benchmark values for the key model parameters other than the substitution elasticity and the distance parameter, which have already been estimated.[22] Their findings can be summarized as follows:

- If the importance of intermediate inputs increases, the incentives of firms to agglomerate rise due to benefits from lower intermediate costs and demand linkages.
- If the elasticity of labor increases, the incentives to agglomerate are reduced, because even relatively low manufacturing wages can persuade workers to move to the manufacturing sector.
- An increase in the share of manufacturing goods will benefit agglomeration, since the relevance of demand linkages increases.
- A decline in the value of substitution elasticity of economies of scale will foster agglomeration, because the importance of firm-specific increasing returns to scale rises.

It is important to note that the values for the breaking points of Φ vary with the parameter settings of the model and seem to be rather sensitive. Comparing the worlds with and without interregional labor mobility, the authors find that the agglomeration range is smaller in the bell-shaped world without labor mobility. They also find that dispersion becomes unstable for low values of Φ. This indicates that economic integration fosters agglomeration more quickly in the NEG world without interregional labor mobility than with interregional labor mobility. From the authors' point of view, one of the most important results imply that

> ...the agglomeration does not extend further than 1-4 times the internal distance of a region. To see this, note that the average internal distance for the NUTSII regions is 42 km. This implies that from the perspective of region r the "critical" or threshold external distance D_{rs} for the model underlying the bell-shaped curve are 87.3 km for Φ_{low}^B and 44.9 for Φ_{high}^B. This means that for any actual $D_{rs} > 87.3$ km we are in (the bell-shaped) figure ... to the left of the first break-point where spreading rules. Along similar lines, it is only when the actual $D_{rs} < 44.9$ km that spreading rules again. In between, that is for 44.9 km $< D_{rs} < 87.3$ km, we are on the part of (the bell shaped) figure ... with (partial) agglomeration. For the Tomahawk ... the threshold external distance $D_{rs} = 161km$. Here, the range of radius of agglomeration forces is thus somewhat stronger but still limited if one considers the fact that the distance between any pair of economic centres for the case of the EU NUTSII regions is often much larger than 161 km. (Brakman et al. (2004) p: 20-21.)

---

[22] For a detailed explanation of the methodology see Brakman et al. (2004).

Put in a nutshell, the main conclusion is that the authors find rather limited spatial reach of agglomeration forces in most of the NUTSII regions of the European Union. This means that agglomeration seems to play a more important role at lower geographical scales. However, a shortcoming of the analysis is that both the Tomahawk and the Bell-shaped figures are only valid for two regions. In the NEG world, no analytic solution yet exists for the break-points in the case of more than two regions.

This might be one of the reasons why various authors use rather the spirit of NEG models for their work, but not a direct derivation of the NEG model. From a European perspective, there are several papers in the spatial spirit of the NEG models, which analyze economic development and convergence at a regional rather than a national level. When taking a look at European regions and their development the question arises as to whether economic convergence at the international level comes at the prices of an increase in divergence at the intranational level. Some empirical works confirm that growth rates of European countries convergence, however, not of European regions - e.g European Commission (2001), and Trondl (1999, 2001). Cappelen et al. (1999) analyze the economic development of European regions for the past two decades and find no convergence among them at all. One can rather see that some groups of regions excel; these are known as the "European Growth Club". These diverging developments are certainly an issue for European regional and cohesion policy.

However, one would not live up to the expectations of the NEG models without considering the spatial allocation of economic activity at a more disaggregated industrial level. Some influential studies concerning the European Union are Midelfart et al. (2000), Amiti (1999), and Bruelhart (1998). The most important results can be summarized as follows:

- Specialization in Western European countries has significantly increased in some manufacturing industries since the 1980s.
- For most industries one can find a significant change in the degree of locational concentration. Labor intensive industries tend to agglomerate mainly in peripheral regions.
- Some significant decrease in concentration can be found for some middle and high technology industries; at the same time there is some tendency for reallocation of these industries into peripheral regions.
- All in all, change in specialization and concentration patterns take place rather slowly.

Furthermore these studies emphasize that the crucial factors for the change in these patterns are endowment with resources and factor inputs of production as described by the Traditional Trade Theories. At the same time, other factors as identified by the New Economic Geography, such as location, transportation and trade costs, scale economies, and backward and forward linkages play an important role. Concerning linkages, central regions seem to have an advantage at attracting those economic activities which are to a great extent reliant on intermediate products and tend to be located at the end of the value added chain. In addition, central regions are often more attractive for scale intensive industries due to their size. Bruelhart (1998) also shows that labor intensive industries increasingly tend to locate in peripheral European regions, but also some intermediate and higher technology intensive industries are relocating activity towards the periphery.

A rather interesting study by Bruelhart, Crozet and Koenig (2004) deals with the impact of the 2004 Eastern enlargement on the former EU 15 member states. They highlight the potentially problematic regions which could benefit less from enlargement. The study analyzes the impact of the new relative market access structure within the enlarged European Union on the Objective 1 regions of the EU 15. These comprise roughly 50 regions which are regarded as being in need of promoting, because their GDP per capita does not exceed 75 % of the EU average, or population density is very low, or location is extremely peripheral. Accordingly, one can find 11 Objective 1 regions in the former EU 15 countries.[23] The model used for this analysis is a 3-region NEG model. It is assumed that two of the three regions are already strongly linked with each other in economic terms - this refers to regions within the EU 15. The analysis focuses on the question of how these regions are affected by opening up towards a third region, i.e. the new EU member states. The empirical model used here, however, does not inherit all the characteristics of above-mentioned NEG models. The main explanatory variable is market potential at a regional level. It is measured as the sum of the economic mass of all European regions, where each of these is weighted with the bilateral distance of the regions. Economic mass is measured as regional GDP in purchasing power parity (PPP). First the relation between regional GDP and market potential is estimated for the 202 European regions. This is done in the following way:

$$M_{i,C} = \sum_c Y_i/d_{ic} \tag{3.62}$$

where i and c denote regions and $c \,\epsilon\, C$. Y denotes the economic mass and d stands for the bilateral distance. C is the relevant set of trading regions. The crucial point of the analysis is the way by which M_i is estimated depending on the different set of countries C. Since our aim is to analyze the impact of Eastern EU enlargement on the EU 15 countries, three different scenarios are used.

1. C is defined as EU 15 countries + the European Free Trade Association (EFTA) countries: Iceland, Liechtenstein, Norway, and Switzerland. This

---

[23] These are found in Germany, France, Spain, Italy, UK, Greece, Ireland, Austria, Portugal, Finland and Sweden. Furthermore there are Objective 1 regions in all new EU member states except for Cyprus. Total population in Objective 1 regions amounts to 155 million. More than 76 million live in the former EU 15 countries, the rest in the new EU member states.

implies a market access to established Western European markets, stating that the impact of Eastern European markets is not relevant.

2. In the second scenario, C includes all EU 25 countries.

3. In the third scenario, C contains 33 countries: EU 25 + potential new EU countries such as Albania, Bosnia-Herzogovina, Bulgaria, Croatia, Macedonia, Romania, Serbia-Montenegro and Turkey.

The regression equation for per capita GDP is the following:

$$(GDP/Pop)_i = \beta_0 + \beta_1 M_{i,C} + \beta_2 Dummy(Obj1Reg)_i + \gamma X_i + \epsilon_i \qquad (3.63)$$

where the coefficient β_2 displays the impact of a dummy variable for Objective 1 regions, and X are country specific fixed effects. The estimation results display a significantly positive impact of market potential on per capita GDP. An increase of the market potential by 10 % yields an increase in the region's per capita income by 1.45 %. The coefficient for the dummy variable is negative and significant, indicating that per capita GDP is significantly lower in Objective 1 regions.

In a second step a simulation study is implemented. Hereby the estimated coefficients from equation 3.63 are used in order to assess the change of per capita income due to the increase of market potential through Eastern enlargement on the EU 15 regions, assuming scenario 2 with EU 25 as the set of trading partners. The results show that the impact on per capita GDP in Objective 1 regions is 0.93 %. For the average of all 152 EU 15 regions the impact is even smaller with 0.65 %. Within the Objective 1 regions Burgenland in Austria benefits most from EU Eastern enlargement with a rise in its per capita GDP by 2.11 %. Geographically remote regions in the UK such as West Wales or Cornwall will benefit the least with roughly 0.5 %. German Objective 1 regions profit between 0.8 % (Magdeburg and Thuringia) and roughly 1.1 % (Dresden and Brandenburg). All in all, one can clearly see an almost linear relationship indicating that the higher the geographical closeness of regions to the new EU member states, the higher the positive impact of EU Eastern enlargement on the regions' per capita GDP. Finally, the study also analyzes the potential impact of a South-East enlargement and finds that its impact would be even stronger when compared to the Eastern enlargement.

3.5 The Relevance of the Main Theories for the New EU Member States

To conclude on the relevance of the main theories for the new EU member states, a study by Hildebradt and Wörz (2005) is extremely applicable. It uses elements of the above-mentioned three main theoretical models - Traditional Trade Theory, New Trade Theory and New Economic Geography - by analyzing concentration and specialization patterns in the new EU member states for

13 manufacturing industries between 1993 and 2000. The authors measure absolute and relative concentration for sectoral output. Absolute concentration displays the distribution of industrial activity among countries. An industry is said to be absolutely concentrated if output is generated in one or in only a few countries. Relative concentration measures the difference between the dispersion in production of one single industry and the average dispersion of production of a whole economy or of total manufacturing industries. An industry is said to be relatively concentrated if output in this industry is generated with a higher concentration as the output of the total economy. Thus relative concentration also means specialization at the country level. Absolute concentration is measured as:

$$CIP_j^A = \sqrt{\frac{1}{c} \sum_i \left(\frac{X_{ji}}{\sum_i X_{ji}} \right)^2} \tag{3.64}$$

where c denotes the number of countries, and X the production of industry j in country i. As a matter of course one must control for the size of countries when measuring relative concentration.

$$CIP_j^R = \sqrt{\frac{1}{c} \sum_i \left(\frac{X_{ji}}{\sum_i X_{ji}} - \frac{\sum_j X_{ji}}{\sum_j \sum_i X_{ji}} \right)^2} \tag{3.65}$$

where the second second term in the brackets shows the share of country i in the manufacturing production of EU10 countries. Comparing concentration measures in 1993 and 2000 shows that absolute concentration has increased in most industries. The results are similar for the relative concentration with the strongest increase being observed in the leather industry. To be able to compare to Western European countries, the authors calculate the same measure for the EU 15 countries for the years 1985, 1993 and 2000. They find that absolute concentration has increased in all industries for the pre-integration period from 1985 to 1993, whereas relative concentration has increased in 11 out of 13 industries. Between 1993-2000, which was strongly shaped by economic integration, the authors find a general tendency for de-concentration in EU 15 industries. Absolute concentration has decreased in 10, relative concentration in 9 industries.

The comparison between East and West Europe shows that the increase of concentration in the years 1993-2000 was much stronger in Eastern Europe than in Western Europe. Next the authors search for the determinants of the changing concentration and specialization patterns. They use different explanatory measures, which are derived from three different theories and were introduced in this section. These are the following:

- Traditional Trade Theory: Technological differences by Ricardo and differences in factor endowments according to Heckscher-Ohlin
- New Trade Theory: Scale Economies and Love of Variety
- New Economic Geography: Transportation costs as well as backward and forward linkages.

Hildebrandt and Wörz (2005) use these explanatory variables within an econometric regression to find out the relevance of the different trade theories when explaining absolute and relative concentration measures in the production of industries in new EU member states. For a further discussion on how these variables are measured, see Hildebrandt and Wörz (2005). The regression results are shown in table 3.1.

Table 3.1. The Impact of Trade Theories on Concentration Patterns in New EU Member States

Theory	Exogenous Variable	Relative Concentration	Absolute Concentration
Neoclassic	FDI	0.0686***	-0.0056
Ricardo	Technological Diff.	0.0279***	-0.2329*
Heckscher-Ohlin	Labor Intensity	-0.0000	0.0000
Heckscher-Ohlin	Human Capital Intensity	-0.0000**	0.0000
New Trade Theory	Domestic Use	0.2652***	0.3797***
New Economic Geography	Scale Economies	-0.0214	0.0261
New Economic Geography	Transportation Costs	-0.0000	0.0003
New Economic Geography	Linkages	0.0014	0.0417
	Quadratic Trend	0.0001***	-0.0008
	Industry Dummy	0.0000***	0.0093***
	Constant	0.0161*	0.0646***
	No. of Obs.	104	104

Source: Hildebrandt and Wörz (2005)

Foreign Direct Investment (FDI) is used as an explanatory variable for concentration measures, because FDI plays an important role for most of the new EU member states in the course of privatization. Since privatization and FDI attracting measures were rather different in the respective countries, FDI can be considered an exogenous variable. By determining relative concentration FDI turns out to have a significant impact, but not by determining absolute concentration.

The Ricardian element of technology differences measured as differences in productivity (more specifically, as differences in labor productivity) plays a significant role both for absolute and for relative concentration. Concerning Heckscher-Ohlin elements, only the impact of human capital intensity can be demonstrated.

The impact of the New Trade Theory variable, domestic use as an indicator for demand, has a strong significant impact, however, this variable cannot solely be distributed to the New Trade Theory. Nevertheless, it has been established in that type of literature as the "home market bias". It is measured here as Output + Import - Export.

The New Economic Geography variables are taken from Forslid et al. (2002). Transportation costs are measured as a share of Western European producer prices and show no significant influence. Linkages are measured as the share of input factors of total production costs and as closeness to consumers. However, neither theses variables have a significant impact. The same is true for scale economies. Since none of the NEG variables plays a role, the question arises as to whether there is a measurement error or whether one might have to use a model which is more closely connected to the NEG theory.

In contrast, some of the Traditional Trade Theory and the New Trade Theory variables show a significant impact. Among others, this exercise and also the previously mentioned direct empirical application of trade models highlight the difficulties which occur when making an effort in directly proving the contents of trade theories. Since data availability is rather poor for the new EU member states and as much of the existing literature shows great deficiencies by directly estimating trade model equations, we will now turn our attention to an empirical analysis of foreign trade specialization, which is rather collaterally connected to the above-explained theoretical models.

4

Analyzing Intra-EU Trade Specialization in Manufacturing

This section analysis intra-EU trade specialization patterns in manufacturing industries in the enlarged EU. First the sources of imitation and innovation are defined, which is important for countries moving from low towards higher technology products' exportation. Then an adequate taxonomy is presented, which will be used to categorize manufacturing goods according to, for example, their factor intensity. This taxonomy is applied to the subsequent analysis of different measures to identify trade specialization patterns such as the Trade Coverage Index, the Grubel-Lloyd Index, and the Revealed Comparative Advantage Index. Moreover these specialization patterns are used to paint a picture of competitiveness of national industries as suppliers on the EU 15 market and to analyze whether there is convergence or divergence among EU 25 countries' trade specialization patterns. Finally, a dynamic panel analysis reveals the main determinants of trade specialization patterns in the new EU member states.

4.1 Imitation and Innovation in Manufacturing

4.1.1 The Importance of Research and Development

Profit-maximizing firms in a dynamic market economy will undertake research and development (R&D) in order to launch process innovations or product innovations. The latter gives the firm a temporary monopoly position in the market and allows it to fetch higher prices in the home market and abroad. With respect to international markets, the development of export unit values over time is interesting as an indicator for technological upgrading. Relatively poor countries will - while catching up after economic opening up - go first through a stage which is mainly characterized by imitation; only later on will innovation gain a strong role.

Different measures can be applied to categorize product groups according to their technology level. From a Schumpeterian point of view, technology intensity of goods plays an important role in specialization patterns. Schumpeterian goods - which are defined as technology intensive goods - can be divided into two categories (Klodt, 1993). Immobile Schumpeterian goods require high research and development (R&D) activities, while R&D and production must be located together at the same geographical location. On the contrary for mobile Schumpeterian goods, production and R&D activity can be located at different places. In the course of catching up the question arises, in the exportation of what kinds of goods do the new EU member states gain more comparative advantages and in the exportation of what kind of goods do they lose comparative advantages? According to the "climbing-up-the-ladder-strategy", technological catching-up first takes place in low-tech industries. Under the assumption that these are likely to be more labor intensive and less capital intensive industrial sectors, the outcome is consistent with the classical Heckscher-Ohlin model. Countries will specialize in labor intensive goods, with the result that catching-up first takes place in those industries. As a result we should observe that the EU 15 countries specialize more in R&D and human capital- intensive goods exportation, whereas the new EU countries specialize in labor intensive goods' exportation. In the course of integration, however, the new EU member states should experience a rise in exports in the low and middle technology fields and in later stages of integration also of higher technology products. One can assume that technology levels and R&D intensities are positively correlated. The two variables are of course no perfect substitutes; to some extent, however, they can be used as alternatives.

Figures 4.1, 4.2 and 4.3 show the R&D intensity in different industrial sectors for selected new EU member countries. The R&D ratio is measured as the relation between sectoral R&D expenditure and sectoral turnover.[1] Note that the underlying figures are not fully comparable with each other. Except for Hungary, R&D expenditure represents total figures; the Hungarian data contains - due to problems with data availability - only in-firm R&D expenditure. R&D expenditure of Hungarian research institutes or Hungarian universities, for example, are not covered. This probably accounts for Hungary's R&D intensity being considerably lower than in the other two countries.

In the new EU countries, R&D expenditure is rather low in most industrial sectors. In Poland and Hungary there is merely one sector each, namely machinery and equipment in Poland, and chemicals in Hungary, and in the Czech Republic two sectors, namely machinery and equipment and other transport equipment, which have significantly higher R&D expenditure ratios. As already mentioned above, the Hungarian figure is not comparable to the other countries, therefore we have to interpret it carefully. The highest in-firm R&D

---

[1] Turnover in the selected new EU countries has kindly been provided by the National Statistical Offices. R&D expenditure in Poland and the Czech Republic are taken from the OECD's Anbert database (OECD, 2004). Data on R&D expenditure in Hungary is taken from Eurostat (2005).

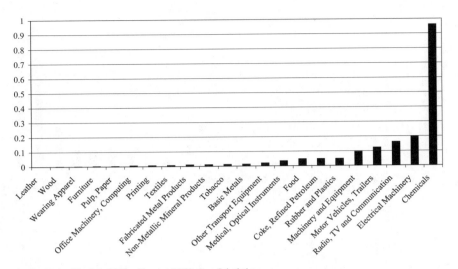

Source: National Statistical Office, Eurostat (2005), Own Calculations

Fig. 4.1. In-Firm R&D Intensity in Hungary, Average of 1998-2001, in %

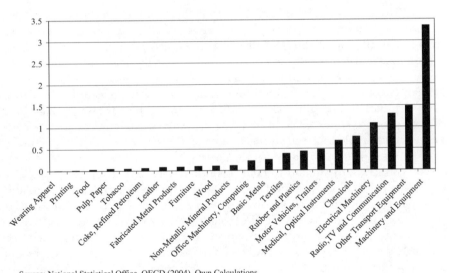

Source: National Statistical Office, OECD (2004), Own Calculations

Fig. 4.2. R&D Intensity in Poland, Average of 1995-2000, in %

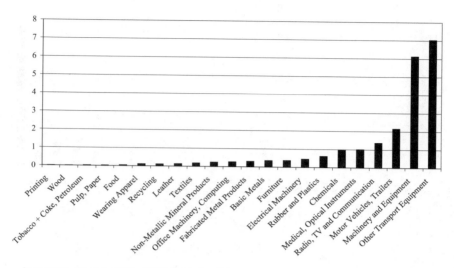

Source: National Statistical Office, OECD (2004), Own Calculations

Fig. 4.3. R&D Intensity in the Czech Republic, Average of 1997-2000, in %

ratio in Hungary does not exceed 1 %, while in most sectors it lies below 0.2 % of turnover, which is rather negligible.[2] However, it is noteworthy that chemicals are at the top of the R&D list in Hungary. Although R&D expenditure represents total figures in the Czech Republic and Poland, only a few sectors exceed the 1 % R&D ratio by far. The most R&D intensive sector shows an R&D ratio of 7 % in the Czech Republic and not even 3.5 % in Poland. However, the distribution of R&D expenditure across the sectors is similar. In all of the countries some of the most R&D intensive sectors are radio, television and communication as well as machinery and other transport equipment.

Figures 4.4 and 4.5 show the respective R&D figures for two of the cohesion countries, Spain and Ireland. Unfortunately data availability problems occur again. For Portugal and Greece, there is no R&D expenditure available. Alternative measures such as investment in tangible assets are informative, though not fully comparable to R&D figures. Therefore Portugal and Greece are left out of this analysis.[3] The Spanish figures are mostly comparable to the Czech Republic. The highest R&D ratios are found in transport equipment, communication and machinery accounting for roughly 4-5 % of the turnover. Concerning the top R&D intensity, Ireland outperforms the countries considered thus far with almost 25 % of R&D expenditure in machinery and

---

[2] Medium technology goods are characterized by R&D intensities between 3.5 and 8.5 %. Below and above we have low technology goods and high technology goods, respectively.

[3] For Spain and Ireland R&D figures are taken from the OECD's Anbert Database (OECD, 2004); turnover is extracted from Eurostat (2005).

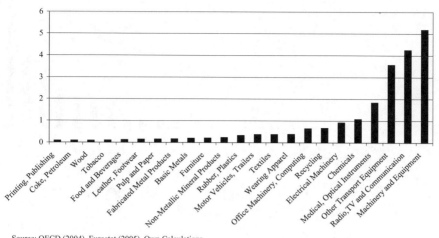

Source: OECD (2004), Eurostat (2005), Own Calculations

Fig. 4.4. R&D Intensity in Spain, 2000, in %

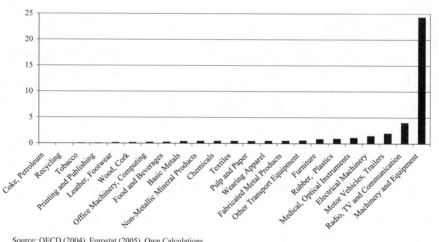

Source: OECD (2004), Eurostat (2005), Own Calculations

Fig. 4.5. R&D Intensity in Ireland, 2000, in %

equipment. This is roughly fourfold the figures of the new EU countries and to some extent is most similar to the situation in Germany (figure 4.6).[4] Also in Germany, the top sector - which is in like manner machinery and equipment - has an R&D ratio of a rather high 15 %. However, in Germany the second and third highest R&D intensive sectors also reach 8-10 % of turnover,

---

[4] R&D expenditure for Germany is extracted from the OECD's Anbert Database (OECD, 2004); data on turnover is taken from Eurostat (2005).

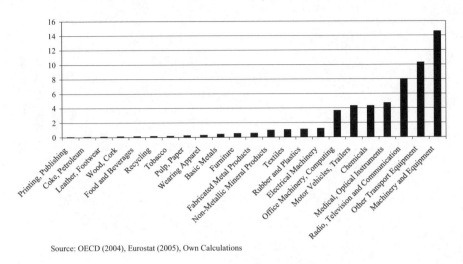

Source: OECD (2004), Eurostat (2005), Own Calculations

Fig. 4.6. R&D Intensity in Germany, 2000, in %

while in Ireland R&D expenditure does not exceed 5 % of turnover in these industries.

Summing up, there are still significant differences in the absolute ratio, which is much higher in some cohesion countries and also in Germany. However, the distribution of R&D expenditure across the sectors is similar if one compares the new EU member states, the cohesion countries, and Germany. In all of the countries some of the most R&D intensive sectors are radio, television and communication as well as machinery and other transport equipment. R&D is, however, not the only source of technological modernization.

4.1.2 Other Factors Influencing Innovation

Other possible measures for technology intensity would be the use of data on capital stock, total factor productivity or investment. However, here we face severe data availability problems for the new EU countries. For many of them - particularly for Poland according to Dyker and Kubielas (2000) -, FDI and imports of goods can be also seen as main sources of technology spill-over and technological modernization. Imports as a source of technology are, however, very hard to measure.

Next we aim to establish whether manufacturing foreign trade patterns, especially exports, in the new EU countries at a disaggregated level are connected to technology intensity in the respective manufacturing sector. To corroborate this hypothesis we will calculate three different indicators of NACE 2-digit-level classified products. One could then order the products according to their national R&D intensity. However, these orders are not fully comparable as shown before. Alternatively one can use a taxonomy.

4.2 Taxonomy: Analytical Sector Classification

Analyzing trends in the composition of foreign trade in manufacturing and making sectoral comparisons among countries requires an appropriate classification of products and industries. One can for instance rely on a traditional method; alternatively new refined approaches could be applied.

4.2.1 Traditional Taxonomy

Traditionally, products were classified according to their ratio of R&D expenditure to sales or turnover and classified as either "low", "middle" or "high" technology products. As indicated earlier medium technology goods are characterized by R&D intensities between 3.5 and 8.5 %. Below and above we deal with low and high technology goods, respectively. More sophisticated analysis further distinguished between "medium-low" and "medium-high" technologies (Fontegné et al., 1999). This taxonomy is especially interesting from a Schumpeterian point of view, however, national differences in R&D intensity of product groups make international comparisons rather demanding and difficult. Although sectoral distribution of R&D intensity is rather similar between the new EU countries and the EU 15 countries, R&D levels are very different. Furthermore, it is not reasonable to assume that most innovation in new EU countries comes from R&D. We will therefore use a different system of taxonomy for the underlying analysis, which is used by the OECD and is widely consistent with the Pavitt taxonomy on the dynamics of technological change and industrial competition.

4.2.2 Pavitt Taxonomy

A major step towards a theoretically based taxonomy was founded by Pavitt (1984). Later developed taxonomies build on his fundament; therefore his taxonomy is introduced briefly in this analysis. In accordance with the Schumpeterian view, the basic unit is the innovating firm. Pavitt's taxonomy of sources of innovation in different sectors can be described as follows. He identifies four categories of firms:[5]

1. Supplier Dominated Firms
   Their main source of innovation is new machinery coming from suppliers of equipment and material. The firm itself makes only a minor contribution to its process or product innovation. Such firms can be found mainly in traditional sectors of manufacturing. They are generally small and have weak R&D capabilities. Technological trajectories are mostly defined in terms of cutting costs.

---

[5] The following description is in the style of Pavitt (1984), and Laursen and Drejer (1997).

2. Science-Based Firms

   R&D activities and linkages among firms, universities and science institutes are the key external sources of innovation within this group. Science-based firms also transfer technology to production intensive firms, for example, in the electronics or the automobile industry. The main internal sources of technology are R&D and production engineering.

3. Specialized Equipment Suppliers

   Incremental innovations take place thanks to cooperation between capital goods suppliers and industrial users. Usually, they are small firms which are producers of production equipment and control instruments. The main internal source of technology is primarily development. External sources are science-based and scale intensive firms as users.

4. Scale Intensive Firms

   Large dimensions of production allow for experience and innovation. Their technological trajectory is described by increasing large-scale fabrication and assembly production. Internal sources of technology are production engineering and R&D departments. External sources are mainly interactive learning with specialized suppliers, but also inputs from science-based firms.

There are of course technological linkages among the different categories of firms, which can go beyond transactions involving the purchase and sale of goods embodying technology. These might include flows of information and skills as well as technological diversification into the main product areas of suppliers and customers. Building upon this taxonomy, the OECD developed its own.

4.2.3 OECD Taxonomy

This approach of the OECD (1987) distinguishes between five groups of products on the basis of the primary factors affecting the competitive process in each economic activity. It was originally used for ISIC classification; here the converted version for NACE rev. 1.1 is presented. Table 4.1 summarizes the taxonomy.

The main advantage of the approach adopted here is that it provides a link between the way product groups are defined and the main types of economic benefits which flow from trade:[6]

- Trade in labor and resource intensive products bring the allocation of resources within industries more closely into line with international patterns of factor endowments.
- Trade in scale intensive products allows firms to increase plant size and lengthen production runs, while at the same time reducing costs.

---

[6] The following description is based on OECD (1987) pp: 274.

Table 4.1. OECD Taxonomy

Grouping	Major factors affecting competitiveness	Examples
Labor intensive	Labor costs	Textiles, leather
Resource intensive	Access to abundant natural resources	Food, wood, refined petroleum
Scale intensive	Length of production runs	Motor vehicles, steel
Science-based	Rapid application of scientific advance	Office machinery and computing, pharmaceutical
Differentiated goods	Tailoring product to highly varied demand characteristics	Electrical machinery and equipment

Source: OECD (1987), p: 272

- Trade in differentiated goods benefits consumers with large product variety without sacrificing the advantages of large-scale production.
- Trade in science-based products makes it likely to spread high fixed costs and risks of R&D over a larger market; this ensures the rapid diffusion of the benefits of new products and processes.

The group of differentiated goods mainly corresponds to the group of specialized suppliers of Pavitt's taxonomy. Furthermore, scale intensive and differentiated goods (or specialized suppliers) increasingly overlap in practice, so that one could aggregate these two groups under production intensive goods, as did Pavitt (1984). For the following empirical analysis we will use the OECD type of taxonomy. NACE 2-digit level product groups are divided into the five categories as follows:[7]

Table 4.2. Relocation of NACE 2-Digit Level Products to Taxonomy Groups

Groups	NACE 2-digit Classification
Labor intensive	17, 18, 19, 28, 36
Resource intensive	15, 16, 20, 23, 26, 27
Scale intensive	21, 22, 27, 24, 25, 34, 35
Science-based	30, 33, 35
Differentiated goods	29, 31, 32

Source: OECD (1987), Soós (2002), Own Modifications

According to table 4.2, two groups cannot be clearly relocated to one taxonomy group. Thus, basic metals (27) belong to both resource- and scale intensive groups. While iron and steel production belongs to the scale intensive group, the production of non-ferrous metals is rather resource intensive. The manufacture of other transport equipment (35) is also situated between two groups: aircraft and spacecraft are clearly science-based, while shipbuild-

---

[7] For an explanation of the NACE two and three digit categories see annex A.

ing and railways belong to the scale intensive group. The following empirical analysis is based on this above-mentioned OECD taxonomy.

4.3 Measures of Intra-EU Trade

The subsequent analysis makes use of three different indicators, the Trade Coverage Index, the Grubel-Lloyd Index of Intra-Industry Trade, and the modified Revealed Comparative Advantage Index to measure foreign trade performance - at a disaggregated level - of three new EU member states and the four cohesion countries. The focus is on trade with the EU 15 countries. Data on exports and imports to the EU 15 in the manufacturing sector is used at a two digit level. Data is classified according to NACE rev.1.1. The list of variables can be found in annex A.

4.3.1 The Role of Exports and Imports: Trade Coverage Index

The Trade Coverage Index (TCI) reveals the ratio of exports (X) to imports (M) at a certain point of time t:

$$TCI_t^j = \frac{X_t^j}{M_t^j} \tag{4.1}$$

where j can represent, for instance, total manufacturing or a certain product group. For a first insight, we calculate the Trade Coverage Index for total manufacturing in different years. Table 4.3 shows the results.

Table 4.3. TCI for Total Manufacturing, 1993-2003

TCI	1993	1994	1995	1996	1997	1998	1999	2000	2001	2002	2003
Hungary	0.77	0.77	0.84	0.86	0.89	0.92	1.03	1.05	1.11	1.17	1.17
Poland	0.75	0.81	0.77	0.60	0.55	0.56	0.59	0.69	0.75	0.77	0.84
Czech R.	0.78	0.79	0.75	0.68	0.73	0.85	0.91	0.93	0.97	1.07	1.11
Spain	0.73	0.76	0.75	0.75	0.74	0.72	0.67	0.70	0.69	0.72	0.69
Ireland	1.39	1.35	1.47	1.55	1.39	1.45	1.51	1.54	1.63	1.72	1.98
Portugal	0.65	0.66	0.68	0.66	0.63	0.60	0.60	0.60	0.63	0.63	0.68
Greece	0.31	0.32	0.30	0.29	0.26	0.24	0.23	0.22	0.22	0.22	0.24

Source: EC (2004), Own Calculations

Only one of the four cohesion countries' and two of the new member states' TCI exceeds unity, namely Ireland, Hungary, and the Czech Republic. TCI in Hungary has increased continually, and has been exceeding unity since 1999, in the Czech Republic since 2002. At the beginning of the sample period Ireland exported roughly 40% more than it imported from the EU 15; at the end of the sample period, this ratio increased to roughly 100%. From this point of

view Ireland is most comparable among the new EU countries to Hungary
and the the Czech Republic, where exports also exceed imports. The other
countries clearly import more from the EU 15 than they export. TCI is closest
to one in Poland, Spain, and Portugal, where exports make up to 70-80% of
imports. Greece is not comparable to any other country considered in the
analysis. The gap between imports and exports is tremendous. Exports make
up only one-fourth of imports, and there is even a slight deterioration of the
situation visible throughout the 1990s.

Let us turn to a more disaggregated view in manufacturing. The following
figures, which contain NACE 2-digit level product categories, are based on
the OECD taxonomy. The product groups are allocated from left to right in
the following order: labor intensive, resource intensive, scale intensive, science-
based and differentiated goods. The two groups, 27 and 35, which belong to
two OECD groups each, are shown separately between the respective product
groups.

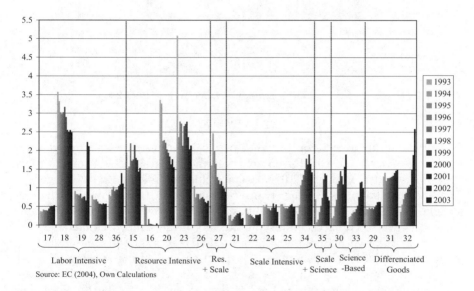

Fig. 4.7. Hungary - Trade Coverage Index, 1993-2003

Figures 4.7- 4.9 confirm the finding of total manufacturing for the new EU
member states. In Hungary - figure 4.7 - many industries basically all along the
technology ladder display TCIs which exceed unity. This is particularly valid
within the labor and the resource intensive industries, but increasingly within
the higher technology groups as well. The highest TCIs can be found for wearing apparel (18) and coke and refined petroleum products (23), followed by

wood and wooden products (20), and some scale intensive and differentiated goods.

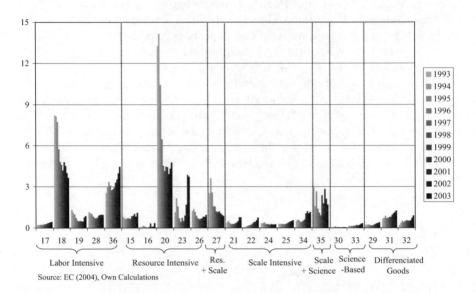

Fig. 4.8. Poland - Trade Coverage Index, 1993-2003

In Poland - figure 4.8 - only a few 2-digit level industries export more than they import with the EU 15, namely wearing apparel (18), furniture (36), wood and wooden products (20), coke and refined petroleum (23), basic metals (27) and manufactures of other transport equipment (35). However, there is a slight rise in TCIs in some differentiated goods; in electrical machinery and apparatus (31), TCI exceeds unity at the end of the sample period.

Also in the Czech Republic - figure 4.9 - there are only some industries for which exports are higher than imports. However, in many, mainly higher technology goods, we see an increase of TCIs in general. Thus by 2003 some scale intensive and differentiated goods show positive net exports. Nevertheless the picture is still dominated by wood and wooden products (20), similar to Poland.

Figures 4.10- 4.13 also confirm the findings of total manufacturing for the cohesion countries. In Spain (figure 4.10) most of the manufacturing sectors show a TCI below one, indicating higher imports than exports. This is especially valid for science-based and differentiated goods. TCIs exceed unity in some labor, resource and scale intensive product groups, such as tanning and dressing of leather (19) - the highest TCI -, food products and beverages (15), non-metallic mineral products (26), publishing and printing (22), and motor vehicles and trailers (34).

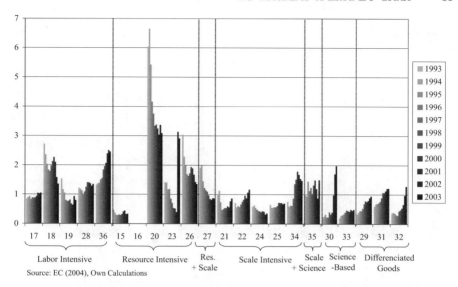

Fig. 4.9. Czech Republic - Trade Coverage Index, 1993-2003

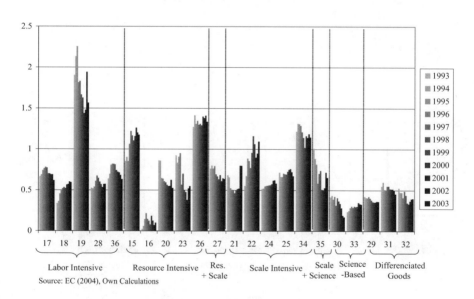

Fig. 4.10. Spain - Trade Coverage Index, 1993-2003

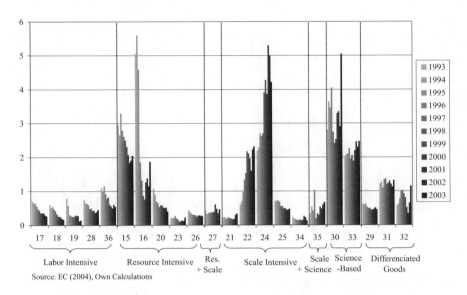

Fig. 4.11. Ireland - Trade Coverage Index, 1993-2003

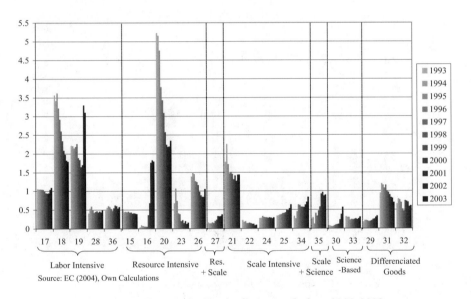

Fig. 4.12. Portugal - Trade Coverage Index, 1993-2003

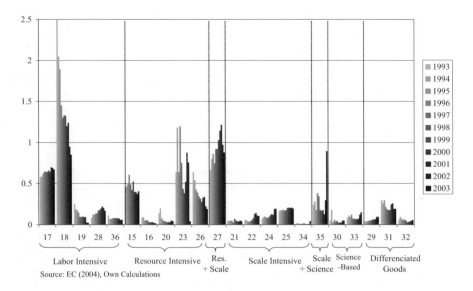

Fig. 4.13. Greece - Trade Coverage Index, 1993-2003

The rather high TCIs for total manufacturing in Ireland (figure 4.11) seem to be generated in only a few branches. By 2003 in more than half of the product groups, imports exceed exports. Thus, TCI is lower than one. Ireland has strongly specialized in the export of only a few products, mostly situated in the middle and the higher end of the technology ladder. Ireland obviously succeeds in the export of science-based products, such as office machinery and computers (30) as well as medical and optical instruments (33). In addition, it exports more than it imports in some differentiated, high technology products like electrical machinery (31) and radio and television equipment (32). Also some products from the scale intensive groups generate positive net exports: publishing and printing (22) and chemicals and its products (24). On the other hand, the export import ratios are very low in many low technology product groups. In the second half of the 1990s, Ireland had no positive net exports in any of the labor intensive sectors, and also TCIs were rapidly declining in the resource intensive production such as in food products and beverages (15), or tobacco (16). To summarize, in most of the lower and lower-middle technology products TCIs are declining in Ireland, whereas TCIs are rising in many higher-middle and higher technology groups. Clearly, Ireland displays a strong focus on exporting high technology products.

The figure for Portugal (figure 4.12) reveals a very different picture with a rather clear message. TCIs exceeding unity by far can mainly be found in labor and resource intensive product groups (thus in low tech production). However, most of the strikingly high TCIs are declining. At the end of the sample period compared to the EU 15, Portugal still excelled in the exportation of five products: cork (20), wearing apparel (18), leather products (19),tobacco (16), and pulp and paper (21). Furthermore, Portuguese exports are higher than imports in other non-metallic mineral products (26), though revealing a declining tendency of TCIs. In most other groups, TCIs are already lower than unity at the end of the sample. Considering technology intensity, one might state that Portugal clearly tends to have positive net exports in lower and lower-middle technology product groups, whereas it imports more from the EU 15 than it exports in higher-middle and high technology product categories.

Figure 4.13 for Greece is rather easy to interpret. In most product groups TCIs do not even exceed the value of 0.5, meaning that imports are more than twice as high as exports. At the end of the sample period, in 2003, TCTs exceeded unity in no product group. Until 2001 this was the case for food and beverages (18). It is striking that in the manufacturing of basic metals (27), Greece's exports tend to gain momentum over imports in the middle of the 1990s; however, TCIs decline again in the last years of observations. Thus, Greece's exports do not exceed imports in any product category at the beginning of the 21st century.

As regards TCI, one should note that cyclical macroeconomic development can affect the picture. In a recession TCI tends to rise while TCI tends to fall in a boom period.

4.3.2 The Role of Intra-Industry Trade: Grubel-Lloyd Index

A great part of trade occurs across countries within the same industries. This is called intra-industry trade, and according to the New Trade Theory it is determined by country characteristics such as demand differences. Generally one also expects that intra-industry trade will rise along with per capita income. High income per capita raises demand for differentiated products, which in open economies translates into rising intra-industry trade. Moreover, the size of intra-industry trade partly indicates the extent of economic integration of a country. Again, we will only use that part of foreign trade of the EU countries associated with the EU 15. Thus, the index directly measures the extent of economic integration with the EU 15. The Grubel-Lloyd Index (GLI) of intra-industry Trade (IIT) for industry j is calculated as follows:

$$GLI_j = \frac{[(X_j + M_j) - |X_j - M_j|]}{(X_j + M_j)} * 100 \qquad (4.2)$$

X stands for exports to the EU 15, M for imports from the EU 15. The index takes values between 0 and 100. The higher the value, the greater the extent of intra-industry trade, the greater the degree of economic integration, and the more one can expect countries to be subject to similar demand side shocks.

For a first insight, we calculate the Grubel-Lloyd Index for total manufacturing in different years. Table 4.4 shows the results.

Table 4.4. GLI for Total Manufacturing, 1993-2003

GLI	1993	1994	1995	1996	1997	1998	1999	2000	2001	2002	2003
Hungary	86.8	87.2	91.5	92.3	94.0	96.0	98.3	97.6	95.0	92.3	92.0
Poland	85.6	89.4	86.7	74.9	70.9	72.1	74.6	81.5	85.4	86.9	91.5
Czech R.	87.7	88.2	85.9	80.9	84.2	91.9	95.3	96.5	98.7	96.8	94.6
Spain	84.5	86.6	85.4	85.9	84.8	84.0	80.4	82.0	81.9	83.5	81.9
Ireland	83.6	85.2	80.0	78.4	83.8	81.5	79.7	78.8	76.1	73.6	67.1
Portugal	78.5	79.2	81.1	79.5	77.1	75.1	75.0	75.0	77.1	77.5	81.2
Greece	47.6	48.0	46.2	45.5	41.2	38.9	37.9	35.8	36.6	36.4	38.5

Source: EC (2004), Own Calculations

Interestingly, the new EU member countries from Eastern Europe are at least as integrated with the EU 15 in terms of trade as the cohesion countries. For Hungary, Poland and the Czech Republic, GLIs have increased in the respective time period from roughly 85 to over 90 %. GLIs are a bit lower in the cohesion countries, and an increase in integration can only be observed in Portugal. Greece, again, is an outlier. Trade integration is rather at a low level and has even declined since the beginning of the 1990s.

Let us now take a look at the sectoral GLIs. In figures 4.14 - 4.20 we will again use the OECD classification for showing the results for NACE 2-digit level manufacturing industries.

Hungary's trade integration with the EU 15 is rather intense all along the technology ladder (figure 4.14). There do not seem to be greater differences between the OECD taxonomy groups. In most industries, GLIs exceed the value of 50, reaching even values around 80 to almost 100 in several industries. Only the tobacco market (16) is less integrated. We can see a clear rise in GLIs in some science-based industries and differentiated goods within the 1990s.

Poland (figure 4.15) is clearly less integrated with the EU 15 than Hungary in terms of foreign trade. Industries with a grade of integration less than 50 % can be found in all five OECD taxonomy groups, but the lack of integration is particulary visible for science-based goods. On the other hand, there are some industries for which GLIs take values exceeding 90, indicating a high share of IIT and a high degree of integration with the EU 15. However, the general picture for Poland clearly tells us that there is still lots of space for an increase in integration.

The relatively low degree of integration in Poland is even more evident if we compare it to the Czech Republic (figure 4.16). With the exception of tobacco (16), integration in the Czech Republic is similarly homogenous across the industries as in Hungary. In most industries GLIs take values around 60-80, or even up to 90 or almost 100. Science-based industries are slightly less integrated, with GLI values around 40-60.

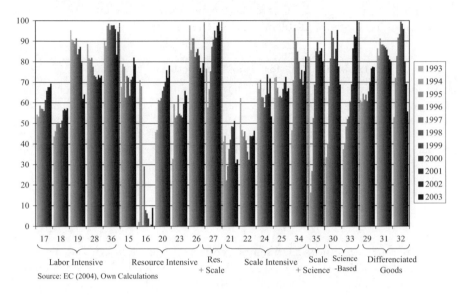

Fig. 4.14. Hungary - GLI for Intra-Industry Trade, 1993-2003

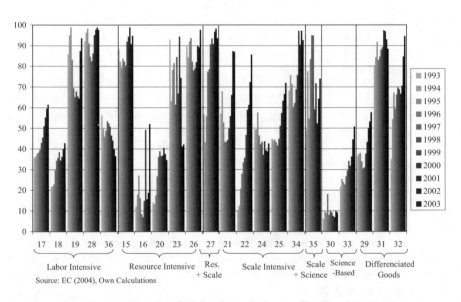

Fig. 4.15. Poland - GLI for Intra-Industry Trade, 1993-2003

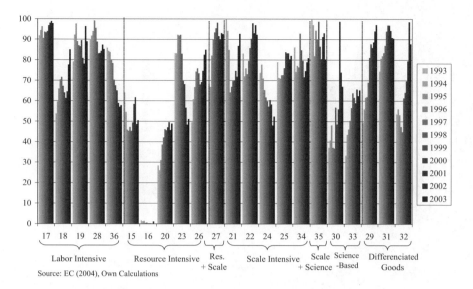

Fig. 4.16. Czech Republic - GLI for Intra-Industry Trade, 1993-2003

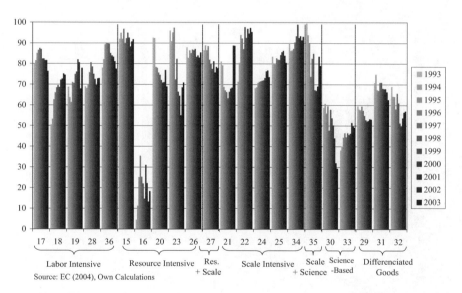

Fig. 4.17. Spain - GLI for Intra-Industry Trade, 1993-2003

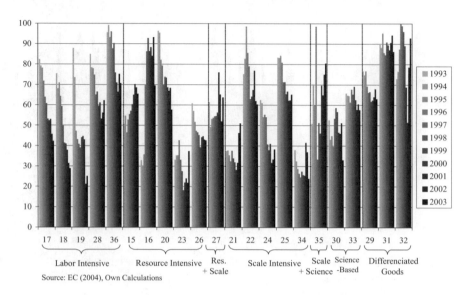

Fig. 4.18. Ireland - GLI for Intra-Industry Trade, 1993-2003

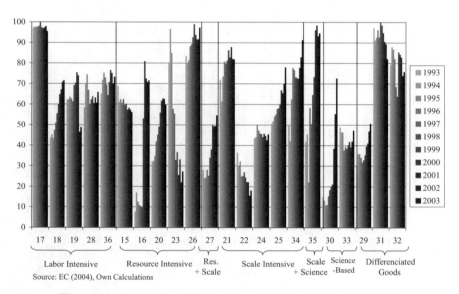

Fig. 4.19. Portugal - GLI for Intra-Industry Trade, 1993-2003

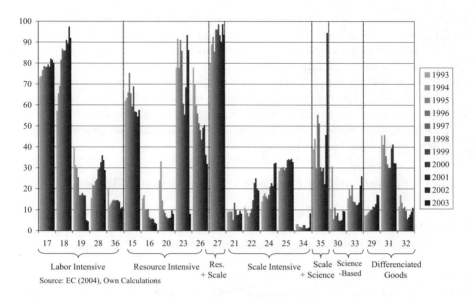

Fig. 4.20. Greece - GLI for Intra-Industry Trade, 1993-2003

Spain is rather intensively integrated with the EU 15 market (figure 4.17). With the major exception of tobacco (16), this is especially valid for labor, resource, and scale intensive product groups. On the contrary, integration is less intense in science-based and differentiated goods' foreign trade.

Compared to Ireland (figure 4.18), the extent of integration is rather stable in Spain. Ireland is facing quite volatile GLIs along the technology ladder. There are groups with quickly declining integration tendencies mainly found in labor intensive sectors, but also groups with quickly rising GLIs in some resource and scale intensive sectors. However, GLIs can generally be characterized with up and down movements without a clear tendency to rise or to fall. Basically, integration is lower than in Spain, while volatility is much higher. Especially the lower and higher-middle technology groups are weakly integrated and tend to record a GLI below 40.

Economic integration is even lower in Portugal (figure 4.19) than in Ireland and Spain. Some resource and scale intensive as well as science-based industries are less than 30 or even 20 % integrated. Similarly to Spain, the tobacco industry displays the lowest extent of integration, but only for the first half of the 1990s. Since then integration has increased to a great extent. Interestingly, some very high technology differentiated goods sectors are highly integrated with the EU 15, indicating that imports also play an important role here. With a high extent of integration both in exports and imports, this may hint towards an assembly line production of electrical machinery and apparatus

(31) and radio, television and communication equipment (32). The highest and most robust degree of integration can clearly be found in textiles (17).

Greece is the least integrated country with the EU 15 among the cohesion countries (figure 4.20), but also as compared with the new Eastern European member states. Although in some labor and resource intensive industries, such as textiles (17), wearing apparel (18), and basic metals (27) GLIs reach higher levels, in most of the product groups integration remains below 20 or even 10 %. Despite some rising GLIs, there does not seem to be an overall tendency for increasing integration since 1993.

4.3.3 The Role of Comparative Advantages: RCA-Balassa

Trade specialization in the sense of the Revealed Comparative Advantage (RCA) of Balassa (1965) reflects sectoral specialization. It reveals a country's sectoral export-import ratio in relation to the export-import ratio of its total economy:

$$RCA_j^{original} = \frac{x_j / \sum_{j=1}^{n} x_j}{m_j / \sum_{j=1}^{n} m_j} \tag{4.3}$$

where x stands for exports, m for imports and $j \in (1...n)$ for the industrial sectors of the economy. There is a wide range of modifications commonly used in the economic literature. The specialization indicator we use in the following is a modification of the classical RCA index, which is often referred to as the ratio of export shares. It reveals the relative comparative advantage of an industry within a country by comparing the share of that particular industry in the country's total exports to the share of that industry in total world exports at a certain point of time. Since we are interested in the question of whether a new EU member state or a cohesion country has a comparative advantage as compared to the EU 15, we take the respective country's exports to the EU 15 instead of total worldwide exports and intra-EU 15 exports instead of worldwide exports. The modified RCA-Balassa for a specific industry j in country c is defined as follows:

$$RCA_{cj}^{modified} = \frac{x_{cj} / \sum_{j=1}^{n} x_{cj}}{x_{ij} / \sum_{j=1}^{n} x_{ij}} \tag{4.4}$$

where c stands for the new EU member or the cohesion country and i for the EU 15. Modified RCA-Balassa has a minimum value of 0 and a maximum value of infinity. If $RCA_{cj} > 1$, country c has a comparative advantage in that industry j as compared to the EU 15. If $RCA_{cj} < 1$, there is a comparative disadvantage of country c in industry j. Instead of exports one could also use different variables, such as patents or value added.

Figures 4.21 - 4.25 show the modified RCA indices for three new EU countries. The horizontal dotted line at 1 (on the left hand scale) indicates the border between comparative advantage and disadvantage. The vertical dotted lines indicate the border between the different product categories according to the OECD taxonomy. At the same time one should take a closer look at export unit values (EUV) on the right hand scale, whose development over time indicates the ability of a country to fetch adequate - if possible higher - prices in world markets. It measures the value (in Euro) of one unit (kg) of exports. Comparing similar products, a higher unit value can be interpreted as an indicator for higher product quality. The black line on the right hand side scale shows the export unit values - expressed in Euro/kg - of the respective product group in the year 2003, the shaded line the export unit values for 1993.

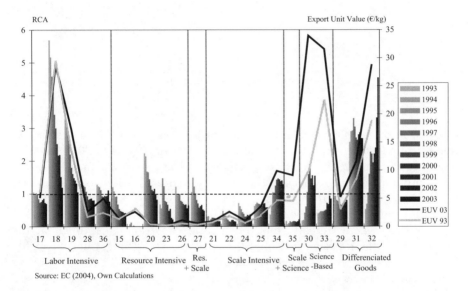

Fig. 4.21. Hungary - RCA of Exports 1993-2003 and Export Unit Values 1993 and 2003

As regards RCA dynamics, figure 4.21 makes clear that some very high and some very low technology intensive products play the most important role in Hungary's comparative advantages in its exports towards the EU 15. RCAs exceed unity in two labor intensive product groups, wearing apparel (18) and leather products (19), with export unit values of 28 and 17 Euro/kg respectively in the year 2003. However, RCAs declined throughout the 1990s in these and in other labor and resource intensive - low and medium technology - product groups. On the contrary, RCAs rose and exceeded unity in the differentiated goods' sectors, especially in electrical machinery and apparatus

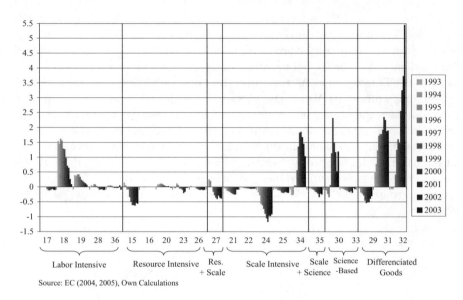

Source: EC (2004, 2005), Own Calculations

Fig. 4.22. Hungary - Weighted and Logarithmic RCA of Exports 1993-2003

(31) and in radio, television and communication equipment (32) industries. In these two industries export unit values rose between 1993 and 2003 reaching more than 11 and 28 Euro/kg, respectively, in the year 2003. In most of the other product groups, especially in resource and scale intensive industries, which mostly belong to medium technologies, both RCAs and export unit values are rather low. One exception might be the manufacturing of motor vehicles (34), where Hungary had a comparative advantage throughout the second half of the 1990s with rising RCAs and an export unit value of roughly 10 Euro/kg in the year 2003. Although there is merely a slight comparative advantage in one science-based product group, namely office machinery and computers (30), export unit values rose considerably between 1993 and 2003.

Concerning the importance of the product groups for the Hungarian industries, figure 4.22 shows the weighted and logarithmic RCAs. The logarithmic transformation is necessary in order to avoid losing the information on comparative advantage or disadvantage through weighting. We use the annual share of the respective industries' exports in the gross value added of the total economy as weights, which are given in the EC's annual database AMECO (EC, 2005). The figure clearly shows the enormous increase in the importance of differentiated goods, such as electrical machinery and apparatus (31), and especially radio, TV and communication equipment (32). In the latter industry, we can observe a very strong and continuous rise in the weighted RCA index. Also motor vehicles and trailers (34), as well as office machinery and computers (30) show rather high weighted RCAs, however, the importance of these two industries does not seem to rise within the observation period. Finally wearing apparel manufacturing (18) displays high, though declining, weighted RCAs. This decline is both due to decreasing RCAs and to decreasing shares in value added. The latter has taken place in particular since 1998.

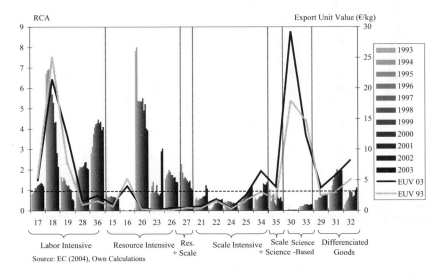

Fig. 4.23. Poland - RCA of Exports 1993-2003 and Export Unit Values 1993 and 2003

Figure 4.23 shows the respective unweighted picture for Poland. Most industries with a relative comparative advantage compared to the EU 15 belong to the labor and resource intensive sectors, meaning that they are positioned rather low on the technology ladder. The highest RCAs are found in wearing apparel (18), furniture (36) and wood and its products (20). However, especially for the latter two, export unit values are extremely low at clearly below 5 Euro/ kg. The value of one kg of exports in wearing apparel is considerably higher at roughly 21 Euro in 2003. In most of the scale intensive, science-based and differentiated goods' sectors Poland still has a comparative disadvantage; however, many RCAs in these sectors seem to have a tendency to increase. Thus, rubber and plastic products (25), motor vehicles (34) and especially electrical machinery and apparatus (31) have reached levels of RCA exceeding unity by the year 2003. Among these categories, export unit values are the highest in the science-based sector with roughly 29 and 12 Euro/kg in the year 2003 and 18 and 15 Euro/kg in the year 1993. Especially in the science-based sector, Poland's comparative disadvantage is nevertheless very distinct.

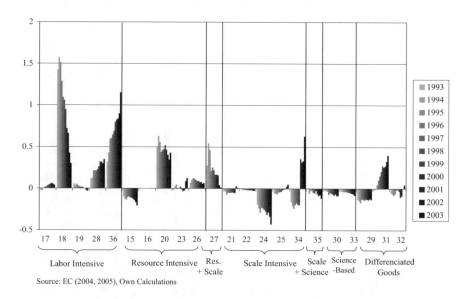

Fig. 4.24. Poland - Weighted and Logarithmic RCA of Exports 1993-2003

Concerning the shares of industries in value added in combination with RCAs, figure 4.24 underlines the importance of labor intensive industries for the Polish economy. Weighted RCAs are the highest in wearing apparel (18), and in furniture (36), though in the former with a strong declining, and in the latter with a rising tendency. A sharp increase is also visible for motor vehicles (34) and electrical machinery and apparatus (31). The predominant position of wood and its products (20), which is shown in the figure of non-weighted RCAs is reduced to a great extent if one takes into account the share of this industry's exports in total value added.

According to figure 4.25 a similar tendency is visible in the Czech Republic as in Hungary. Many of the RCAs in the lower technology sectors have been declining and many in the higher technology intensive sectors have been rising in the course of 1993-2003. At the same time rather strong comparative advantages can be found all along the technology ladder. Within the labor intensive category, wearing apparel (18) has lost comparative advantage despite an export unit value of 32 Euro/kg in 2003, as did leather products (19), which have an export unit value of 15 Euro per kg. All in all, export unit values are similar to the other two countries mainly in the labor intensive, in the resource intensive and in the differentiated goods' sectors. There was a very sharp decline in RCAs as well as in export unit values within the resource intensive categories, where export unit values were extremely low in 2003. Similar to the other new EU member countries, the Czech Republic also has a relative comparative disadvantage in science-based product groups,

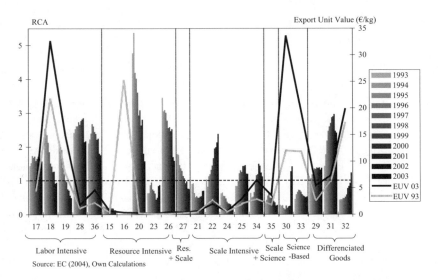

Fig. 4.25. Czech Republic - RCA of Exports 1993-2003 and Export Unit Values 1993 and 2003

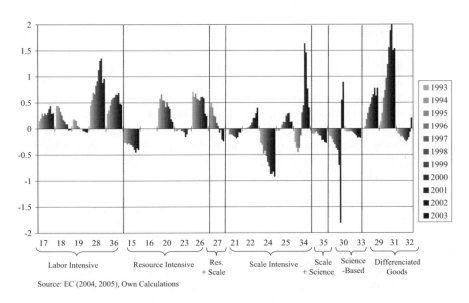

Fig. 4.26. Czech Republic - Weighted and Logarithmic RCA of Exports 1993-2003

although export unit values grew considerably up to 34 Euro per kg in 2003 in office machinery and computers. This rise has been accompanied by a jump in RCAs exceeding unity in the last two years of observations. Also the sharp rise in RCA in electrical machinery and apparatus (31) is remarkable, despite its low export unit value.

The highest shares of manufacturing exports in total value added are to be found in the year 2003 in electrical machinery and apparatus (31), motor vehicles (34), followed by fabricated metal products (28), and office machinery and computers (30). The latter displays a sharp rise in weighted RCAs in the last two years of observation. It is, however, striking that the Czech Republic did not have a weighted comparative advantage in office machinery and computers (30) until 2002. The fifth most important industry is machinery and equipment (29), where the continuous rise in RCAs has been interrupted since 2002. The same is valid for the manufacture of fabricated metal products (28), motor vehicles (34), and electrical machinery and apparatus (31). All in all the message of the non-weighted and the weighted RCAs does not differ extraordinarily in the case of the Czech Republic.

Figures 4.27 - 4.33 show the RCA indexes for the four cohesion countries. Spain (figure 4.27) has a comparative advantage compared to the EU 15 in 5 out of 22 product groups in the year 2003. This is exactly the number of product groups with an RCA exceeding one in 1993, which is in line with the observation that there is not many dynamics in the development of Spanish exports to the EU. At the same time RCAs are dominated by only three lower and middle technology product groups: tanning and dressing of leather (19), non-metallic mineral products (26) and motor vehicles and trailers (34). Each of these three product groups belong to a different OECD category, including labor intensive, resource intensive and scale intensive production. There is no comparative advantage to be found in high technology product groups, neither in the science-based nor in the differentiated goods category. Thus, Spain clearly has specialized in the export of some middle and low technology product groups and has a strong comparative disadvantage in the export of high-technology products.

At the same time science-based products have the highest export unit values with one kg exports of office machinery and computers (30) being worth roughly 97 Euro in 1993, declining to only 39 Euro in 2003. One labor intensive sector also shows rather high figures; the value of 1 kg Spanish wearing apparel export (18) amounted to 33 Euro in 2003. Most of the other product groups' export unit values were below 10 Euro/kg.

Taking into account the industries' shares in total value added as shown in figure 4.28, there is only one industry left with a dominant RCA position: motor vehicles and trailers (34). Its exports amount to 4.6 % of total value added, which is by far the highest share among all manufacturing industries.

In contrast to Spain, Irish exports are dominated by science-based products; especially in the exportation of office machinery and computers (30) Ireland has a very strong comparative advantage compared to the EU 15

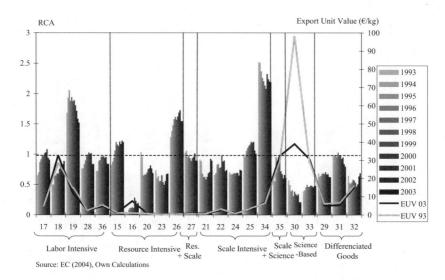

Fig. 4.27. Spain - RCA of Exports 1993-2003 and Export Unit Values 1993 and 2003

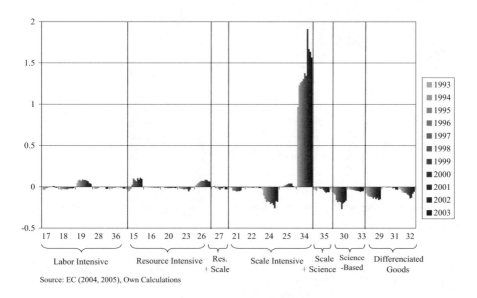

Fig. 4.28. Spain - Weighted and Logarithmic RCA of Exports 1993-2003

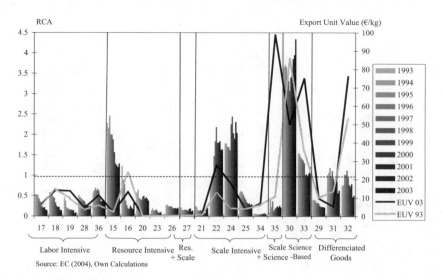

Fig. 4.29. Ireland - RCA of Exports 1993-2003 and Export Unit Values 1993 and 2003

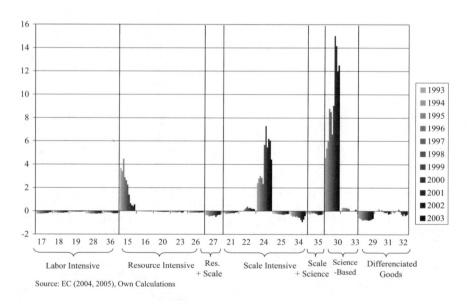

Fig. 4.30. Ireland - Weighted and Logarithmic RCA of Exports 1993-2003

(figure 4.29). Similar to Spain, the value of some science-based exports has declined sharply. One kg of office machinery and computers (30) exported from Ireland to the EU 15 was worth 86 Euro in 1993, and declined to 49 Euro in 2003. The scale intensive product group plays an important role in Irish foreign trade. Not only in chemicals (24), but also in publishing and printing (22), Ireland has a strong comparative advantage as measured by the unweighted RCA. These product groups mostly belong to the higher-middle and high technology intensive classes. In the course of the 1990s, some product groups experienced considerable changes. While in the first half of the 1990s, Irish food and beverages exports had RCAs exceeding unity, their importance decreased considerably towards the end of the sample period.

Taking a look at figure 4.30, which displays the weighted RCAs clearly indicates the increasing dominance of two sectors, namely office machinery and computers (30), where exports were worth 19.6 % of value added in the year 2003 (raising from 8.1 % in 1993), and chemicals and chemical products (24) with 14.3 % of value added in 2003 (raising from 9.5 % in 1993). Food and beverages (15) had a value added share of 5.0 % in 2003 (down from 10.2 % in 1993). Although printing and publishing (22) seem to be an important sector according to the unweighted RCAs, the weighted measures show no sign of this.

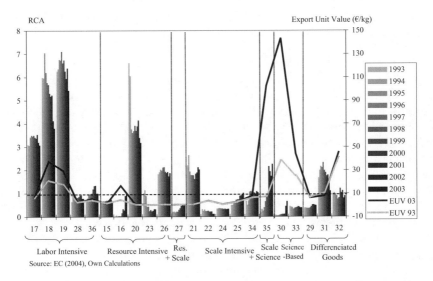

Fig. 4.31. Portugal - RCA of Exports 1993-2003 and Export Unit Values 1993 and 2003

Figure 4.31 shows that Portuguese export patterns are dominated by sectors with a strong comparative advantage in mostly the low and lower-middle

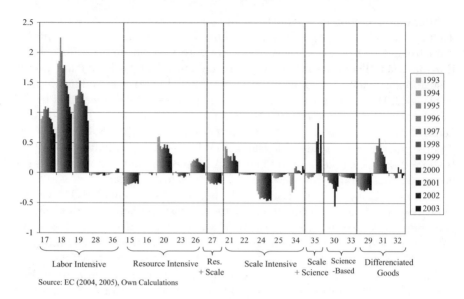

Fig. 4.32. Portugal - Weighted and Logarithmic RCA of Exports 1993-2003

technology product groups. Most RCAs exceeding unity belong to labor intensive industries, such as textiles (17), wearing apparel (18), and leather products (19). In the resource intensive industries Portugal is also competitive on the EU 15 market with wood and cork products (20) and non-metallic mineral products (26). In most of the scale intensive and science-based product groups, there is a clear disadvantage in terms of exports. Some exceptions are pulp and paper products (21), and other transport equipment (35). At the same time export unit values have clearly risen both in low and in higher technology intensive goods between 1993 and 2003. This may indicate the increasing importance of quality of the Portuguese exports. One kg of wearing apparel exports (18) was worth 37 Euro in 2003, up from 21 Euro/kg in 1993, and export unit values of some science-based products increased from 38 Euro/kg in 1993 to 143 Euro/kg in 2003. Most other groups' export unit values remained below 10-15 Euro/kg throughout the 1990s.

According to figure 4.32, the differences are not too large between the weighted and the unweighted RCAs. Basically all industries that show a comparative advantage with the unweighted RCA can keep these magnitudes when weighting with value added shares. At the same time the three most important industries (17, 18, and 19) are slightly losing importance in terms of shares in the total economy's value added.

The Greek situation is rather puzzling (figure 4.33). RCAs are dominated by very high values of comparative advantages in wearing apparel (18), combined with rather low export unit values of 29 Euro, rising from 23 Euro/kg

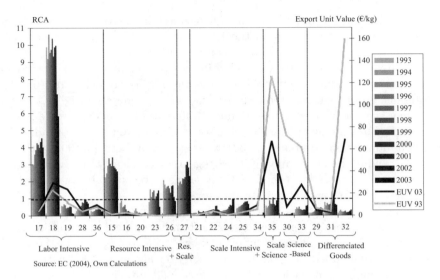

Fig. 4.33. Greece - RCA of Exports 1993-2003 and Export Unit Values 1993 and 2003

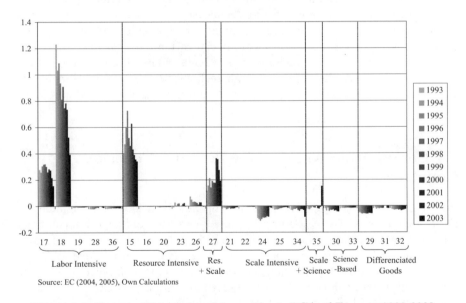

Fig. 4.34. Greece - Weighted and Logarithmic RCA of Exports 1993-2003

in 1993. There are also other labor and resource intensive goods, which enjoy a comparative advantage on the EU 15 market. These are textiles (17), food and beverages (15), and non-metallic mineral products (26) as well as the resource and scale intensive production of basic metals (27). It is striking that export unit values in all of these categories lay clearly below 10 Euro/kg. In product groups where export unit values are considerably higher, though declining, such as in science-based and in differentiated goods, Greece has no comparative advantage on the EU 15 market. Export unit values of radio, TV and communication equipments (32) were strikingly high in 1993 with 159 Euro/kg, sliding down to only 69 Euro/kg in 2003. Clearly, in the evolution of Greece's foreign trade to the EU 15, it seems to be specializing in low tech industries and often in low quality products.

Taking into account the shares of value added in figure 4.34 it is striking that these are generally very low compared to any other country considered in this analysis. Total manufacturing exports are worth only 3.8 % of the Greek economy's value added in 2003, and was slightly higher in 1993 with 4.5 %. This is the main explanation, why weighted and unweighted RCAs hardly differ from each other, since none of the manufacturing industries strikes out with a relatively high value added share.

Concerning the dynamic development of RCAs we conclude that Poland exports rather low and some medium technology (or labor intensive) products to the EU 15 just like Greece and Portugal and to a lesser extent Spain. The Czech Republic, however, shows clear specialization patterns also in the field of medium and even high technology products, while Hungary and Ireland mainly specialize in the export of high technology, whereas in Hungary we also find export specialization in some very low technology products in the 1990s.

4.4 Competition Among New EU and Cohesion Countries

How does the new competitive landscape of the EU 25 look? Having analyzed EU trade patterns of selected new EU member states and cohesion countries, a major question remains to be answered. Against which cohesion countries will the new EU countries compete on the single European market? Will it be the cohesion countries? Will the cohesion countries lose competitive power on the EU market in the course of European integration and EU enlargement? Building on the idea of the Traditional Trade Theory, one would expect the new EU member states to compete with the less developed EU 15 countries - the cohesion countries - because they tend to specialize in the same industries due to similar factor endowments and comparative advantages.

Since foreign trade competition always concerns at least two countries, we will now turn to a comparative analysis of country results. From the focus of countries' specialization as suppliers of goods on the EU 15 market, one has to proceed in at least two steps to be able to draw conclusions on the competitive landscape of the Single European Market and compare:[8]

1. the RCAs, and
2. the export unit values.

First of all, two countries face competition on the EU 15 market if both countries have a comparative advantage of exports in this specific industry. Thus, the national share of a product group in total manufacturing exports to the EU 15 is higher than the respective share in total intra-EU manufacturing exports. This implies that a country is more specialized in exporting a specific industrial good than the EU 15 average. This might be a necessary condition, but is this sufficient for competition? The answer is probably no.

If the export shares of one specific industry in at least two countries are higher than the respective export share of that industry on the EU market, these countries compete in terms of quantity, but do they compete in terms of quality as well? They still might export goods of completely different quality, which finally do not compete against each other due to differences in consumers' preferences and to differences concerning purchasing power of consumers. Therefore it seems necessary to also look at the export unit values of the products in order to establish whether they belong to the same quality of goods and thus compete against each other. This is done by using the quartiles of the export unit value distribution of the EU 15 countries. Hereby the quartiles of the distribution are assumed to represent the borders between the different quality classes of products: low quality products are situated below the 25 %-quartile, lower-middle up to the 50 %- quartile, higher-middle up to the 75 %-quartile, and high quality products are found above the 75 %- quartile of the distribution. To simplify, middle quality compiles all values between the 25 % and the 75 %-quartiles. New EU countries' export unit values are not included in calculating the quartiles, because the main focus lies on the supplier position of the countries on the EU 15 market; therefore the point of reference is the quality of EU 15 exports.

From a theoretical perspective, one can distinguish between different quality groups and then find out whether countries show overlaps in one or several of the quality categories. This is particularly interesting if one analyzes over time. As regards EUVs in absolute terms, one might have to look at inflation dynamics as well, which could distort the picture, as a country's export in a product category might move towards higher EUVs which, however, could reflect an inflation phenomenon. In the 1990s, however, the inflation rate was rather low in the EU and the OECD countries, leading one to possibly ignore these inflation aspects. We will now turn to analyzing the competitive structure in the five main product categories of the OECD taxonomy taking

---

[8] If needed, one could additionally take a look at the importance of specific sectors and industries for the economy as a whole, for example by analyzing the sectoral export shares to GDP or to value added as done in the previous section.

into account three new EU member states and four cohesion countries. We compare the situation in the years 1993 and 2003 and analyze the shifts that have taken place.

4.4.1 Labor Intensive Industries

Recalling the figures on RCAs, it is striking that Ireland does not compete in any labor intensive sectors as a supplier on the EU 15 market. Spain only competes in one product group - leather -, whereas all other countries in at least two or three. The situation in each product group is described in the following.

Textiles (17)

Three competitors were present on the market in both years, namely the Czech Republic, Greece and Portugal. All three raised their RCAs from 1993 to 2003, thus strengthening their competitive position on the EU 15 market. Greece and the Czech Republic provided low quality textiles in both years, whereas Portugal lost in quality measures from high to medium. In addition, Hungary was competitive in 1993 with high quality textiles, but no longer in 2003; Poland entered the market in 2003 with low quality instead. Table 4.5 summarizes the outcomes; the export unit values shown refer to the EU 15 as a benchmark for quality determination.

Table 4.5. Textiles (17) - Low, Middle and High Quality Product Suppliers within the EU 15 Market Measured by Intra-EU 15 Export Unit Values

	EUV (EUR/kg) 1993	EUV (EUR/kg) 2003	Competitors 1993	Competitors 2003
Low Quality	< 4.9	< 5.0	Czech Rep. Greece	Czech Rep. Greece Poland
Middle Quality	4.9 - 6.2	5.0 - 7.1		Portugal
High Quality	> 6.2	> 7.1	Hungary Portugal	

Source: Own Calculations

Wearing Apparel (18)

Five countries had a comparative advantage in wearing apparel in 1993: Portugal, Greece, Hungary, Poland and the Czech Republic (table 4.6). From

1993 to 2003 in all three new EU countries, comparative advantages were considerably reduced, in the Czech Republic to such an extent that it had lost its advantage by 2003. At the same, time Poland also lost by quality of exports; by 2003 it provided low quality wearing apparel, whereas it had provided middle quality in 1993. Greece's RCAs also decreased, but at the same time it could remain in the middle quality segment. On the contrary, Portugal was able to climb up the quality ladder and provided high quality wearing apparel in 2003; the rise in Portuguese export unit values from 21.1 Euro/kg in 1993 to 37.7 Euro/kg in 2003 is remarkable.

Table 4.6. Wearing Apparel (18) - Low, Middle and High Quality Product Suppliers within the EU 15 Market Measured by Intra-EU 15 Export Unit Values

	EUV (EUR/kg) 1993	EUV (EUR/kg) 2003	Competitors 1993	Competitors 2003
Low Quality	< 19.8	< 22.3		Poland
Middle Quality	19.8 - 29.7	22.3 - 32.7	Hungary Greece Poland Czech Rep. Portugal	Hungary Greece
High Quality	> 29.7	> 32.7		Portugal

Source: Own Calculations

Leather, Luggage, Footwear (19)

The new EU countries' market position has clearly deteriorated since 1993; in the year 2003 only Hungary was left on the market with a comparative advantage in low quality products (table 4.7). Poland and the Czech Republic no longer competed. In addition, Spain and Portugal were competitive on the EU 15 market, where Portugal remained in the high quality segment in both years, and Spanish quality deteriorated from high to low quality.

Fabricated Metal Products (28)

In both years considered, only Poland and the Czech Republic competed against each other with low quality products of below 2.6 Euro/kg value (table 4.8). In 1993, Hungary was also a competitor for low quality. Neither of the three new EU member states nor any of the cohesion countries competed with middle or high quality fabricated metal products on the EU 15 market.

Table 4.7. Leather (19) - Low, Middle and High Quality Product Suppliers within the EU 15 Market Measured by Intra-EU 15 Export Unit Values

	EUV (EUR/kg) 1993	EUV (EUR/kg) 2003	Competitors 1993	Competitors 2003
Low Quality	< 10.0	< 22.6	Poland Czech Rep.	Hungary Spain
Middle Quality	10.0 - 14.6	22.6 - 29.0	Hungary	
High Quality	> 14.6	> 29.0	Spain Portugal	Portugal

Source: Own Calculations

Table 4.8. Fabricated Metal Products (28) - Low, Middle and High Quality Product Suppliers within the EU 15 Market Measured by Intra-EU 15 Export Unit Values

	EUV (EUR/kg) 1993	EUV (EUR/kg) 2003	Competitors 1993	Competitors 2003
Low Quality	< 2.5	< 2.6	Poland Czech Rep. Hungary	Poland Czech Rep.
Middle Quality	2.5 - 3.4	2.6 - 4.2		
High Quality	> 3.4	> 4.2		

Source: Own Calculations

Furniture (36)

Again, only Poland and the Czech Republic had a comparative advantage in both years considered; both offered low quality furniture to the EU 15 market(table 4.9). Furthermore, Hungary was still competitive in 1993 with low quality furniture, but not in 2003. Instead, Portugal entered as a competitor for middle quality goods. High quality furniture was not offered by any of the seven countries considered in this analysis.

Figure 4.35 provides a graphical analysis of the competitive structure in the labor intensive industrial sector as a whole, comparing the years 1993 and 2001. To conclude, the competitive position of three countries did not change; Portugal, Greece and Ireland remained in the same position, whereas the latter was not competing in the labor intensive sectors at all. Portugal

Table 4.9. Furniture (36) - Low, Middle and High Quality Product Suppliers within the EU 15 Market Measured by Intra-EU 15 Export Unit Values

	EUV (EUR/kg) 1993	EUV (EUR/kg) 2003	Competitors 1993	Competitors 2003
Low Quality	< 4.4	< 4.7	Poland Czech Rep. Hungary	Poland Czech Rep.
Middle Quality	4.4 - 6.0	4.7 - 6.8		Portugal
High Quality	> 6.0	> 6.8		

Source: Own Calculations

remained competitive in high and middle quality, while Greece in middle and low quality. No country was able to move up the quality ladder from 1993 to 2003. On the contrary, Hungary left the high quality sector and provided only middle and low quality goods by 2003. Spain moved from high to low quality, the Czech Republic and Poland from middle and low quality to merely low quality. The general observation can be made that the new EU and the cohesion countries are rather extensively present on the EU 15 market with labor intensive products. Furthermore, these countries seem to specialize more and more on the middle and lower end of the quality ladder, yielding to other suppliers of higher quality labor intensive goods.

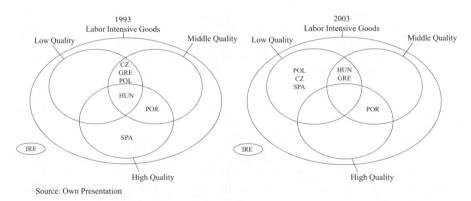

Source: Own Presentation

Fig. 4.35. Structure of Competitiveness within the Labor Intensive Industrial Sectors

4.4.2 Resource Intensive Industries

For the sake of simplicity, the two product groups which belong to two of the OECD product categories each, 27 as resource + scale intensive and 35 as scale + science intensive, have been put into either category. Therefore basic metals (27) are included in the resource intensive industries.

Tobacco (16)

Except for Ireland in 1993, neither the cohesion nor the new EU countries had a comparative advantage in exporting tobacco (table 4.10). This is probably due to the geographical location and the climate of all these countries, which do not favor the cultivation of tobacco. At the same time, Denmark and the Netherlands had quite robust comparative advantages, which is probably due to their having harbor cities.

Table 4.10. Tobacco (16) - Low, Middle and High Quality Product Suppliers within the EU 15 Market Measured by Intra-EU 15 Export Unit Values

	EUV (EUR/kg) 1993	EUV (EUR/kg) 2003	Competitors 1993	Competitors 2003
Low Quality	< 3.1	< 8.9		
Middle Quality	3.1 - 10.5	8.9 - 17.0		
High Quality	> 10.5	> 17.0	Ireland	

Source: Own Calculations

Food and Beverages (15)

Greece and Ireland were competitors in both years, where Ireland competed with high quality and Greece with middle quality. According to table 4.11, Hungary was also competitive with middle quality in 1993 and was replaced in 2003 by Spain.

Wood and Cork (20)

In 1993, Poland and the Czech Republic competed against each other in low quality wooden exports, Hungary and Portugal in medium quality, and Spain

Table 4.11. Food and Beverages (15) - Low, Middle and High Quality Product Suppliers within the EU 15 Market Measured by Intra-EU 15 Export Unit Values

	EUV (EUR/kg) 1993	EUV (EUR/kg) 2003	Competitors 1993	Competitors 2003
Low Quality	< 1.0	< 1.0		
Middle Quality	1.0 - 1.4	1.0 - 1.4	Greece Hungary	Greece Spain
High Quality	> 1.4	> 1.4	Ireland	Ireland

Source: Own Calculations

was present on the market with high quality wood and cork. By 2003, Hungary and Spain exited the market; Portugal and the Czech Republic remained competitive in the respective quality segment (table 4.12).

Table 4.12. Wood and Cork (20) - Low, Middle and High Quality Product Suppliers within the EU 15 Market Measured by Intra-EU 15 Export Unit Values

	EUV (EUR/kg) 1993	EUV (EUR/kg) 2003	Competitors 1993	Competitors 2003
Low Quality	< 0.3	< 0.4	Czech Rep. Poland	Czech Rep.
Middle Quality	0.3 - 0.7	0.4 - 0.9	Hungary Portugal	Poland Portugal
High Quality	> 0.7	> 0.9	Spain	

Source: Own Calculations

Coke, Refined Petroleum, Nuclear Fuel (23)

The only competitor in 1993 was Portugal, in 2003 Poland. Both were competitive with low quality coke and petroleum products (table 4.13).

Other Non-metallic Mineral Products (26)

There was intense but declining competition between the new EU member states and the cohesion countries in this sector. Six out of seven countries

Table 4.13. Coke, Refined Petroleum, Nuclear Fuel (23) - Low, Middle and High Quality Product Suppliers within the EU 15 Market Measured by Intra-EU 15 Export Unit Values

	EUV (EUR/kg) 1993	EUV (EUR/kg) 2003	Competitors 1993	Competitors 2003
Low Quality	< 0.1	< 0.2	Portugal	Poland
Middle Quality	0.1 - 0.2	0.2 - 0.4		
High Quality	> 0.2	> 0.4		

Source: Own Calculations

competed in 1993 (with the exception of Ireland), and four in 2003 (with the exception of Ireland, Greece and Hungary). Two of the new EU countries, namely the Czech Republic and Poland, moved up the quality ladder from low quality in 1993 to middle quality in 2003, while Portugal slid down from a middle to low quality supplier. Spain remained in the middle quality segment in both years. High quality non-metallic products were exported to the EU 15 by other groups outside the new EU members and the cohesion countries (table 4.14).

Table 4.14. Other Non-metallic Mineral Products (26) - Low, Middle and High Quality Product Suppliers within the EU 15 Market Measured by Intra-EU 15 Export Unit Values

	EUV (EUR/kg) 1993	EUV (EUR/kg) 2003	Competitors 1993	Competitors 2003
Low Quality	< 0.3	< 0.4	Czech Rep. Poland Greece	Portugal
Middle Quality	0.3 - 0.6	0.4 - 0.7	Hungary Portugal Spain	Czech Rep. Poland Spain
High Quality	> 0.6	> 0.7		

Source: Own Calculations

Basic Metals (27)

In 1993, five countries were competitive in the manufacture of basic metals: the Czech Republic, Hungary, Poland, Greece and Spain. Only Poland and Spain offered middle quality, the other countries low quality. By 2003, merely two countries remained competitive, Poland and Greece. Greece upgraded in quality from low to high, whereas Poland downgraded from middle to low quality (table 4.15).

Table 4.15. Basic Metals (27) - Low, Middle and High Quality Product Suppliers within the EU 15 Market Measured by Intra-EU 15 Export Unit Values

	EUV (EUR/kg) 1993	EUV (EUR/kg) 2003	Competitors 1993	Competitors 2003
Low Quality	< 0.5	< 0.6	Hungary Czech Rep. Greece	Poland
Middle Quality	0.5 - 0.6	0.6 - 0.8	Poland Spain	
High Quality	> 0.6	> 0.8		Greece

Source: Own Calculations

Figure 4.36 provides a graphical analysis of the competitive structure in the resource intensive industrial sectors as a whole, comparing the years 1993 and 2003. One country, namely Hungary, completely exited competition in resource intensive industries by 2003. Three countries remained as suppliers in the same type of quality: Poland, Portugal and Ireland. Thus three countries altered their competitive position on the EU 15 market. The Czech Republic partially upgraded and provided medium quality goods in addition to low quality by 2003; this comes from providing medium quality non-metallic mineral products. Greece also upgraded and supplied the EU 15 with middle and high quality by 2003; Greece exported basic metals of high quality and food and beverages of medium quality. Spain partially downgraded and provided medium quality resource intensive goods by 2003, instead of medium and high quality in 1993. The task of finding an overall trend of development within the resource intensive sectors is rather challenging. However, it seems that the peripheral EU countries tend to move up the quality ladder in supplying resource intensive goods.

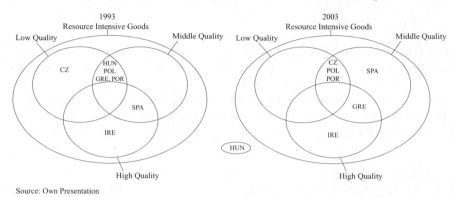

Source: Own Presentation

Fig. 4.36. Structure of Competitiveness within the Resource Intensive Industrial Sectors

4.4.3 Scale Intensive Industries

Other transport equipment (35) is included here, as airspace is the only item which belongs to science-based goods, while most of the other transport equipment is rather scale intensive in production. The situation in each product group in described below.

Pulp and Paper (21)

The only country with a relative comparative advantage in both years was Portugal. It supplied the EU 15 with low quality pulp and paper products (table 4.16). In addition, Poland gained a comparative advantage with medium quality pulp and paper products by 2003.

Table 4.16. Pulp and Paper (21) - Low, Middle and High Quality Product Suppliers within the EU 15 Market Measured by Intra-EU 15 Export Unit Values

	EUV (EUR/kg) 1993	EUV (EUR/kg) 2003	Competitors 1993	Competitors 2003
Low Quality	< 0.6	< 0.6	Portugal	Portugal
Middle Quality	0.6 - 0.9	0.6 - 0.8		Poland
High Quality	> 0.9	> 0.8		

Source: Own Calculations

Publishing and Printing (22)

This is one of the very few product groups for which export unit values of the EU 15 declined between 1993 and 2003 (table 4.17). Both in 1993 and 2003, the Czech Republic had a revealed comparative advantage in low quality goods. By 2003, Ireland entered the market with high quality products; its export unit value development is remarkable. In 2003 it amounted to 12.6 Euro/kg, which already was rather high compared to the EU 15 average of 5.1 Euro/kg. Moreover, EUVs rose to 51.3 Euro/kg in 1999; in the same year the EU 15 average amounted to 7.3 Euro/kg. Then EUV fell and resulted in 27.7 Euro/kg in 2003, which was still five times higher than the EU 15 average of 5.4 Euro/kg.

Table 4.17. Publishing and Printing (22) - Low, Middle and High Quality Product Suppliers within the EU 15 Market Measured by Intra-EU 15 Export Unit Values

	EUV (EUR/kg) 1993	EUV (EUR/kg) 2003	Competitors 1993	Competitors 2003
Low Quality	< 3.8	< 2.6	Czech Rep.	Czech Rep.
Middle Quality	3.8 - 5.5	2.6 - 5.0		
High Quality	> 5.5	> 5.0		Ireland

Source: Own Calculations

Chemicals and Chemical Products (24)

On the chemicals market, Ireland appeared as the sole competitor among the cohesion countries and the selected new EU member states, supplying high quality products. Again, it struck out with a remarkable increase in export unit values, which rose from 4.4 Euro/kg in 1993 to more than 17 Euro/kg in 2003. The latter is an extreme outlier, since the EU 15 average EUV amounted to merely 2.5 Euro/kg in 2003 (table 4.18).

Rubber and Plastic Products (25)

While no country had a comparative advantage in 1993, the Czech Republic competed in middle quality goods, and Poland, Portugal and Spain competed against each other with low quality products in 2003 (table 4.19). The EUV distribution of the EU 15 countries hardly changed between 1993 and 2003.

Table 4.18. Chemicals and Chemical Products (24) - Low, Middle and High Quality Product Suppliers within the EU 15 Market Measured by Intra-EU 15 Export Unit Values

	EUV (EUR/kg) 1993	EUV (EUR/kg) 2003	Competitors 1993	Competitors 2003
Low Quality	< 0.6	< 1.0		
Middle Quality	0.6 - 1.4	1.0 - 1.9		
High Quality	> 1.4	> 1.9	Ireland	Ireland

Source: Own Calculations

Table 4.19. Rubber and Plastic Products (25) - Low, Middle and High Quality Product Suppliers within the EU 15 Market Measured by Intra-EU 15 Export Unit Values

	EUV (EUR/kg) 1993	EUV (EUR/kg) 2003	Competitors 1993	Competitors 2003
Low Quality	< 2.9	< 2.9		Poland Portugal Spain
Middle Quality	2.9 - 3.4	2.9 - 3.5		Czech Rep.
High Quality	> 3.4	> 3.5		

Source: Own Calculations

Motor Vehicles and Trailers (34)

In this product group the new EU and the cohesion countries gained a lot of ground in the course of the 1990s. While only Spain competed in the market in 1993, by 2003 Poland and the Czech Republic entered the market with low quality products, Portugal with medium quality, and Hungary even with high quality motor vehicles and trailers. At the same time, Spain downgraded its supply to low quality by 2003 (table 4.20).

Other Transport Equipment (35)

This group has been included in the scale intensive category, although some of its products (aircraft and spacecraft) are rather science-based. This might

Table 4.20. Motor Vehicles and Trailers (34) - Low, Middle and High Quality Product Suppliers within the EU 15 Market Measured by Intra-EU 15 Export Unit Values

	EUV (EUR/kg) 1993	EUV (EUR/kg) 2003	Competitors 1993	Competitors 2003
Low Quality	< 6.2	< 7.0		Czech Rep. Poland Spain
Middle Quality	6.2 - 7.6	7.0 - 8.8	Spain	Portugal
High Quality	> 7.6	> 8.8		Hungary

Source: Own Calculations

be an explanation for the rather interesting findings shown in table 4.21 and raises the question of whether one should use more disaggregated data for such industries, where allocation to an OECD category at 2-digit level is not clear. In 1993, Poland had a comparative advantage in other transport equipment with low quality goods, and in 2003 Portugal and Greece competed with high quality supplies. These last two cases are rather mysterious in the sense that it is difficult to find a coherent explanation, since Greek EUVs showed extreme volatility in the time period of 1993 to 2003; Portuguese EUVs rose in the same time period from 7 Euro/kg to more than 103 Euro/kg.

Table 4.21. Other Transport Equipment (35) - Low, Middle and High Quality Product Suppliers within the EU 15 Market Measured by Intra-EU 15 Export Unit Values

	EUV (EUR/kg) 1993	EUV (EUR/kg) 2003	Competitors 1993	Competitors 2003
Low Quality	< 10.4	< 22.3	Poland	
Middle Quality	10.4 - 27.5	22.3 - 62.8		
High Quality	> 27.5	> 62.8		Portugal Greece

Source: Own Calculations

Figure 4.37 provides a graphical analysis of the competitive structure in the scale intensive industrial sectors as a whole, comparing the years 1993 and 2003. Both the new EU member states and the cohesion countries managed to place themselves well on the scale intensive markets. Already in 1993 the situation was rather beneficial, because only Hungary and Greece were not competitive. In 1993 Ireland provided high quality scale intensive goods, Spain medium quality. The two new EU countries Poland and the Czech Republic, together with Portugal, were suppliers for low quality products. By 2003, Hungary and Greece also gained comparative advantages, even in the high quality segment where they competed against Ireland. The Czech Republic and Poland upgraded to low and middle quality, whereas Portugal even to low, medium and high quality scale intensive goods. On the contrary, Spain's supplied quality downgraded to merely low. In general the case can then be made that the EU periphery is rather successful as a supplier of scale intensive goods on the EU 15 market and does so in all three quality segments. Especially in high quality goods, their position seems to be much stronger as compared to other OECD product categories.

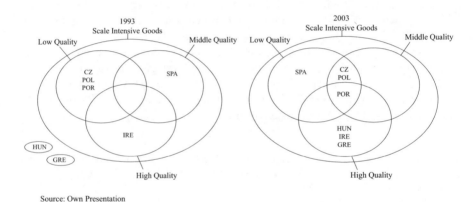

Source: Own Presentation

Fig. 4.37. Structure of Competitiveness within the Scale Intensive Industrial Sectors

4.4.4 Science-Based Industries

Office Machinery and Computers (30)

In this sector, there was a global fall in absolute prices in the 1990s due to enormous technological progress, which might impair quality ladder analysis. However, we assume that relative quality groupings are not affected by this phenomenon. In 1993, Ireland was the only country with a relative comparative advantage on the EU 15 market for office machinery and computers.

It provided high quality products. By 2003, export unit values declined to middle quality. At the same time, Hungary and the Czech Republic entered the market with low quality products (table 4.22).

Table 4.22. Office Machinery and Computers (30) - Low, Middle and High Quality Product Suppliers within the EU 15 Market Measured by Intra-EU 15 Export Unit Values

	EUV (EUR/kg) 1993	EUV (EUR/kg) 2003	Competitors 1993	Competitors 2003
Low Quality	< 50.4	< 44.9		Czech Rep. Hungary
Middle Quality	50.4 - 85.1	44.9 - 64.1		Ireland
High Quality	> 77.8	> 64.1	Ireland	

Source: Own Calculations

Medical and Optical Instruments (33)

Participation in this sector was very scarce. In both years only Ireland had a comparative advantage on the EU 15 market. In 1993, this advantage existed for middle quality products, and by 2003 Ireland was able to upgrade quality, see table 4.23.

Table 4.23. Medical and Optical Instruments (33) - Low, Middle and High Quality Product Suppliers within the EU 15 Market Measured by Intra-EU 15 Export Unit Values

	EUV (EUR/kg) 1993	EUV (EUR/kg) 2003	Competitors 1993	Competitors 2003
Low Quality	< 30.4	< 32.1		
Middle Quality	30.4 - 62.4	32.1 - 75.1	Ireland	
High Quality	> 62.4	> 75.1		Ireland

Source: Own Calculations

Figure 4.38 provides a graphical analysis of the competitive structure in the science-based industrial sectors as a whole comparing the years 1993 and 2003. It is striking that hardly any of the analyzed countries competed within the science-based sectors. In 1993, only Ireland was competitive with middle and high quality goods and this remained the case through 2003. In addition, Hungary and the Czech Republic also entered the market with low quality goods in 2003.

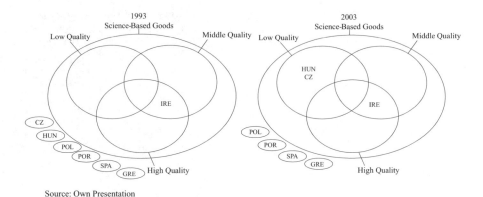

Source: Own Presentation

Fig. 4.38. Structure of Competitiveness within the Science-Based Industrial Sectors

4.4.5 Differentiated Goods

Machinery and Equipment (29)

Only a few words are required to describe the competitive situation in machinery and equipment. Only the Czech Republic was competitive both in 1993 and 2003 with low quality products (table 4.24).

Electrical Machinery and Apparatus (31)

This is the only product group within the differentiated goods for which participation was rather high among the the EU countries and the cohesion countries. Hungary, the Czech Republic and Portugal had a comparative advantage in both 1993 and 2003. Hungary and the Czech Republic were able to upgrade quality, whereas Portugal downgraded from high to medium quality. In addition Ireland was competitive in 1993 with high quality goods, and Poland in 2003 with medium quality goods (table 4.25).

Table 4.24. Machinery and Equipment (29) - Low, Middle and High Quality Product Suppliers within the EU 15 Market Measured by Intra-EU 15 Export Unit Values

	EUV (EUR/kg) 1993	EUV (EUR/kg) 2003	Competitors 1993	Competitors 2003
Low Quality	< 6.8	< 6.7	Czech Rep.	Czech Rep.
Middle Quality	6.8 - 9.5	6.7 - 9.5		
High Quality	> 9.5	> 9.5		

Source: Own Calculations

Table 4.25. Electrical Machinery and Apparatus (31) - Low, Middle and High Quality Product Suppliers within the EU 15 Market Measured by Intra-EU 15 Export Unit Values

	EUV (EUR/kg) 1993	EUV (EUR/kg) 2003	Competitors 1993	Competitors 2003
Low Quality	< 6.9	< 5.8	Czech Rep.	
Middle Quality	6.9 - 9.8	5.8 - 10.4	Hungary	Czech Rep. Poland Portugal
High Quality	> 9.8	> 10.4	Ireland Portugal	Hungary

Source: Own Calculations

Radio, Television and Communications (32)

Interestingly, none of the cohesion nor any of the new EU countries was competitive with radio, television and communications equipment in 1993. Even more interestingly, by 2003 all three new EU member states, Hungary, Poland and the Czech Republic, gained a comparative advantage with low quality products. The cohesion countries remained non-competitive. Medium and high quality goods were, however, not supplied by the new EU countries (table 4.26).

Finally, figure 4.39 summarizes the competitive structure of differentiated goods in both years. It is difficult to claim that the EU peripheral countries per se gained competitive power in the sectors of differentiated goods in the course of the 1990s. Both in 1993 and 2003, three countries were not com-

Table 4.26. Radio, Television and Communications (32) - Low, Middle and High Quality Product Suppliers within the EU 15 Market Measured by Intra-EU 15 Export Unit Values

	EUV (EUR/kg) 1993	EUV (EUR/kg) 2003	Competitors 1993	Competitors 2003
Low Quality	< 21.4	< 32.2		Czech Rep. Hungary Poland
Middle Quality	21.4 - 40.5	32.2 - 68.5		
High Quality	> 40.5	> 68.5		

Source: Own Calculations

petitive, namely Poland, Greece and Spain in 1993, and Ireland, Greece and Spain in 2003. However, it seems that the new EU member states successfully placed themselves on the EU 15 market. They could mostly upgrade supplied quality or increase competitiveness, whereas the cohesion countries were not as successful. Still, hardly any of the countries considered in the analysis were competitive with high quality differentiated products.

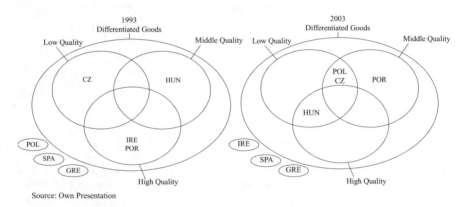

Source: Own Presentation

Fig. 4.39. Structure of Competitiveness within the Differentiated Goods

Concerning the picture of the competitive structure of suppliers on the EU 15 market we can summarize the results from two points of view. Firstly, we can compare each country's position in all industries throughout the 1990s to reveal the following picture. The Czech Republic never had a comparative advantage with a high quality product. Poland seems to have remained in the same quality segments with its export products; both in 1993 and 2003 it supplied the EU 15 with low and medium quality products. Thus, the Czech Republic and Poland seem to have specialized on the EU 15 market in low and middle quality products. Hungary, on the other hand, also competed with high quality products in both years, thus competing along the entire length of the quality ladder. On the contrary, in 1993 Spain and Ireland did not have a relative comparative advantage with low quality products; for Ireland this was still valid in 2003. Thus, Spain and Ireland seem to have specialized on the EU 15 market as suppliers of middle and higher quality goods. Portugal spread its comparative advantages across the range of low, middle and high quality products in both years. Greece did so as well in 2003, whereas it was only competitive with low and medium quality products at the beginning of the 1990s. From this point of view, Poland, Hungary, and the Czech Republic were competitors mainly of Portugal and Greece in the lower and middle quality goods, but for some middle quality goods also Spain and Ireland were potential competitors. In addition, Hungary faced competition from Spain and Ireland in some higher quality products, and in a few industries also from Portugal and exceptionally from Greece.

Secondly, we can analyze each product category separately, leading to the following conclusions. In labor and resource intensive industries there was an intensive market participation of new EU and cohesion countries. With the exception of Spain in labor intensive goods and Ireland in resource intensive goods, these countries tend to have specialized in medium and lower quality goods, scarcely competing in high quality. Ireland did not participate much in the market for labor intensive goods, whereas Hungary's only field of non-participation was in resource intensive goods at the end of the sample period. In scale intensive product groups, the EU peripheral countries gained more and more ground in the 1990s and subsequently, not only in terms of competitiveness, but also in terms of quality upgrading. By 2003, four of the seven countries analyzed were competitive within the high quality segment. Accession and cohesion countries were very weak in competing in science-based industries. Most countries did not compete in that market segment at all; only Ireland and later on Hungary and the Czech Republic were able to enter, however only with low quality products. The situation looks much better for the new EU countries in differentiated goods, however, not for the cohesion countries. In 2003, all new EU countries competed, but only one cohesion country, Portugal. Greece and Spain remained outside in both years. Nevertheless, the competitive countries lost in terms of quality, and hardly competed with high quality any more in 2003. Supply of high quality differentiated goods was mainly left to other European countries.

The comparative analysis of specialization within the EU market with a special focus on the EU periphery, the cohesion and new EU countries is rather complex to put it in a nutshell. However, there appears to be some findings which are rather robust for the time period 1993-2003 and which can be seen as general conclusions drawn from the analysis:

- New EU countries are gaining competitive power and improving quality in scale intensive industries.
- Most new EU and cohesion countries have a strong disadvantage in science-based industries.
- Ireland does not compete in labor intensive industries.
- Hungary no longer competes in resource intensive industries, but gains a comparative advantage in scale intensive industries.
- Spain and Greece do not compete in science-based and in differentiated goods.
- The Czech Republic, Poland, and Hungary when supplying low and middle quality products tend to compete against Greece and Portugal; for medium quality, sometimes against Spain and Ireland as well.
- Hungary, in addition, supplies higher quality goods competing against Spain and Ireland, in some product groups since the end of the 1990s also against Portugal and Greece.
- With the exception of scale intensive and some resource intensive industries, high quality goods are, however, mostly not supplied by the EU peripheral countries on the EU 15 market.

To gain a complete picture of the competitive structure of suppliers on the EU 15 market, one might include other European countries and some non-European suppliers of the EU market, as well. Due to the focus of this analysis on competitiveness within the EU periphery, the approach of looking at new EU and cohesion countries is appropriate. We find the hypothesis to hold that both the new EU and the cohesion countries compete mostly within the same product categories mainly with lower and medium quality goods. Thus, most higher quality products, and especially science-based products of all qualities, are still supplied on the EU 15 market by countries other than the EU periphery. Having analyzed competitiveness, we will now turn our attention to the development of foreign trade patterns in the enlarged European Union and will test whether EU 25 trade specialization patterns have converged or diverged since the beginning of the 1990s.

4.5 Do Intra-EU Trade Patterns Converge?

Much has been written in the economic literature about convergence among countries, mostly in terms of income. In the course of EU enlargement this subject has become even more relevant in the European context. One main tool to test for convergence is the concept of of β- and σ-convergence for which Barro and Sala-i-Martin (1991, 1992, and 1995) pioneered. In the economic growth context, β-convergence states that poor countries grow faster than rich ones implying catching-up of the poor countries, and σ-convergence states that income variance between poor and rich countries is diminishing. Some papers, for example, Quah (1993) and Evans (1998), question the econometric validity of these models, thus enhancing the use of the properties of time-series analysis considering convergence as a stochastic process just like Bernard and Durlauf (1995).

More recently, two main approaches have been proposed for testing convergence. One main line of the literature focuses on using and developing cross-section and panel estimation methods to identify convergence (e.g. Islam, 1995). The other line of the literature works on extending the process of unit root tests (originally coming from the time series literature) to the analysis of (dynamic) panel models (e.g. Im, Pesaran, Shin, 1995). These procedures can be distinguished according to the models they use and the restrictions they impose under the panel unit root zero hypothesis.

Some papers in the literature analyze the role of foreign trade in income convergence (e.g. Gaulier, 2003). While a lot has been written about income convergence, the topic of convergence in trade structures has been treated in the empirical literature to a much lesser extent. This is where the following analysis contributes. It adopts the methods of β- and σ-convergence, widely used in the growth literature, to identify convergence in trade patterns within the EU.[9] The main idea behind the analysis of convergence in trade patterns is that similarity in production and trade structures among EU 25 countries will ease the integration process. From a macroeconomic point of view, one may state that when integration extends far beyond trade, as is the case in the European Union, convergence in production and trade structures will help smooth the integration process. The more similar countries are in terms of sectoral specialization, the more likely it is that they will face symmetric shocks and an increase in business cycle co-movements. Correlation in business cycles is even more important if countries aim to have a common monetary policy, as is relevant for countries eager to join the Eurozone. Furthermore, from a theoretical point of view, similar countries integrate more easily, because they are likely to show very similar diversification patterns, thus achieving factor price equalization through trade. Trade in products can, at least to some extent, replace trade in production factors and lead to convergence in factor prices. Thus, incentives to factor mobility, especially to migration, will be reduced. This is extremely important in the European context, since there are many concerns about potential migration flows within the EU 25.

4.5.1 Methodology

In this context we distinguish between (1) specialization or de-specialization in trade patterns on the one hand, and (2) between concentration and de-concentration in trade patterns on the other. The methodologies for testing (1) whether countries are stable across sectors or whether they tend to become more or less specialized at an intra-country level (intra-country/cross

---

[9] We do not use a panel unit root test, because the standard estimation method of β- and σ-convergence fits our data better.

sectoral analysis), and (2) whether countries tend to converge within the same sectors or whether a specific sector tends to become more or less concentrated (intra-sectoral/cross-country analysis) are basically analogous. This distinction is more or less by definition two sides of the same coin. It is nevertheless important, because the two kinds of processes might not always move in the same direction, and also the speed of the processes might differ significantly. Therefore, we will deal with the two sides of the coin successively, starting with the intra-country/cross-sectoral analysis.

Country-Wise Regression

The following testing method for technological specialization patterns is based on Pavitt (1989) and Cantwell (1989). They were inspired by a Galtonian regression model of Hart (1974). Further discussion can be found in the context of convergence in Hart (1994). Specialization patterns are tested by the following regression:

$$logRCA_{ij}^{t_1} = \alpha_j + \beta_j logRCA_{ij}^{t_0} + \varepsilon_{ij}^{t_1} \tag{4.5}$$

where i stands for a country and j for an industrial sector. The initial year of observations is referred to by t_0, whereas t_1 represents the final year. Note that within this analytical framework nothing can be said about the determinants of the initial export specialization patterns.

Concerning (de-)specialization, we are interested in the value of β. If $\beta = 1$, specialization patterns of the respective country i across all industries j have not changed from t_0 to t_1. If $\beta > 1$, the country tends to become more specialized in sectors where it has initially been specialized and less specialized where initial specialization is low. Thus the existing patterns of specialization have strengthened. Since we measure the direct comparative (dis-)advantage towards the EU 15, we can also say that $\beta > 1$ implies a divergence from the EU 15 specialization patterns between the initial and the final period of time. In analogy to the convergence literature in the growth theory we might term this β-specialization. If $0 < \beta < 1$, the initial patterns have changed: sectors with an initially low RCA tend to increase over time and initially high RCAs tend to decrease. This implies a convergence of the country's export patterns towards the EU 15 patterns and might be called β-de-specialization. The case of $\beta < 0$ would mean a reversed ranking: sectors with RCAs below the country's average in the initial period would be above the average in the final period and visa versa.

Hereby we will need to test firstly, whether β is significantly different from zero ($H_0 : \beta = 0$ versus $H_1 : \beta \neq 0$) and secondly, whether β is significantly different from one ($H_0 : \beta = 1$ versus $H_1 : \beta \neq 1$). To generalize: ($H_0 : \beta = b$ and $H_1 : \beta \neq b$). This is done by a simple two-sided t-test, where the definition of the t-distribution is given by equation 4.6:

$$t_\beta = \frac{\beta - b}{s_\beta} \sim t(n - 2) \tag{4.6}$$

where t_β follows the Student t-distribution with n-2 degrees of freedom and t_β is called the t-value of β. Furthermore, s_β is the standard error of β.

Another question raised within this regression analysis is a test whether the degree of specialization changes. β-de-specialization is a necessary, but not sufficient condition for a decline in the degree of overall national specialization patterns measured by a decrease in the dispersion of the distribution. Although dispersion of the RCAs is reduced within a country in case of $0 < \beta < 1$ for the time being, but new shocks seized by the error term could lead to an increase again. Thus the degree of change in specialization also depends on the R^2 (i.e., on the relative importance of random errors). According to Hart (1974), it is shown that:

$$\frac{\sigma_j^{2t_1}}{\sigma_j^{2t_0}} = \frac{\beta_j^2}{R_j^2} \tag{4.7}$$

This is equivalent to:

$$\frac{\sigma_j^{t_1}}{\sigma_j^{t_0}} = \frac{|\beta_j|}{|R_j|} \tag{4.8}$$

The standard deviation is referred to by σ, and R^2 represents the measure of quality in the regression. If $\beta = R$, which is equivalent to $\beta/R = 1$, the dispersion (standard deviation) is unchanged. If $\beta > R$ (or $\beta/R > 1$), the standard deviation has increased over time, thus the degree of specialization has increased. In analogy to above, this is termed as σ-specialization. If $\beta < R$ (or $\beta/R < 1$), the standard deviation has decreased over time, thus the degree of specialization has decreased. Likewise, this can be described as σ-de-specialization.

Sector-Wise Regression

Let's turn to the other side of the coin and deal with the intra-sectoral/cross-country analysis. Here we focus on the question of whether specialization patterns tend to converge within the same sector across countries. To put it differently, we analyze whether concentration within one sector has decreased or increased across countries over the time period. In analogy to equation 4.5, the regression is as follows:

$$logRCA_{ij}^{t_1} = \alpha_i + \beta_i logRCA_{ij}^{t_0} + \varepsilon_{ij}^{t_1} \tag{4.9}$$

Again, if $\beta = 1$, it corresponds to unchanged patterns from the initial to the final time period. If $\beta > 1$, countries tend to become more specialized in sectors where they initially were specialized and less specialized where initial specialization was low. This leads to a higher concentration within the respective sector. One might call this β-concentration (or β-divergence) in trade patterns. If $0 < \beta < 1$, countries initial specialization patterns tend to weaken, thus concentration within industries is decreasing. One might call this β-de-concentration (or β-convergence).[10] The special case of $\beta < 0$ again means a reversed ranking. According to equation 4.6 we test additionally whether the coefficient is significantly different from one.

β-concentration is again a necessary, but not sufficient condition for an increase in the degree of concentration as measured by an increase in the dispersion of the distribution. According to equation 4.7 it is shown that:

$$\frac{\sigma_i^{2t_1}}{\sigma_i^{2t_0}} = \frac{\beta_i^2}{R_i^2} \tag{4.10}$$

This is equivalent to:

$$\frac{\sigma_i^{t_1}}{\sigma_i^{t_0}} = \frac{|\beta_i|}{|R_i|} \tag{4.11}$$

If $\beta = R$, the dispersion (standard deviation) is unchanged. If $\beta > R$, the standard deviation has increased over time, thus the degree of concentration has increased. In analogy to the above-mentioned, this is termed as σ-concentration. If $\beta < R$, the standard deviation has decreased over time, thus the degree of concentration has decreased. Likewise, this can be described as σ-de-concentration.

Table 4.27 summarizes the expressions used both in the growth and in the trade specialization literature and shows that basically the same phenomenon is described by different terms depending on which framework is used.

Table 4.27. Overview on Expressions Used in the Literature

	Trade Literature		Growth Lit.
	Intra-country/ cross-sector	Intra-sector/ cross-country	
$\beta = 1$ or $\beta = R$	no change	no change	no change
$\beta > 1$ or $\beta > R$	Specialization	Concentration	Divergence
$0 < \beta < 1$ or $0 < \beta < R$	De-specialization	De-concentration	Convergence

Source: Borbèly (2004)

Table 4.27 reveals that from a technical point of view the same process is meant by talking about specialization, concentration, or divergence on the one hand; and de-specialization, de-concentration and convergence on the other.

---

[10] At some points in the literature, this second side of the coin is described as divergence/convergence case (Dalum et al., 1996). However, in our point of view the description concentration/de-concentration fits to the analysis much better, since within this framework, we look through the window of a single sector across all countries.

4.5.2 Country-Wise Export Specialization Patterns

In accordance with the methodology, we will deal with the regression results of the two sides of our coin successively. Firstly, we present the results from the inter-country/cross-sectors perspective. We are interested in whether each of the countries considered has reinforced export specialization where it already has been highly specialized in the initial period, or whether there is a tendency to de-specialization. The latter also implicates moving towards the EU 15 average patterns of specialization. Table 4.28 summarizes the results for all EU 25 countries starting with the 10 new EU-Member States, followed by four cohesion countries and the rest of the European Union. For each country there are two lines of coefficients: the upper line shows the regression results considering 22 NACE 2-digit classified industries, the bottom line for the 95 NACE 3-digit classified industries. As indicated above, it is tested in the first step whether the coefficient is significantly different from zero with the corresponding level of significance, in the second step whether it is significantly different from one. If the former is not the case, the table shows the value zero; if the latter is not the case, the table shows the value one.

Table 4.28. Country-Wise Stability of EU 15 Export Specialization Patterns (First Line: 2-Digit Level with 22 Industries, Second Line: 3-Digit Level with 95 Industries)

Country	1993-2003			1993-1997			1997-2003		
	β	R	β/R	β	R	β/R	β	R	β/R
Poland	0.74**	0.93	0.79	1			1		
	0.65***	0.72	0.90	0.84***	0.87	0.97	1		
Czech R.	0.50**	0.63	0.79	1.21***	0.96	1.27	1		
	0.68***	0.69	0.98	1			0.80***	0.93	0.86
Hungary	0.72*	0.91	0.79	0.64***	0.85	0.75	0.71***	0.91	0.78
	0.61***	0.69	0.88	0.80***	0.87	0.92	0.87**	0.87	0.99
Cyprus	0.70*	0.40	1.77	0.40***	0.70	0.57	0.24*	0.40	0.59
	0.58***	0.62	0.92	0.63***	0.76	0.83	0.862**	0.76	0.81
Estonia	0			0.37**	0.41	0.89	1		
	0.31***	0.39	0.80	0.45***	0.48	0.94	1		
Latvia	0.54***	0.70	0.77	0.81**	0.90	0.90	0.63**	0.70	0.90
	0.37***	0.43	0.86	0.61***	0.68	0.91	0.54***	0.68	0.79
Lithuania	0.57***	0.80	0.72	0.73***	0.87	0.83	0.77*	0.80	0.97
	0.47***	0.54	0.88	0.72***	0.75	0.96	0.82**	0.75	1.11

Table 4.28 (continued)

Country	1993-2003 β	1993-2003 R	1993-2003 β/R	1993-1997 β	1993-1997 R	1993-1997 β/R	1997-2003 β	1997-2003 R	1997-2003 β/R
Malta	0.66*	0.82	0.80	1			1		
	0.43***	0.46	0.94	0.71***	0.71	1.00	0.78***	0.71	1.10
Slovenia	0.78**	0.89	0.87	0.88***	0.98	0.90	1		
	0.72***	0.77	0.93	0.88**	0.83	1.05	1		
Slovakia	0.48***	0.69	0.70	0.66***	0.85	0.77	0.63**	0.69	0.91
	0.77***	0.74	1.03	0.84***	0.85	0.99	0.80***	0.85	0.94
Spain	0.44***	0.94	0.47	0.57***	0.87	0.65	1		
	0.37***	0.64	0.59	0.36***	0.60	0.61	1		
Portugal	0.38***	0.72	0.53	0.89*	0.96	0.93	1		
	0.64***	0.66	0.97	0.74***	0.88	0.84	0.59***	0.88	0.67
Ireland	1			1			0.81**	0.92	0.89
	0.73***	0.77	0.95	1			0.82***	0.92	0.89
Greece	0.61**	0.64	0.97	1			1		
	0.77***	0.79	0.97	0.80***	0.89	0.91	0.78***	0.89	0.88
Belg.+Lux.	0.60***	0.88	0.68	0.58***	0.77	0.76	0.82*	0.88	0.93
	0.79***	0.78	1.01	0.78***	0.88	0.88	0.75***	0.88	0.85
Denmark	1			0.81**	0.93	0.87	0.70**	0.80	0.88
	0.75***	0.87	0.87	0.88***	0.92	0.95	1		
Finland	1			0.60***	0.86	0.70	0.58***	0.77	0.75
	0.76***	0.87	0.87	0.76***	0.91	0.84	0.82***	0.91	0.91
France	0.60**	0.69	0.87	1			0.69*	0.69	1.01
	0.84**	0.79	1.06	0.83***	0.84	0.98	0.77***	0.84	0.91
Germany	0.71***	0.85	0.84	1			1		
	0.75***	0.84	0.90	0.82***	0.87	0.95	1		
Italy	1			0.82***	0.95	0.87	0.81***	0.96	0.85
	0.85***	0.87	0.98	0.84***	0.92	0.92	0.88***	0.92	0.96
Netherlands	0.80*	0.92	0.87	1			1		
	1			0.78***	0.85	0.92	0.62***	0.85	0.74
Sweden	0.57***	0.97	0.59	0.60***	0.95	0.63	1		
	0.56***	0.86	0.65	0.61***	0.90	0.67	1		
UK	0.80**	0.91	0.87	1			1		
	0.79***	0.84	0.94	0.79***	0.90	0.88	0.82***	0.90	0.91

Source: EC (2004), Own Calculations

As shown in table 4.28, the β-values are generally significantly different from zero and are positive, rejecting the hypothesis that export specialization patterns are random or reverse.[11] In the longest time horizon considered, 1993-2003, the results show a tendency towards de-specialization, because in most cases β takes a value between zero and unity, meaning an increase of RCAs in industries where countries have been relatively less specialized and a decrease in industries where they have been rather highly specialized. In the context of relative export shares compared to the EU 15 this implies a tendency to move towards the EU 15 average patterns of specialization. At first sight, export specialization patterns seem to harmonize within the EU. However, for the subsamples, especially the one for 1997-2003 indicates that specialization figures became more rigid in the second half of the 1990s as compared to the first half.

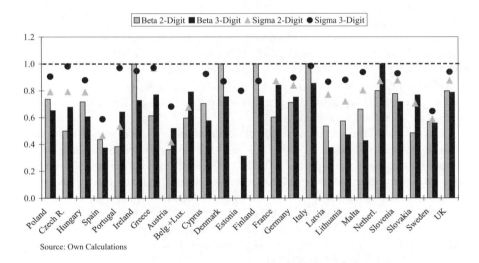

Source: Own Calculations

Fig. 4.40. Country-Wise De-specialization in EU 25, 1993-2003

Figure 4.40 summarizes the results concerning convergence for the total time horizon on the two digit level and on the three digit level, whereas the latter seems to be superior within these regressions. The picture displays rather clearly the general tendency to β-de-specialization within the EU. For most countries, β-values are below one, indicating a move towards the EU 15 average of export specialization patterns. For each country the left beam indicates

---

[11] Note for table 4.28: all β-coefficients with one star have a significance level of 90 %, with two stars 95 % and with three stars 99 %. The value 1 means that there is no change within the specialization patterns; neither can we find convergence, nor divergence.

the β-coefficient as the result of a regression with 22 NACE 2-digit level industries, whereas the right beam shows the result of a regression with 95 NACE
3-digit level industries. The direction of change moving from 2 to 3 digits is
not clear. In some cases the β-coefficient rises, in some it declines. For a range
of countries, however, the results seem to be rather sensitive to the degree
of disaggregation. For four countries we find no change in the specialization
patterns if we consider 2-digit level industries; only the Netherlands, however,
show sticky patterns if we consider 3-digit level industries. Furthermore,we
never find diverging patterns from EU 15 specialization based on either the 2
or the 3-digit level of industries. This is very much in line with the analysis
for 20 OECD countries and 60 industries, conducted by Dalum et al. (1996),
who find the same kind of slow trend towards de-specialization both for 2 and
3-digit SITC classified industries.

β-de-specialization often, but not always, goes hand in hand with σ-
de-specialization, meaning a decrease in the overall national specialization
patterns measured as a decrease in the dispersion of the distribution. σ-de-
specialization is indicated in figure 4.40 with the shaded triangles at the 2-
digit level and with the black-filled circles for NACE 3-digit level industries.
At the 3-digit level, in Belgium and Luxembourg, France, and Slovakia, a
development of specialization towards the EU 15 average specialization was
not accompanied by a decrease in the dispersion; in all the other countries
σ-de-specialization was found.

One can also find significant differences comparing the results for the three
time horizons (see figure 4.41). It is striking that β-coefficients are mostly
higher in the later time period of 1997-2003 than in the earlier 1993-1997 or
the total time horizon of 1993-2003. In the second half of the 1990s, many
more countries show rather sticky export specialization patterns, while in the
earlier and the total period this is rather the exception. One might state that
for the new EU member states this outcome is generated by the change of the
initial conditions of specialization patterns at the beginning of the transition
period.[12] Until the mid 1990s the change in specialization patterns - when
moving away from the initial extent and volume of foreign trade in CMEA
times - might have been the driving force determining de-specialization. After
this process had come to an end, there is more space for deepening trade
patterns, which makes specialization more stable and sticky, since a high beta,
which is not significantly different from one indicates a high degree of stickiness
and stability of the relative export structure. Figure 4.41 shows the results
at the 3-digit level. Here we find that most countries converge in the total
time period, and only some show rather sticky patterns. Towards the end of
the time horizon more and more countries reveal unchanged specialization
patterns. The Netherlands is the only country with an outspoken reversed
development. For the total time period we find no significant change in the
specialization patterns, however, the β-value is significantly lower for the first

---

[12] See also Hoekman and Djankov (1997), as well as Kaminski (1999).

half of the 1990s, and even lower for the second half. At the same time no country's specialization patterns diverge from the EU 15 average.

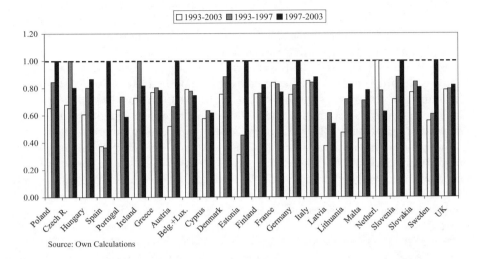

Source: Own Calculations

Fig. 4.41. Country-Wise De-specialization in EU 25 in Three Time Periods at the 3-Digit Level

Dalum et al. (1996) find that less-developed OECD countries show low β-coefficients, whereas most of the small high-income countries show high β-coefficients. We cannot confirm these findings within the EU 25 countries. Neither the new member states nor the cohesion countries do generally show lower β-coefficients; nor does for instance Belgium, Luxembourg, or Denmark have higher β-coefficients than the rest of the EU.

Beelen and Verspagen (1994) suggest that convergence in specialization patterns would level off with a time lag, as convergence in per capita income has more or less come to an end. Once countries have reached the same per capita income, some time after convergence in specialization patterns will be completed, thus foreign trade patterns remain sticky. That means that β should not be significantly different from one in countries with a per capita income close to the average of the EU 15 such as Germany, Italy or France. We cannot really confirm this with our calculation.

4.5.3 Sector-Wise Export Concentration Patterns

There is strong evidence in the literature that markets for manufactured products tended to converge in the course of the 1980s and the early 1990s in OECD countries.[13] In our context, this would mean a de-concentration of industries

---
[13] See Soete and Verspagen (1994) and Dalum et al. (1996).

across countries. In our analysis we consider another time period and also deal with a different set of countries, still there is some overlap in both aspects.

In this section we analyze the degree of concentration of each industry across countries. Hereby we differentiate between EU 15, EU 18 (EU 15 + Hungary + Poland + Czech Republic) and EU 25 countries. Tables 4.31, 4.32 and 4.33 present the results for these three groups of countries at NACE 2-digit level. For the 95 industries of NACE 3-digit level, only the group of EU 25 countries has been analyzed and the results are shown in table 4.35.

Our findings confirm just to some extent that there is an overall tendency in industries towards de-concentration both in EU 15 and EU 18 as well as in EU 25 countries. Although most β-coefficients of the 2-digit level regressions shown in tables 4.31, 4.32 and 4.33 are significantly different from zero, only some of them are significantly different from one. For the longest time period considered, there are ten industries in the EU 15 where concentration decreased (convergence) between 1993 and 2003. These industries are spread across the technology ladder including resource intensive and scale intensive industries, science-based, as well as differentiated goods. For the total time period one industry can be found with an increase in concentration (divergence): office machinery and computers (30). De-concentration is roughly as often found in the EU 15 in the time period 1993-1997 as in the total time period, whereas concentration increased in the motor vehicle industry. In the time period of 1997-2003, 15 out of 22 industries show sticky concentration patterns.

Expanding the set of countries by adding Hungary, Poland and the Czech Republic, an increase in concentration in motor vehicles can no longer be found, but the strong increase in concentration in office machinery and computer (30) remains. However, de-concentration has taken place in more industries as compared to the EU 15. Again, the time period 1997-2003 shows the most sticky concentration patterns. The β-coefficient is not significantly different from unity in 16 out of 22 industries.

Considering all the EU 25 countries, it is not surprising that concentration can be found less often when more countries are included in the analysis. Put differently, we find de-concentration more often when we include more countries. For the EU 25 countries, sticky patterns are rather the exception for the total time period of 1993-2003, as in most industries we find de-concentration. This is to a lesser extent also the case for 1993-1997 and the least for 1997-2003. Whereas for the EU 15 and EU 18 the dispersion of the distribution mostly decreased when we observed de-concentration, for the EU 25 there are a couple of more exceptions.

Table 4.31. Sector-Wise Concentration of EU 15 Export Specialization Patterns of EU 15 Countries at NACE 2-Digit Level with 22 Industries

Group Classification	Nace	Name	1993-2003			1993-1997			1997-2003		
			β	R	β/R	β	R	β/R	β	R	β/R
Labor Intensive	17	Textiles	1			1			1		
	18	Wearing apparel	1			0.87*	0.92	0.94	1		
	19	Leather, luggage…	1			1			1		
	28	Metal products	1			0.73**	0.95	0.77	1		
	36	Furniture	1			1			1		
Resource Intensive	15	Food, beverages	0.60***	0.93	0.65	0.74***	0.98	0.76	0.82***	0.98	0.84
	16	Tobacco	0.45**	0.65	0.68	0.44***	0.58	0.76	1		
	20	Wood and cork	0.92*	0.99	0.93	0.94**	0.99	0.94	1		
	23	Coke, petroleum, fuel	1			1			1		
	26	Non-met. mineral products	1			1			1		
Res. + Scale Int.	27	Basic metals	0.77***	0.97	0.79	1			0.81***	0.98	0.82
Scale Intensive	21	Pulp, paper	1			1			0.70***	0.78	0.89
	22	Publishing	0.65**	0.78	0.83	0.84***	0.85	0.99	1		
	24	Chemicals	0.56*	0.55	1.00	0.78*	0.85	0.92	0.75**	0.91	0.83
	25	Rubber, plastic products	1			1.09*			1		
	34	Motor vehicles	0.49**	0.54	0.92	0.69**	0.64	1.09	0.61*	0.68	0.88
Scale + Science	35	Other transport equipment	2.79**			1			1		
Science Based	30	Office machinery, computer	0.72*	0.89	0.80	1			0.78**	0.94	0.82
	33	Medical, optical instruments	0.73*	0.84	0.87	0.85**	0.94	0.90	1		
Differentiated Goods	29	Machinery and equipment	0.53*	0.53	1.00	1			0.53**	0.64	0.83
	31	Electrical machinery	1			1			1		
	32	Radio, TV, communication	1			1			1		

Source: EC (2004), Own Estimations

Note: one star denotes a significance level of 90 %, two stars 95 % and three stars 99 %.

Table 4.32. Sector-Wise Concentration of EU 15 Export Specialization Patterns of EU 18 Countries (EU 15+Hungary, Poland, Czech Republic) at NACE 2-Digit Level with 22 Industries

Group Classification	Nace	Name	1993-2003 β	1993-2003 R	1993-2003 β/R	1993-1997 β	1993-1997 R	1993-1997 β/R	1997-2003 β	1997-2003 R	1997-2003 β/R
Labor Intensive	17	Textiles	1			1			1		
	18	Wearing apparel	0.59***	0.89	0.66	0.82***	0.97	0.85	0.80*	0.89	0.90
	19	Leather, luggage…	0.65*	0.88	0.73	1			1		
	28	Metal products	1			0.83*	0.90	0.91	1		
	36	Furniture	1			1			1		
Resource Intensive	15	Food, beverages	0.66**	0.95	0.69	0.77***	0.93	0.83	1		
	16	Tobacco	1			0.62**	0.74	0.84	1		
	20	Wood and cork	0.89**	0.98	0.91	0.95*	0.99	0.96	1		
	23	Coke, petroleum, fuel	1			1			1		
	26	Non-met. mineral products	0.72**	0.92	0.78	1			0.80**	0.92	0.87
Res. + Scale Int.	27	Basic metals	1			1			1		
Scale Intensive	21	Pulp, paper	0.79**	0.95	0.83	0.93*	0.99	0.94	0.85*	0.95	0.90
	22	Publishing	0.50**	0.81	0.61	1			1		
	24	Chemicals	1			1			1		
	25	Rubber, plastic products	0.45*	0.79	0.56	0.76**	0.85	0.90	0.77**	0.91	0.85
	34	Motor vehicles	1			1			1		
Scale + Science	35	Other transport equipment	0.51**	0.69	0.74	0.70*	0.76	0.91	1		
Science Based	30	Office machinery, computer	3.26**		0.74	1			0.67*	0.71	0.94
Differentiated Goods	33	Medical, optical instruments	0.66***	0.94	0.77	0.84**	0.96	0.88	0.77**	0.90	0.86
	29	Machinery and equipment	0.72**	0.94	0.77	0.84**	0.95	0.89	1		
	31	Electrical machinery	1			1			1		
	32	Radio, TV, communication	1			1			1		

Source: EC (2004), Own Estimations
Note: one star denotes a significance level of 90 %, two stars 95 % and three stars 99 %.

Table 4.33. Sector-Wise Concentration of EU 15 Export Specialization Patterns of EU 25 Countries at NACE 2-Digit Level with 22 Industries

Group Classification	Industry Nace	Name	1993-2003 β	R	β/R	1993-1997 β	R	β/R	1997-2003 β	R	β/R
Labor Intensive	17	Textiles	1			1			1		
	18	Wearing apparel	0.60**	0.67	0.90	1			0.79**	0.88	0.90
	19	Leather, luggage…	0.68*	0.62	1.11	0.58***	0.79	0.73	1		
	28	Metal products	0.34***	0.60	0.57				0.68***	0.79	0.86
	36	Furniture	1			1			1		
Resource Intensive	15	Food, beverages	0.76**	0.85	0.90	0.88*	0.92	0.96	1		
	16	Tobacco	1			0.59***	0.78	0.76	1		
	20	Wood and cork	1			1			0.89**	0.97	0.91
	23	Coke, petroleum, fuel	0.68*	0.65	1.04	0.52***	0.38	1.36	0.41***	0.61	0.68
	26	Non-met. mineral products	0.33***	0.61	0.54	0.72***	0.61	1.18	1		
Res. + Scale Int.	27	Basic metals	0.54***	0.70	0.77	0.61***	0.84	0.73	0.69***	0.92	0.75
Scale Intensive	21	Pulp, paper	0.72***	0.92	0.78	1			0.69*	0.77	0.89
	22	Publishing	0.33**	0.50	0.65	0.53***	0.77	0.69	1		
	24	Chemicals	0.65*	0.58	1.12	0.69***	0.86	0.81	0.51***	0.71	0.72
	25	Rubber, plastic products	0.29***	0.53	0.55	0.71***	0.71	1.00	0.64***	0.87	0.73
	34	Motor vehicles	0.59***	0.79	0.75	1			1		
Scale + Science	35	Other transport equipment	0.73***	0.81	0.91	0.68***	0.79	0.87	0.61***	0.70	0.87
Science Based	30	Office machinery, computer	5.49***			0.53***	0.70	0.76	0.66***	0.92	0.72
	33	Medical, optical instruments	0.49***	0.84	0.58	0.77***	0.92	0.84	1		
Differentiated Goods	29	Machinery and equipment	0.57***	0.81	0.71	0.69***	0.88	0.78	0.56***	0.59	0.95
	31	Electrical machinery	0			0.33***	0.59	0.56			
	32	Radio, TV, communication	0			0.77***	0.92	0.84			

Source: EC (2004), Own Estimations

Note: one star denotes a significance level of 90 %, two stars 95 % and three stars 99 %.

Figure 4.42 summarizes the outcomes of tables 4.31, 4.32 and 4.33 for the total period of 1993-2003 at the 2-digit level. It is rather challenging to differentiate the results between the five groups of industries with different technology levels: labor intensive, resource intensive, scale intensive, science-based industries and differentiated goods.[14] All along the technology ladder we find industries with both a strong de-concentration and with sticky patterns. At this point there does not seem to be a strong correlation between technology intensity and concentration within an industry. Office machinery and computers (30) clearly serve as an outlier, since β-coefficients are significantly higher than unity for all three subsamples (2.7 for EU 15, 3.2 for EU 18, and 5.4 for EU 25). Concentration has strongly increased in office machinery and computers since the beginning of the 1990s.

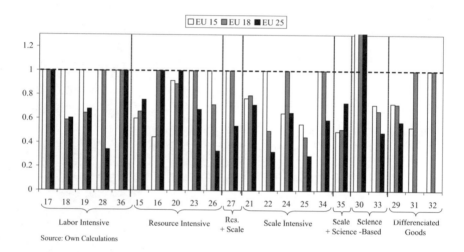

Fig. 4.42. Sector-Wise Concentration of Industries Across Countries at the 2-Digit Level, 1993-2003

However, in accordance with the country-wise regression results, stickiness is much more distinct taking into account the results for subperiods. Again, we find sticky patterns in many more industries in the second half of the 1990s than in the first half and in the total period.

From theoretical considerations, traditional labor intensive industries are expected to show rather higher β-de-concentration (lower values of β- coefficients), if one assumes labor to be mobile. For sectors using components of natural resources, one would generally expect rather stable concentration patterns, since production and exports in these industries rely on factors that do

---

[14] As indicated before, this grouping is based on Pavitt's taxonomy (1984) and OECD (1987).

not change quickly over time, and where capital intensity is often high. The expectation is straight forward for scale intensive industries; for science-based sectors and for differentiated goods like computers, electronics, and telecommunications equipment one would also expect rather strong concentration at first, meaning β-values exceeding unity. This might evidently be due to the exploitation of economies of scale for instance by big multinational companies, but also due to the advantages of concentration of research & development activities for high-tech industries. However, due to the increasing importance of outsourcing and globalization, having production sites in several countries or regions fosters de-concentration from an exportation point of view, at least for mobile Schumpeterian goods.

Table 4.35 presents the regression results for 95 NACE 3-digit level industries for the EU 25 countries. It turns out that sector-wise regressions are more sensitive to the degree of aggregation than country-wise regressions. Table 4.34 sums up the share of 2 and 3-digit level industries with an increase in de-concentration within each of the five product categories for the EU 25 countries.

Table 4.34. Share of 2 and 3-Digit Level Industries with an Increase in De-concentration for EU 25, in % of the Respective Product Group

	1993-2003		1993-1997		1997-2003	
	2-dig.	3-dig.	2-dig.	3-dig.	2-dig.	3-dig.
Labor Intensive Industries	60	73	20	73	40	50
Resource Intensive Industries	66	59	66	70	33	44
Scale Intensive Industries	100	69	66	48	66	69
Science-Based Industries	50	100	100	83	100	83
Differentiated Goods	33	81	66	81	33	68

Source: Own Calculations

For the total time period, the highest de-concentration is found in science-based industries at the 3-digit level and for scale intensive industries at the 2-digit level (see table 4.34). In the first half of the 1990s, de-concentration is also rather high in in most industries except for labor intensive at the 2-digit level; at the 3-digit level de-concentration is lowest for scale intensive industries. In the second half of the 1990s de-concentration occured the most frequently in science-based industries both at the 2- and at the 3-digit level. The numbers show rather clearly that the level of aggregation matters immensely. The differences are rather large between NACE 2-digit and 3-digit level industries for all three time periods considered.

Table 4.35. Sector-Wise Concentration of EU 15 Export Specialization Patterns of EU 25 Countries at NACE 3-Digit Level with 95 Industries

Class	Nace	Sector name	1993-2003			1993-1997			1997-2003		
			β	R	β/R	β	R	β/R	β	R	β/R
Labor	171	Spinning of textile fibres	1			1			1.21*		
	172	Textile weaving	1			1			1		
	173	Finishing of textiles	NA			NA			NA		
	174	Manufacture of made-up textile articles	0.51***	0.61	0.84	0.73***	0.87	0.84	1		
	175	Manufacture of carpets and rugs	0.29**	0.50	0.58	0.75***	0.89	0.85	0.49***	0.71	0.69
	176	Manufacture of knitted and crocheted fabrics	0.40**	0.46	0.86	0.57***	0.74	0.77	1		
	181	Manufacture of leather clothes	0.50***	0.71	0.71	0.81**	0.93	0.88	0.69***	0.85	0.81
	182	Manufacture of other wearing apparel and accessories	0.38***	0.66	0.58	0.66**	0.83	0.80	0.54***	0.75	0.72
	183	Dressing and dyeing of fur; articles of fur	0.61**	0.68	0.90	1			0.79**	0.88	0.90
	191	Tanning and dressing of leather	0.36*	0.38	0.95	0.61***	0.72	0.84	0.53**	0.47	1.13
	192	Manufacture of luggage, handbags, saddlery	0.35**	0.42	0.81	0.58**	0.71	0.82	1		
	193	Manufacture of footwear	0.57***	0.60	0.94	0.77***	0.86	0.89	1		
	281	Manufacture of structural metal products	0***	0.56	0.82	0.53***	0.80	0.66	0.58***	0.73	0.80
	282	Manufacture of tanks, reservoirs, containers of metal	0.46***	0.84	0.80	0.65***	0.80	0.81	0.70*	0.69	1.02
	283	Manufacture of steam generators	0.67***	0.84	0.77	0.73***	0.86	0.85	0.67***	0.78	0.86
	286	Manufacture of cutlery, tools and general hardware	0.65***	0.61	0.61	0.56***	0.93	0.60	1		
	287	Manufacture of other fabricated metal products	0.37***			0.58***	0.85	0.69	0.72**	0.82	0.89
	361	Manufacture of furniture	1			1			1		
	362	Manufacture of jewellery and related articles	0.65**	0.68	0.95	0.69*	0.66	1.04	0.84**	0.92	0.91
	363	Manufacture of musical instruments	0.65**	0.68	0.96	0.68***	0.80	0.85	1		
	364	Manufacture of sports goods	0.78***	0.85	0.91	1			0.82*	0.90	0.92
	365	Manufacture of games and toys	1			1			1		
	366	Miscellaneous manufacturing n.e.c.	0			0.32***	0.55	0.59	0		
Resource	151	Production, processing and preserving of meat	1			0.68***	0.86	0.79	1.36**		

Table 4.35 (continued)

Class	Nace	Sector name	1993-2003			1993-1997			1997-2003		
			β	R	β/R	β	R	β/R	β	R	β/R
	152	Processing and preserving of fish and fish products	1			1			1		
	153	Processing and preserving of fruit and vegetables	1			1			1		
	154	Manufacture of vegetable and animal oils and fats	0.39*	0.36	1.09	0.62*	0.53	1.17	0.64**	0.68	0.93
	155	Manufacture of dairy products	0.66***	0.80	0.82	1			1		
	156	Manufacture of grain mill products, starches	1			1			0.70**	0.82	0.86
	157	Manufacture of prepared animal feeds	0.37*	0.40	0.93	0.50***	0.52	0.95	1		
	158	Manufacture of other food products	0.69***	0.86	0.81	0.88*	0.93	0.94	0.76***	0.88	0.86
	159	Manufacture of beverages	0.72***	0.89	0.81	0.83**	0.94	0.88	0.87*	0.94	0.93
	160	Manufacture of tobacco products	1			0.59**	0.66	0.89	1		
	201	Sawmilling and planing of wood, impregnation of wood	1			1			0.89*	0.96	0.92
	202	Manufacture of veneer sheets; plywood, laminboard	0.70**	0.81	0.87	0.67***	0.90	0.74	1		
	203	Manufacture of builders carpentry and joinery	0.55***	0.67	0.83	0.83*	0.88	0.95	0.78**	0.89	0.87
	204	Manufacture of wooden containers	0.71*	0.70	1.02	0.78*	0.81	0.96	1		
	205	Manufacture of other products of wood; cork	1						0.83***	0.93	0.89
	231	Manufacture of coke oven products	1			0.77*	0.85	0.90	1		
	232	Manufacture of refined petroleum products	0			0.59***	0.80	0.73	0		
	233	Processing of nuclear fuel	0.69*	0.73	0.94	0.54***	0.72	0.74	1		
	261	Manufacture of glass and glass products	0.42***	0.74	0.56	0.51***	0.85	0.59	0.80*	0.85	0.95
	262	Manufacture of non-refractory ceramic goods	0.63***	0.84	0.75	0.66***	0.91	0.73	1		
	263	Manufacture of ceramic tiles and flags	0.75**	0.83	0.90	0.84*	0.90	0.93	1		
	264	Manufacture of bricks, tiles and construction products	1			0.73**	0.84	0.88	1		
	265	Manufacture of cement, lime and plaster	0.47***	0.54	0.88	0.80***	0.89	0.90	0.66**	0.73	0.90
	266	Manufacture of articles of concrete, plaster and cement	0.22***	0.69	0.32	0.31***	0.72	0.43	0.60***	0.80	0.76
	267	Cutting, shaping and finishing of stone	0.59***	0.73	0.80	1			0.67***	0.83	0.80
	268	Manufacture of other non-metallic mineral products	1			1			1		
	274	Manufacture of basic precious and non-ferrous metals	0.30**	0.45	0.67	0.43***	0.60	0.72	0.61***	0.65	0.93

Table 4.35 (continued)

Class	Nace	Sector name	1993-2003			1993-1997			1997-2003		
			β	R	β/R	β	R	β/R	β	R	β/R
Scale	271	Manufacture of basic iron and steel and of ferro-alloys	1			0.88*	0.95	0.93	1		
	272	Manufacture of tubes	0.68***	0.91	0.75	1			0.51***	0.83	0.62
	273	Other first processing of iron and steel	0.51***	0.70	0.74	0.65***	0.83	0.79	0.81*	0.87	0.94
	211	Manufacture of pulp, paper and paperboard	1			1			0.82**	0.89	0.92
	212	Manufacture of articles of paper and paperboard	0.72***	0.85	0.85	0.55***	0.77	0.72	0.65***	0.90	0.73
	221	Publishing	0.29***	0.53	0.55	0.38***	0.52	0.72	0.55***	0.72	0.76
	222	Printing and service activities related to printing	0.22*	0.34	0.64	0.62***	0.92	0.68	0.70**	0.78	0.90
	241	Manufacture of basic chemicals	0.55***	0.74	0.75	1			1		
	242	Manufacture of pesticides and agro-chemical products	0.49**	0.48	1.03	1			0.53**	0.52	1.01
	243	Manufacture of paints, varnishes, printing ink	0.72**	0.84	0.86	1			0.60***	0.70	0.86
	244	Manufacture of pharmaceuticals and medicinal chemicals	1			0.45***	0.86	0.52	1		
	245	Manufacture of soap and detergents and perfumes	0.38***	0.80	0.47	1			0.72**	0.80	0.90
	246	Manufacture of other chemical products	0.68***	0.81	0.83	1			0.71***	0.84	0.85
	247	Manufacture of man-made fibres	1			1			1		
	251	Manufacture of rubber products	0.50***	0.65	0.76	0.64***	0.92	0.70	0.45***	0.66	0.68
	252	Manufacture of plastic products	0.25**	0.49	0.51	1			0.50***	0.68	0.74
	341	Manufacture of motor vehicles	0.57***	0.77	0.75	0.84*	0.91	0.93	0.61***	0.86	0.71
	342	Manufacture of bodies for motor vehicles; (semi-) trailers	0.67**	0.72	0.93	0.55***	0.66	0.83	0.80**	0.89	0.90
	343	Manufactures of parts for motor vehicles and engines	0.67***	0.78	0.86	0.68*	0.71	0.95	1		
	351	Building and repairing of ships and boats	1			1					
	352	Manufacture of railway and tramway locomotives	0.68*						1		
	354	Manufacture of motorcycles and bicycles	0.57***	0.78	0.74	1			0.58***	0.75	0.77
	355	Manufacture of other transport equipment	1			0.79*	0.86	0.93	0.69***	0.70	0.99

Table 4.35 (continued)

Class	Nace	Sector name	1993-2003			1993-1997			1997-2003		
			β	R	β/R	β	R	β/R	β	R	β/R
Science	353	Manufacture of aircraft and spacecraft	0.50***	0.74	0.68	0.46***	0.69	0.66	1		
	300	Manufacture of office machinery and computers	0.46***	0.76	0.61	0.53***	0.75	0.70	0.61***	0.70	0.87
	331	Manufacture of medical and surgical equipment	0.55***	0.82	0.67	0.73***	0.93	0.79	0.79***	0.94	0.84
	332	Instruments for measuring, checking, testing, navigating	0.41***	0.74	0.55	0.72***	0.95	0.76	0.61***	0.83	0.72
	334	Optical instruments and photographic equipment	0.28**	0.42	0.66	0.57***	0.85	0.67	0.71*	0.73	0.98
	335	Manufacture of watches and clocks	0.50***	0.58	0.86	1			0.45***	0.61	0.74
Different.	291	Manufacture of machinery for mechanical power	0.54***	0.79	0.68	0.64***	0.95	0.68	1		
	292	Manufacture of other general purpose machinery	0.39***	0.79	0.50	0.63***	0.95	0.66	0.64***	0.85	0.76
	293	Manufacture of agriculture and forestry machinery	0.58***	0.73	0.79	0.63***	0.86	0.73	1		
	294	Manufacture of machine tools	0.48***	0.70	0.69	0.53***	0.84	0.63			
	295	Manufacture of other special purpose machinery	0.52***	0.70	0.74	0.70***	0.90	0.77	0.79*	0.82	0.96
	296	Manufacture of weapons and ammunition	1			1			0.67***	0.74	0.90
	297	Manufacture of domestic appliances	0.73**	0.74	0.99				0.75***	0.92	0.82
	311	Manufacture of electric motors, generators, transformers	0.75**	0.80	0.94	0.5***	0.69	0.82	1		
	312	Manufacture of electricity distribution, control apparatus	0.22***	0.54	0.41	0.41***	0.87	0.47	0.64***	0.74	0.86
	313	Manufacture of insulated wire and cable	0.26*	0.38	0.69	0.44***	0.63	0.71	0.60***	0.68	0.89
	314	Manufacture of accumulators, primary cells, batteries	0.48***	0.67	0.72	0.56***	0.72	0.79	0.64***	0.78	0.82
	315	Manufacture of lighting equipment and electric lamps	0.49***	0.76	0.65	0.83*	0.90	0.92	0.57*	0.81	0.70
	316	Manufacture of electrical equipment	0			0.27**	0.43	0.62	0.78***	0.87	0.90
	321	Manufacture of electronic valves and tubes	0.21*	0.38	0.56	0.70**	0.84	0.83	0.38***	0.57	0.66
	322	TV, and radio transmitters, apparatus for line telephony	0.38***	0.53	0.73	0.51***	0.73	0.70	1		
	323	TV and radio receivers, sound or video recording	0			0			0.63**	0.64	1.00

Source: EC (2004), Own Estimations
Note: one star denotes a significance level of 90 %, two stars 95 % and three stars 99 %.

Concerning EU 25 countries, a significant increase in concentration (β-value exceeding unity) can rarely be found. At the 2-digit level there is no industry at all with a significant increase in concentration; this is also valid at the 3-digit level considering the total time horizon of 1993-2003 and 1993-1997. In the second half of the 1990s, a significant increase in concentration was found at the 3-digit level for two industries, namely preparation of spinning of textile fibres (171) and production, processing and preserving of meat and meat products (151). Furthermore, for the total time period there are five industries at the 3-digit level, where RCAs of the previous period do not play a significant role in explaining RCAs of the present period, thus the β-coefficient is not significantly different from zero: manufacture of structural metal products (281), miscellaneous manufacturing (366) - where the insignificance does make sense -, manufacture of refined petroleum products (232), manufacture of electrical equipment (316), and manufacture of television and radio services (323). For the latter this is also the case for the time period 1993-1997. For the industry groups 366 and 232, the insignificance appeared yet again in the time period 1997-2003.

To conclude, carrying over the well known concepts of β and σ-convergence from the growth into the trade literature we ask two questions: (1) whether EU countries EU 15 export specialization patterns are stable across sectors or whether these countries tend to become more or less specialized on an intra-country cross sectoral level, and (2) whether specific sectors tend to become more or less concentrated in an intra-sectoral, cross-country level. We hereby consider three groups of countries, EU 15, EU 18 (+ Hungary, Poland and the Czech Republic) and EU 25. Note that the two questions are basically analogous, comparable to two sides of the same coin. Comparing these two sides means that countries with relatively high betas in the country-wise specialization patterns tend to be specialized in those industries which show rather high beta values (low degree of β-convergence) in the sector-wise patterns. Countries with rather sticky export patterns are specialized in industries which are rather highly concentrated.

We find a strong tendency toward de-specialization at the intra-country cross sectoral level. Most countries have moved closer to the EU 15 average export specialization patterns in the time period between 1993 and 2003. Only the Czech Republic diverges from the EU 15 if we consider 2-digit level industries in the subsample 1993-1997, however, all countries show converging patterns if we consider 3-digit level industries. Thus we never find diverging patterns from EU 15 specialization in regressions based on the more disaggregated level of industries. The dispersion of the distribution does not always decrease, if de-specialization is found. Comparing part-time regressions, we find that in the second half of the 1990s, more countries show rather sticky export specialization patterns, while in the earlier and the total period this is rather the exception.

At the inter-sectoral cross country level, our findings confirm the main body of the literature, which finds that there is an overall tendency in industries towards de-concentration (in the OECD and also) in the EU countries. We test this hypothesis for all three groups of countries, EU 15, EU 18 and EU 25. It is rather challenging to differentiate the results between industries along the technology ladder. At least at the more disaggregated industry level we find one of the lowest de-concentration in scale intensive industries exploiting economies of scale and in resource intensive industries. In labor, science-based industries, as well as for differentiated goods, de-concentration is slightly higher.

Focusing on the three new EU countries, it seems that Hungary to a slightly greater and Poland as well as the Czech Republic to a slightly lesser extent show convergence toward the EU 15 export specialization patterns. Polish and Czech trade patterns seem rather sticky and have not fully converged to the EU 15 average since 1993.

Having seen that de-specialization dominates the picture of intra-EU exports, which means that most countries initial trade patterns change, indicating that sectors with initially low RCAs tend to increase over time and initially high RCAs tend to decrease, one main question remains to be answered. What drives export specialization patterns?

4.6 Determinants of Export Specialization in New EU Member States: A Dynamic Panel Analysis

Although there is great body of literature on RCAs, there is hardly any complete and comprehensive explanation of national comparative advantages for the countries considered. Therefore we will deal with the determinants of comparative advantages in the last section of this chapter, focusing on the new EU member states.

Several factors play a major role in explaining export specialization patterns. Mainly they depend on the production structure of an economy, which again is dependent on factor endowments (e.g., labor and capital) and factor prices according to the Traditional Trade Theory. Other theoretical models such as the New Trade Theory models stress the importance of distance and explain why intra-industry trade exists. Furthermore interregional demand differences and trade costs are emphasized by the New Economic Geography. In addition, newer theories show the major role played by investments, especially foreign direct investments, innovation and technological development. In this section we will analyze the impact of different variables on sectoral modified RCAs, as shown in detail in the previous sections. Unfortunately, such a sectoral analysis is strongly restricted by data unavailability for Eastern European countries. Even if data is available from different sources, one has to control for unmatch in the data. To minimize such measurement and incomparability problems, it is advisable not to use too many different data sources.

4.6.1 The Data

The choice of the exogenous variables for explaining the modified RCAs is unfortunately strongly influenced by the restrictions that data availability imposes. Since the main idea of this analysis is to stick to industry levels, some severe data availability restrictions appear.

The endogenous variable is the modified RCA as already used in the previous part of this chapter, which can also be called the relative export share of industries on the EU 15 market (data source: COMEXT trade database from the European Commission, 2004). The choice of the exogenous variables for explaining the modified RCAs is unfortunately strongly influenced by the restrictions that the data availability imposes.

Sectoral industrial production as a percentage of GDP, indicating the size of the respective industrial sector, is expected to be one of the most robust explanatory variables. Ignoring pure trade with final products, exported products are usually generated domestically, thus they appear in the sectoral industrial output. It is reasonable to assume that an increase in the sectoral industrial production will lead to a rise in the relative export position. Hence the expected sign of the coefficient is positive. In this analysis, we use nominal industrial production as a percentage of nominal GDP for 22 NACE 2-digit level manufacturing industries in Eastern European EU countries, provided from the WIIW Industrial Database Eastern Europe (2004).

Wage differentials are one of the main driving forces for the European division of labor, thus enhancing export specialization patterns in Eastern European countries. Especially for labor intensive industries, high wage countries from Western Europe see possibilities to adjust. They can either relocate the labor intensive part of their production to a lower wage country (e.g. in Eastern Europe) which is called offshoring and which mechanisms would also be included in the FDI variable, or such a company can buy parts or intermediate products from a lower wage country and import it. This mechanism is called outsourcing. Both enhance the exports of the respective lower wage country (e.g. in Eastern Europe). From a European perspective, the greater the wage differential is between West and East, the larger the incentives for outsourcing and offshoring and the stronger the enhancing effect for Eastern European exports towards Western Europe. In this analysis we use relative wages to capture wage differentials. More precisely we use average nominal monthly wages in Euro per employee for Eastern European countries, provided by the WIIW (2004) and relate it to average nominal monthly wages in Euro in the aggregate of 12 Euroland countries. The wages for the individual Euroland countries are published in the OECD Stan Industrial Database (2005), whereas the aggregate of the 12 countries is calculated by the author using nominal GDP weights from the year 2000. By definition, a rise in the Eastern European country's wage lowers the wage differential; more precisely, it raises our variable, the relative wage share, which hampers relative export shares of Eastern European countries. Thus we expect the sign of this variable to be negative.

Furthermore in the basic specification of our regression, we expect the impact of export unit values (source: European Commission, 2004) to appear with a positive sign. Export unit values are measured - identical to the beginning of this chapter - as the value measured in Euro of one unit exports. Thus we use Euro/kg. If you are successful in raising the value of one unit of your exports, for most products this tends to be a sign for an increase in quality. For some high quality clothing and products such as a down jacket, a decline in weight, however, implies a rise in quality. Also for products with very fast technological development such as the computer industry, there is a general tendency to lower prices while increasing quality at the same time. Although these effects are not captured by the export unit value variable, for the total of 22 industries we expect to see a positive correlation between EUV and modified RCAs.

Last but not least imports are expected to have a significant impact on export shares as measured by the modified RCA. Due to knowledge and technology spillover, export shares are expected to rise when import shares rise, especially in industries with a rather high share of intermediate imports. Imports as an explanatory variable are measured according to the endogenous variable, namely as the share of sectoral imports on total imports in a country c relative to the same share in intra-EU 15 trade.

So far we have introduced all the variables that are used in the baseline specification of the panel setting. As indicated, our panel comprises eight countries c, 22 industries j and 11 years t, 1993-2003. Since data on industrial production and wages are not available for the Czech Republic and Slovakia at the two digit level, these two countries drop out of the panel, giving a number of potential maximum observations of $6 * 22 * 11 = 1452$. Besides data problems, the choice of estimation method is also challenging, which will be dealt with in the following.

4.6.2 The Methodology of the Dynamic Panel Estimation

Let us reduce the three dimensions of our data set to merely two dimensions, namely a cross-section dimension i - which is a combination of country c and industry j - and a time dimension t. Still we deal with a typical panel data setting of the following type:

$$y_{i,t} = c + \delta X_{i,t} + \epsilon_{i,t} \tag{4.12}$$

where we generally must assume an error-components structure in panels of the following type:

$$\epsilon_{i,t} = \mu_i + \eta_{i,t} \tag{4.13}$$

where μ_i denotes the unobservable, time-invariant individual specific effect, which accounts for any individual-specific effect that is not included in the regression, and $\eta_{i,t}$ denotes the remainder (white-noise) disturbance. The dependent variable is denoted by y, and X stands for various purely exogenous variables. Depending on the structure of the individual effects μ_i, one can estimate such a panel model either as fixed effects or as random effects model.

Given that μ_i are fixed parameters to be estimated, and $\eta_{i,t}$ are the remainder disturbances, which are stochastically independent and identically distributed $IID(0, \sigma_\eta^2)$, the appropriate specification is a fixed effects model. Furthermore $X_{i,t}$ must be independent of $\eta_{i,t}$ for all i and t. In this case we can directly estimate the fixed effects with dummy variables for each cross section; thus the model is the following:

$$y_{i,t} = c + \delta X_{i,t} + \theta \mu_i + \eta_{i,t} \tag{4.14}$$

If, however, μ_i are assumed to be random and distributed $IID(0, \sigma_\mu^2)$, in addition to $\eta_{i,t}$ being distributed $IID(0, \sigma_\eta^2)$, and μ_i are independent of $\eta_{i,t}$, we deal with a random effects model which can be written as in equations 4.12 and 4.13. Furthermore, $X_{i,t}$ must be independent of $\eta_{i,t}$ and $\mu_{i,t}$ for all i and t. The question then arises as to whether we have to apply a fixed or a random effects model. This can be tested with the so-called Hausman-test. Under the H_0-hypothesis, both estimators are consistent and should not differ systematically, thus the fixed effects are not significant. Under the H_1-hypothesis, however, fixed effects exist, so one has to control for this heterogeneity of data in the estimation. For our data set, the H_0-hypothesis cannot be accepted; therefore we have to control for fixed effects in our model.

Controlling for the fixed effects is done most simply (in accordance with equation 4.14) by including dummy variables for all three dimensions: time t, country c, and industry j. This estimator is called Least-Squares Dummy Variables (LSDV) in the literature, because for each individual (in this case time period, country and industry) one dummy is included in the regression (Baltagi, 2001).[15] This estimator is also known as the Fixed Effect (FE) least squares or the Within-Estimator, which describes the variation within the individuals such as describing their deviation from the individual averages. Including a set of exogenous variables X, and estimating the logarithmic transformation of RCAs in levels as the endogenous variable y, the regression can be described as follows:

$$y_{c,j,t} = \alpha_c + \beta_j + \gamma_t + \delta X_{c,j,t} + \eta_{c,j,t} \tag{4.15}$$

The first two coefficients display the time invariant dummy variables, the individual fixed effects; the third dummy displays the time fixed effects. However, due to these dummies, there is a large loss of degrees of freedom in the

---

[15] As a matter of course one reference individual is left out of the regression for all three types of dummies.

estimation. Furthermore, one cannot include any time-invariant variables such as dummies for groups of industries (e.g., labor intensive, science-based, etc.), because this would result in perfect multicollinearity. Yet there is also a more severe problem with the LSDV/ FE estimator, which is in principle the best linear unbiased estimator (BLUE), if the fixed effect model is the true model and $\eta_{c,j,t}$ is the classical white noise error term, which means that $X_{c,j,t}$ are independent of $\eta_{c,j,t}$ for all c, j, and t (Baltagi, 2001). Still, the LSDV is only consistent if $t \to \infty$, which is clearly not the case for our data set with t=11. If t is fixed and $c \to \infty$ as well as $j \to \infty$, only the coefficient for the purely exogenous variables X is consistent, but not the coefficients for the individual effects (Baltagi, 2001; Lancester, 2000). Neither is this the case for our estimation, since both c=6 and j=22 are small numbers, far from infinity. To conclude, the LSDV is not consistent when applied to our set of data.

In addition, the Durbin-Watson test statistics of the LSDV estimation indicates autocorrelation in all specifications. As expected, the development of RCA depends to a great extent on its values in the previous period, thus showing a strong autoregressive character. This urges us to include the lagged endogenous variable as an explanatory variable. Since we are interested in explaining the dynamics of the adjustment of RCAs, the main idea has been the inclusion of the lagged endogenous variable as an explanatory variable anyway. At the same time this introduces basic problems for the panel estimation method, which will be dealt with below. Using the combination of country c and industry j as the cross-section identifier i, the fixed effect dynamic panel data model - with the lagged endogenous variable - is specified in the following way:

$$y_{i,t} = c + \lambda y_{i,t-1} + \delta X_{i,t} + \theta \mu_i + \eta_{i,t} \qquad (4.16)$$

where $\eta_{i,t}$ denotes the white-noise disturbance. Since $y_{i,t}$ is correlated with μ_i, and μ_i is time-invariant, it is obvious that also $y_{i,t-1}$ is correlated with μ_i. Thus the lagged endogenous variable as a regressor is correlated with the fixed effects. This makes clear that any simple ordinary least squares (OLS) regression will render biased/ inconsistent estimates. How about the LSDV/ FE estimator? Although it eliminates the μ_i by subtracting the mean (Within-estimator) such as

$$y_{i,t} - \bar{y}_i = \lambda(y_{i,t-1} - \bar{y}_{i.-1}) + \delta(X_{i,t} - \bar{X}_i) + \theta(\mu_i - \bar{\mu}_i) + (\eta_{i,t} - \bar{\eta}_i) \quad (4.17)$$

or

$$y_{i,t} - \bar{y}_i = \lambda(y_{i,t-1} - \bar{y}_{i.-1}) + \delta(X_{i,t} - \bar{X}_i) + (\eta_{i,t} - \bar{\eta}_i) \qquad (4.18)$$

where

$$\bar{y}_{i,-1} = \frac{\sum\limits_{t=2}^{T} y_{i,t-1}}{T-1} \tag{4.19}$$

still $(y_{i,t-1} - \bar{y}_{i,-1})$ is correlated with $(\eta_{i,t} - \bar{\eta}_i)$, because $y_{i,t-1}$ is correlated with $\bar{\eta}_i$. This is easy to see if one visualizes that $\bar{\eta}_i$ contains $\eta_{i,t-1}$, which is correlated with $y_{i,t-1}$. Therefore the LSDV/ FE estimator renders biased results also in a dynamic panel setting, and its consistency depends upon t being large (Baltagi, 2001; Nickell, 1981; Kiviet, 1995)[16], which is not the case for our set of data. Only if $t \to \infty$ are the coefficients for the lagged endogenous and the exogenous variables estimated in a consistent way, thus the bias decreases with t. Nevertheless if t is not too small relative to the number of cross-sections, there might be reasons to choose the Within-estimator, arguing that the bias is not too large (Baltagi, 2001). According to Monte-Carlo simulations by Judson and Owen (1999), the bias can be as much as 20 % for t=30. Since our sample only includes 11 years, one has to assume that the bias in our Within-Estimation would be much higher than that.

Another alternative is the use of a Generalized Method of Moments (GMM) estimation, although it is also biased in a dynamic panel model setting. Nevertheless, one should note that GMM is usually preferable to LSDV for samples with a relative small t. Within this framework, Anderson and Hsio (1981) suggest the method of first differencing for eliminating the fixed effects. The estimation in first differences has the form:

$$y_{i,t} - y_{i,t-1} = \lambda(y_{i,t-1} - y_{i,t-2}) + \delta(X_{i,t} - X_{i,t-1}) + (\eta_{i,t} - \eta_{i,t-1}) \tag{4.20}$$

or

$$\Delta y_{i,t} = \lambda \Delta y_{i,t-1} + \delta \Delta X_{i,t} + \Delta \eta_{i,t} \tag{4.21}$$

Since $\Delta y_{i,t-1}$ is correlated with the error term $\Delta \eta_{i,t}$, because $y_{i,t-1}$ is correlated with $\eta_{i,t-1}$, one has to instrument for it. It has been suggested in the literature (Anderson and Hsiao, 1982) to use further lags of y (such as $y_{i,t-2}$) as instruments. Further lags of y are not correlated with the error term, however, such an instrumental variable method results in consistent but not always efficient estimates, because it does not use all the available moment conditions, and does not take into account the differenced structure on the residual disturbances $\Delta \eta_{i,t}$ (Ahn and Schmidt, 1995; Baltagi, 2001). It turns out that adding extra moment conditions by using an extended system, which additionally estimates equations in levels using instruments in first differences increases efficiency. This is what the "system GMM" (Generalized Method of

---

[16] A more extensive discussion on this bias, which is prominently called in the literature as the "Nickell-Bias", can be found in Hsiao (1986) and in Anderson and Hsiao (1982).

Moments) estimator by Blundell and Bond (1998) does, which will be applied to our set of data.

According to Roodman (2005) from the Boston College Department of Economics, which provides a STATA modul for this estimator, it fits two related dynamic panel models together quite well.[17] The first is the Arellano-Bond (1991) estimator, which is often called the "difference GMM". While first differencing the equation, the individual fixed effects are removed, which eliminates a potential source of omitted variable bias in the estimation. At the same time predetermined variables become endogenous. The authors develop a GMM estimator, which treats the model as a system of equations, one for each time period. The only difference between the equations is the use of their set of instruments. The endogenous and predetermined variables in first differences are instrumented with lags of their own levels. However, it is shown in the literature that lagged levels are often bad instruments for first differences. Exogenous variables enter the instrument matrix in first differences with one column per instrument.

Here the second model steps in, which is an extended version of a model by Arellano and Bover (1995), further developed by Blundell and Bond (1998) and called the "system GMM" estimator. Arellano and Bover show that efficiency of the estimator can be increased by adding the original equations in levels to the system, thus having additional moment conditions. In these equations in levels predetermined and endogenous variables are instrumented with lags of their own first differences. Blundell and Bond develop the necessary assumptions for this model augmentation and test it with Monte Carlo simulations.

The "system GMM" as a linear estimator implements both estimations. Especially for small t, the "system GMM" has enormous efficiency gains as compared to the basic GMM estimator in first differences, which is at the same time a strong support for the use of extra moment conditions (Baltagi, 2001). Furthermore, the "system GMM" is available as a one- and two-step estimator. The two-step estimator is asymptotically more efficient, but at the same time its standard errors are often downward biased (Arellano and Bond, 1991, Blundell and Bond, 1998). However, this is controlled for in the two-step "system GMM" estimation. A finite-sample correction is available and used here for the two-step covariance matrix as described by Windmeijer (2000), which dramatically improves the accuracy as shown in Monte Carlo simulations. Therefore the two-step estimator used here shows better properties for small samples than the one-step estimator in the "system GMM".

In accordance with our data, the set of instruments used in the following analysis includes the second, third, and fourth lagged differences of y and all exogenous variables of the regression. For total manufacturing we always

---

[17] Source: Official STATA command provided for free to the research community by Roodman, D. (2005). The following describtion of the estimator is based upon the description by Roodman (2005).

use these three lagged differences, because the larger number of observations allows us to have a larger number of instruments. For subsamples, however, we use a maximum number of two lagged differences as instruments in order to avoid the problem of having too many instruments relative to the number of observations.

To conclude, both LSDV and GMM estimators are inconsistent for the dynamic panel model setting with the underlying data, because the time dimension of the sample is too small. However, it seems that the bias is smaller when implementing the GMM estimator, and asymptotic efficiency can be increased by using the "system GMM" estimator. As time passes by and a larger time dimension t can be used for the Eastern European countries, the bias of such estimates will also be reduced. For the time being, the only alternative would be to renounce such estimates which would not make sense from a research point of view. Bearing in mind the benefits and the shortcoming of the "system GMM" estimator, its results will now be presented.

4.6.3 Estimation Results

The basic specification of the model includes those variables, which have been explained at the beginning of this section. The estimation results show the parameters, which determine the development of modified RCAs as shown in table 4.36. Dummy variables for the different groups of industries as described by the OECD (1987) - such as labor, resource, scale intensive, science-based and differentiated goods - are also included into the basic specification. However, the only dummy with a significant impact is the one for labor intensive industries.

Due to already mentioned data unavailabilities, only 935 observations could be realized from the potentially available 1452 in the basic specification. However, the results are meaningful. As expected, the lagged endogenous variable is highly significant with a positive coefficient, which is below unity. That indicates that a one percent increase (decline) in the modified RCA of the previous period leads to an increase (decline) of the RCA in the current period by 0.72 percent. Thus there is a relatively strong adjustment process of RCAs in the time dimension. Also the sectoral industrial production has a positive impact on RCAs. This impact is the most distinctive considering the one year lagged industrial output. Accordingly, a one percent rise in output as a percentage of GDP results in 0.12 percent increase in the RCA one year later. As a matter of course, the coefficient for the industrial production is much lower then the coefficient for the lagged endogenous variable. The expected positive influence of the export unit value as an indicator for the quality of exports is only significant with an error probability of ten percent. Accordingly, a one percent increase in the export unit value brings about a 0.04 percent rise in the relative export share. However, since this coefficient is rather low, one can also see from table 4.36 that the 95 percent confidence

Table 4.36. Dynamic Panel Regression Results for RCAs - Basic Specification for Total Manufacturing

Arellano-Bond Dynamic Panel-Data Estimation, Two-Step System GMM Results

Group variable: cross		Number of obs = 935				
Time variable: time		Number of groups = 122				
Number of instruments: 35		Obs per group: min = 3				
$F(6,121) = 191.73$		avg = 7.66				
Prob > F = 0.000		max = 9				
Dep.var:	Coef.	Corr.	t	P>|t|	95 % Conf.Intervall	
$lnrcamod_t$		Std.Error				
$lnrcamod_{t-1}$	0.726	0.047	15.19	0.000	0.631	0.820
$lnip_{t-1}$	0.120	0.042	2.83	0.005	0.036	0.205
$lneuv$	0.042	0.025	1.65	0.103	-0.008	0.092
$lnwagerel$	-0.088	0.065	-1.35	0.179	-0.217	0.041
$lnimportrca$	0.159	0.078	2.02	0.046	0.002	0.315
$dlab$	0.233	0.069	3.36	0.001	0.095	0.370
$constant$	0.179	0.172	1.04	0.298	-0.160	0.520

Hansen test of overid. restrictions: chi2(28)=36.56 Prob >chi2=0.129
Arellano-Bond test for AR(1) in first differences: z = -2.09 pr>z =0.036
Arellano-Bond test for AR(2) in first differences: z = 1.36 pr>z =0.174

Source: Own Estimations

interval includes negative values for the coefficient of the export unit value.[18] Surprisingly, relative wages in Eastern Europe do not turn out to be significant in determining comparative export advantages. A one percent rise in the relative wage of Eastern European EU countries, which corresponds to a decline in the wage differential, implicates a 0.08 percent decline in the sectoral revealed comparative advantage considering all 22 industrial sectors only if one would allow for an error probability of 17%. Unfortunately, this is no empirical proof for the widely spread expectation that comparative advantages of the new EU member states result to some extent from the fact that they have sufficiently lower wages then the Western European EU countries. As indicated, dummy variables for the five OECD industry groups are also included. The only dummy variable proving significant is the one for the labor intensive industries. It shows that the relative export shares in the labor intensive industries are still significantly higher than the RCAs in the other industries. Although RCAs are clearly declining in the labor intensive industries in some Eastern European countries such as Hungary, a strong specialization in those industries is still present. This result remains robust even if one runs

---

[18] Furthermore, the reversed impact has also been tested. One could image that RCAs could have a positive impact on the export unit value. The explanation would be that with an increasing comparative advantage in one sector, this industry is able to rise its quality and thus rise the export unit value. However, we find no empirical evidence for this kind of relationship.

the regression without Poland, which shows one of the highest RCAs in the labor intensive industries among the six countries considered in the analysis. At the end of the table some tests are included to assess the validity of the specification. The Hansen test rejects the hypothesis of over-identifying restrictions. That means that the instruments as a group appear as exogenous. Furthermore the Arellano-Bond test for autocorrelation of first and second order delivers the expected results. Per construction we should find first order autocorrelation in the regression, because $\epsilon_{i,t-1}$ is both contained in $\Delta\epsilon_{i,t}$, and $\Delta\epsilon_{i,t-1}$. However, second order autocorrelation should be avoided, since this would imply that the instruments for the lagged endogenous variable are not exogenous. Both autocorrelation tests deliver the correct and expected results for our basic specification.

It is worth testing the robustness of our results for subsamples by excluding some countries, industries or years. Since the number of years and also of countries is already very limited, the most reasonable, and from an economic point of view the most interesting, appears to be to run the regression for specific industries or groups of industries. Especially the impact of relative wages, imports and maybe also of export unit values might differ among industries. Therefore we now run the basic regression just for the five labor intensive industries according to the OECD classification, which include manufacture of textiles; of wearing apparel and dressing; of leather, luggage, handbags and footwear; of fabricated metal products; and manufacture of furniture. The results are shown in table 4.37.

Table 4.37. Dynamic Panel Regression Results for RCAs - Basic Specification for Labor Intensive Manufacturing Industries

Arellano-Bond Dynamic Panel-Data Estimation, Two-Step System GMM Results						
Group variable: cross			Number of obs = 221			
Time variable: time			Number of groups = 29			
Number of instruments: 28			Obs per group: min = 5			
F(5,28) = 537.21			avg = 7.62			
Prob > F = 0.000			max = 9			
Dep.var:	Coef.	Corr.	t	P>|t|	95 % Conf.Intervall	
$lnrcamod_t$		Std.Error				
$lnrcamod_{t-1}$	0.899	0.120	7.47	0.000	0.652	1.145
$lnip_{t-1}$	0.117	0.081	1.45	0.158	-0.048	0.284
$lneuv$	0.018	0.055	0.33	0.744	-0.095	0.131
$lnwagerel$	-0.177	0.038	-4.58	0.000	-0.256	-0.098
$lnimportrca$	0.079	0.050	1.57	0.128	-0.024	0.183
$constant$	0.191	0.359	0.53	0.597	-0.543	0.927
Hansen test of overid. restrictions: chi2(22)=25.99 Prob >chi2=0.252						
Arellano-Bond test for AR(1) in first differences: z = -2.54 pr>z =0.011						
Arellano-Bond test for AR(2) in first differences: z = -1.23 pr>z =0.217						

Source: Own Estimations

First of all it is striking that the number of observations declines to 221 if one excludes all non-labor intensive manufacturing industries. Still, all tests on the validity of the specification indicate no problem. Note that the number of instruments has also been reduced. The lagged endogenous variable is still highly significant; the coefficient is, however, closer to unity than in the respective estimation for all industries, indicating lower dynamics. At the same time the impact of the lagged industrial production - though displaying roughly the same coefficient - would only be significant if one allowed for an error probability of 15 percent. Interestingly, the coefficient for the export unit variable has turned out to be insignificant, indicating that competition on the EU 15 market in labor intensive products is not to a great extent influenced by quality competition. Importantly, the impact of relative wages on comparative advantages in labor intensive industries is significant with an error probability of less than one percent. Also the coefficient is clearly higher than in the estimation for total manufacturing. For labor intensive industries, a one percent increase in relative wages results in a 0.17 percent decrease in comparative advantages. Surely, this is perfectly in line with the Heckscher-Ohlin theorem, which focuses on the importance of relative endowments in shaping foreign trade patterns. Finally, the importance of imports is much lower for the labor intensive industries than for total manufacturing; the coefficient is lower and the error probability is higher. This underlines the fact that (intermediate) imports do not play such an important role for labor intensive industries.

In the next step we only consider the upper end of the technology ladder and do the basic regression for just science-based and differentiated goods. According to the OECD classification these include manufacture of office machinery and computers; of medical precision and optical instrument; of machinery and equipment; of electrical machinery and apparatus; and manufacture of radio, television and communication equipment and apparatus. The results are displayed in table 4.38.

With 258, the number of observations in the high technology groups is very similar to the labor intensive industries regressed above. Also here, the Hansen test for overidentifying restrictions as well as both Arellano-Bond tests for AR(1) and AR(2) indicate no problem in the estimation. The results clearly correspond to prior expectations. The coefficient for the lagged endogenous variable is highly significant and lower than in the previous estimations. Thus adjustment dynamics are the highest in high technology industries as compared to total manufacturing and to labor intensive industries. Furthermore, a one percent increase in the industry output in the previous year brings about a 0.37 percent higher RCA in the current period. For high technology industries, export unit values as indicators for quality matter a lot. This is shown in the highly significant and positive coefficient for the EUV. A rise in the EUV by one percent improves the revealed comparative advantage in high technology industries by 0.17 percent. It seems that in these industries competitiveness is much more influenced by quality differences than in lower technology industries. This might also be explained by the fact that export

Table 4.38. Dynamic Panel Regression Results for RCAs - Basic Specification for High Technology Industries

Arellano-Bond Dynamic Panel-Data Estimation, Two-Step System GMM Results						
Group variable: cross			Number of obs = 258			
Time variable: time			Number of groups = 34			
Number of instruments: 28			Obs per group: min = 3			
F(5,33) = 119.04			avg = 7.59			
Prob > F = 0.000			max = 9			
Dep.var: $lnrcamod_t$	Coef.	Corr. Std.Error	z	P>|z|	95 % Conf.Intervall	
$lnrcamod_{t-1}$	0.381	0.064	5.92	0.000	0.250	0.512
$lnip_{t-1}$	0.372	0.083	4.44	0.000	0.201	0.543
$lneuv$	0.173	0.066	2.59	0.014	0.037	0.309
$lnwagerel$	0.147	0.137	1.07	0.291	-0.132	0.428
$lnimportrca$	0.372	0.185	2.01	0.053	-0.004	0.749
$constant$	1.204	0.421	2.86	0.007	0.346	2.062
Hansen test of overid. restrictions: chi2(22)=21.61 Prob >chi2=0.483						
Arellano-Bond test for AR(1) in first differences: z = -1.81 pr>z =0.070						
Arellano-Bond test for AR(2) in first differences: z = 0.24 pr>z =0.812						
Source: Own Estimations						

unit values show much higher and much more diverging figures at the higher end than at the lower end of the technology ladder as shown in the previous part of this chapter. Advancing comparative advantages in science-based and differentiated goods apparently depends to a great extent on the ability of upgrading quality. Considering fast technological change and tough competition in these industries, this finding is to a great extent reasonable. So are the findings on the impact of relative wages on comparative advantages in high technology industries, which is basically non-existent. The coefficient is not significant, indicating that wages do not play an important role for export advantages in these industries. Finally, a rise in the relative import share by one percent yields a rise in the relative export share by 0.37 percent, which clearly demonstrates that success and competitiveness of high-technology industries depend to a great extent on imports. The impact is significant with an error probability of 5 percent and is roughly as strong as the influence of industrial production and of the lagged endogenous variable. This is a strong indicator for a bazaar kind of activity as explained before or for assembly type of production. Still, this does not hinder competitiveness of high-tech export industries.

In the next step we will modify the basic specification by adding other exogenous variables which are expected to have an impact. First of all one should take a look at labor productivity in explaining comparative advantages. Although firms should have an incentive to locate labor intensive activities in areas with relatively low labor costs such as the Eastern European countries, low wages do not necessarily reflect low production costs, because labor productivity might also be low in these countries. Therefore we shall now control for relative labor productivity, which is measured as sectoral industrial output in million Euro per employee in Eastern European countries in relation to the same measure in Euroland. Output for Eastern European countries is provided by the WIIW (2004) in national currency and has been converted to Euro using annual average exchange rates to the Euro published by Eurostat. The number of employees at a sectoral level is also provided by WIIW (2004). Output for Euroland is taken from the OECD STAN Industry Database (2005) such as the number of employees. Again, the Euroland aggregate is calculated using GDP shares of 2000. Using this measure one might at first sight expect a positive coefficient in explaining revealed comparative advantages. If labor productivity in Eastern Europe rises, assuming Euroland productivity to remain stable, relative productivity rises and is expected to enhance comparative advantages.

However, before running the modified regression, which is denoted as Specification I, one has to check for possible multicollinearity among the exogenous variables. Supposing that wages reflect productivity to some extent, one must assume that relative wages and relative labor productivity are correlated. A simple correlation test reveals a coefficient of 0.80, which is highly significant, and a Fixed Effect estimator shows a highly significant positive coefficient of 0.70. Thus the relation between RCA, wages and productivity is pictured according to the following simple model.

$$RCA = \alpha * wage + \epsilon \qquad\qquad \alpha < 0$$

and

$$wage = \beta * productivity + \epsilon \qquad\qquad \beta > 0$$

Thus combining the two simple equations gives:

$$RCA = \gamma * productivity + \epsilon \qquad\qquad \gamma = \alpha * \beta < 0$$

Assuming a strong positive correlation between wages and labor productivity, these simple equations show that the expected sign for our labor productivity variable is negative. Thus we proceed with Specification I, where wages are replaced by labor productivity. Again first total manufacturing industries are analyzed, followed by labor intensive and finally by high technology industries. Table 4.39 displays the results.

Including total manufacturing, the number of observations amounts to 930. The explanatory variables already used in the basic specification show rather robust characteristics. The fortitude of the impact both from the lagged endogenous variable and the lagged industrial production is very close to the impact shown in the basic specification, as are the significance levels. This is also valid to some extent for the impact of export unit values, however, the

Table 4.39. Dynamic Panel Regression Results for RCAs - Specification I for Total Manufacturing

Arellano-Bond Dynamic Panel-Data Estimation, Two-Step System GMM Results						
Group variable: cross			Number of obs = 930			
Time variable: time			Number of groups = 123			
Number of instruments: 35			Obs per group: min = 5			
$F(6,122) = 224.96$			avg = 7.56			
Prob > F = 0.000			max = 9			
Dep.var: $lnrcamod_t$	Coef.	Corr. Std.Error	t	P>|t|	95 % Conf.Intervall	
$lnrcamod_{t-1}$	0.742	0.043	16.96	0.000	0.655	0.829
$lnip_{t-1}$	0.129	0.051	2.53	0.013	0.028	0.231
$dlab$	0.169	0.075	2.25	0.026	0.020	0.317
$lneuv$	0.040	0.023	1.72	0.087	-0.005	0.086
$lnlprel$	-0.100	0.064	-1.57	0.120	-0.227	0.026
$lnimportrca$	0.167	0.076	2.19	0.030	0.016	0.318
$constant$	0.233	0.160	1.46	0.148	-0.084	0.551
Hansen test of overid. restrictions: chi2(28)=36.06 Prob >chi2=0.141						
Arellano-Bond test for AR(1) in first differences: z = -2.15 pr>z =0.032						
Arellano-Bond test for AR(2) in first differences: z = 1.36 pr>z =0.172						

Source: Own Estimations

error probability declines from 10 to 8 percent. The new explanatory variable, relative labor productivity, shows the right sign with an error probability of 12 percent. A one percent rise in the relative labor productivity yields higher relative wages, which depresses modified RCAs by 0.10 percent. The impact of imports is rather robust. A one percent increase in relative import shares results in a 0.16 percent rise in the relative export shares. If we - in the next step - consider only labor intensive industries, we expect a stronger impact of labor productivity. The results are shown in table 4.40.

There should be no doubt by now about the importance of the lagged endogenous variable and the lagged industrial production, since their impact seems very stable throughout the different modification in the model specification. Similar to the basic regression, export unit values do not influence comparative advantages in labor intensive industries. However, the assumption on the positive correlation between relative wages and relative labor productivity - as explained in the simple small model earlier - gains ground on the basis of Specification I in the labor intensive industries. Accordingly, a one percent increase in relative labor productivity, bringing forward a rise in relative wages, results in a decline of comparative advantages in the labor intensive industries by 0.15 percent. The negative wage effect is shown to overtop the positive productivity effect on RCAs. We also find evidence of the hypothesis that imports do not play an important role for labor intensive industries, the coefficient turning out to be insignificant. Finally, also in this

Table 4.40. Dynamic Panel Regression Results for RCAs - Specification I for Labor Intensive Manufacturing Industries

Arellano-Bond Dynamic Panel-Data Estimation, Two-Step System GMM Results

Group variable: cross		Number of obs = 217				
Time variable: time		Number of groups = 29				
Number of instruments: 28		Obs per group: min = 5				
$F(5,28) = 297.33$		avg = 7.48				
Prob > F = 0.000		max = 9				

Dep.var: $lnrcamod_t$	Coef.	Corr. Std.Error	t	P>|t|	95 % Conf.Intervall	
$lnrcamod_{t-1}$	0.884	0.125	7.07	0.000	0.628	1.141
$lnip_{t-1}$	0.136	0.074	1.83	0.078	-0.016	0.289
$lneuv$	-0.010	0.058	-0.17	0.864	-0.130	0.110
$lnlprel$	-0.150	0.048	-3.10	0.004	-0.249	-0.051
$lnimportrca$	0.062	0.051	1.23	0.229	-0.041	0.167
$constant$	0.377	0.362	1.04	0.306	-0.364	1.119

Hansen test of overid. restrictions: chi2(22)=27.75 Prob >chi2=0.184
Arellano-Bond test for AR(1) in first differences: z = -2.59 pr>z =0.010
Arellano-Bond test for AR(2) in first differences: z = -1.17 pr>z =0.240

Source: Own Estimations

estimation there is no sign of any meaningful concern according to the Hansen and the Arellano-Bond tests. We now proceed by estimating the impact of labor productivity on high technology industries' RCAs. The results are shown in table 4.41.

The lagged endogenous variable and the lagged industrial output repeatedly show a robust positive impact. The rise of these variables by one percent causes comparative advantages in high technology industries to rise by 0.40 and 0.35 percent respectively. It is striking that the impact of these two variables is only that homogenous for the high technology subsample. For both the total manufacturing sample and the labor intensive sample, the impact of the lagged endogenous variable outperforms the impact of the industrial output by far. It is clear that adjustment dynamics in RCAs are the fastest for high technology industries. Moreover, it seems that industrial production as a percentage of GDP indicating the size of an industry and exports are more strongly connected at the higher end than at the lower end of the technology ladder. Table 4.41 also reinforces the strong impact of export unit values for the high technology industries. With a significance level of 90 percent, a one percent increase in export unit values leads to an increase in RCAs by 0.14 percent. Unsurprisingly, the impact of labor productivity on comparative advantages in the high technology sectors is strongly rejected by the panel estimation. Put in a nutshell, quality determines competitiveness of high technology industries, not wages. Moreover, export shares strongly depend on imports with a highly significant coefficient of 0.38.

Table 4.41. Dynamic Panel Regression Results for RCAs - Specification I for High Technology Industries

Arellano-Bond Dynamic Panel-Data Estimation, Two-Step System GMM Results						
Group variable: cross			Number of obs = 258			
Time variable: time			Number of groups = 34			
Number of instruments: 28			Obs per group: min = 5			
F(5,33) = 119.13			avg = 7.59			
Prob > F = 0.000			max = 9			
Dep.var: $lnrcamod_t$	Coef.	Corr. Std.Error	t	P>|t|	95 % Conf.Intervall	
$lnrcamod_{t-1}$	0.403	0.055	7.28	0.000	0.290	0.516
$lnip_{t-1}$	0.357	0.085	4.16	0.000	0.182	0.531
$lneuv$	0.146	0.079	1.86	0.072	-0.014	0.308
$lnlprel$	0.066	0.106	0.63	0.534	-0.149	0.282
$lnimportrca$	0.384	0.151	2.54	0.016	0.076	0.691
$constant$	1.052	0.384	2.74	0.010	0.270	1.834
Hansen test of overid. restrictions: chi2(22)=21.68 Prob >chi2=0.479						
Arellano-Bond test for AR(1) in first differences: z = -1.66 pr>z =0.098						
Arellano-Bond test for AR(2) in first differences: z = 0.40 pr>z =0.692						

Source: Own Estimations

It is not only wages and labor productivity that might play an important role in explaining comparative advantages, but also relative unit labor costs. They are calculated as the ratio of wages to productivity. On the one hand, the intuitive impact of relative unit labor costs would be negative, since a rise would deteriorate competitiveness especially in labor intensive industries. On the other hand, since wages and productivity are strongly correlated in our sample, one could expect that in the combination of these two variables there is no movement, no explanatory power left in the data. Indeed, the regression results including relative unit labor costs show no significant impact of it in any of the three samples. The other coefficients remain robust, but since there is no additional information provided by the estimations, the results are not reported.

After having analyzed several variables concerning labor as a factor input, we shall move on and try to control for the impact of some variables, which are possibly able to catch information on explaining comparative advantages in the higher technology industries. It would be very interesting to use sectoral data on capital endowments. However, data on capital formation at a 2-digit level classification is hardly available for most of the Eastern European EU member countries. We therefore use data on gross capital formation at current prices for the total economy as percentage of GDP instead.[19] Furthermore we use a relative measure to the capital intensity of EU 15 countries. Note that

---

[19] Data is taken from the European Commission's AMECO Database (European Commission, 2005).

assuming capital intensity of the total economy to have an impact on sectoral RCAs is still in line with the Heckscher-Ohlin model, which states that a strong overall endowment with capital will boost capital intensive industries. Accordingly, those industries which use capital intensively shall see a rise in RCAs if capital endowment at the macroeconomic level increases. First we check for multicollinearity among the explanatory variables and find that relative capital intensity is correlated with relative wages. We therefore drop the wages from the basic specification when including capital. Surprisingly, the capital variable never appears with a significant coefficient neither for the total sample nor for the two subsamples. One would have expected that capital endowments play an important role for high-technology industries, but we find no empirical evidence. This might be due to the information shortage of the capital variable, since it does not reveal any information on the allocation of capital among the industrial sectors.

We now turn our attention to the role of investment and innovation. We try to capture these influences by using two variables, foreign direct investment and expenditure on research and development. One main hypothesis concerns the role of foreign direct investment in the export specialization patterns of industries along with their competitiveness and comparative advantages on the EU market. Not only according to the theoretical literature is FDI an important driving force for economic catching-up and development. Carstensen and Toubal (2004) analyze econometrically the determinants of foreign direct investment in Eastern European countries at an aggregated macroeconomic level using a dynamic panel data method for the time period from 1993 to 1999. They show that the traditional determinants such as market potential, low relative unit labor costs, skilled workforce and relative endowments have a significant and expected effect. Furthermore they show that transition-specific variables such as the method of privatization and country risk play an important role.

It seems clear that foreign direct investment is an important factor driving economic development in Eastern European countries, however the question arises as to whether investors assess an industry as promising once it has a comparative advantage as measured by the RCA, or does the existence of foreign investors drive the profitability and success of an industry? To put it more clearly, what comes first: foreign direct investment or comparative advantage? Answering these questions one must bear in mind that it is the stock of FDI which determines RCAs, but RCAs can rather influence FDI flows, not stocks. We will start with analyzing the impact of FDI on RCAs. FDI stock in million Euro is provided from the WIIW FDI Database (2005), and we calculate FDI stocks as a percentage of GDP using GDP in million Euro taken from Eurostat. We test whether FDI's expected positive impact on revealed comparative advantage can be proved in a dynamic panel setting. However, before running the estimation several problems appear. Sectoral FDI data in percent of GDP as described above is not only correlated with RCAs, the endogenous variable of the panel, but also with several exogenous variables of the basic specification such as relative wages, export unit values, import shares, and even with industrial output. This is not surprising, because FDI is expected to drive industrial production and to contribute to quality upgrading as measured by the export unit value through technology and know-how spillovers. The impact of FDI on wages is not that straight forward. One could, on the one hand, expect FDI to foster technological development and human capital formation and therefore have a positive impact on wages. On the other hand, intensified use of machinery might depress wage levels, so that a negative impact of FDI on wages is imaginable. Against this background it is not surprising that FDI is also correlated with the labor productivity variable of Specification I. In order to bring clarity to the situation, we prefer to run the dynamic panel regression just for RCAs and FDI. Table 4.42 displays the results for total manufacturing industries.

Table 4.42. Dynamic Panel Regression Results for RCAs and FDI for Total Manufacturing

Arellano-Bond Dynamic Panel-Data Estimation, Two-Step System GMM Results

Group variable: cross			Number of obs = 1127			
Time variable: time			Number of groups = 153			
Number of instruments: 35			Obs per group: min = 1			
F(2,152) = 84.73			avg = 7.37			
Prob > F = 0.000			max = 10			
Dep.var: $lnrcamod_t$	Coef.	Corr. Std.Error	t	P>|t|	95 % Conf.Intervall	
$lnrcamod_{t-1}$	0.873	0.085	10.16	0.000	0.703	1.042
$lnfdigdp_t$	0.006	0.009	0.71	0.480	-0.012	0.025
constant	0.008	0.057	0.15	0.885	-0.106	0.122

Hansen test of overid. restrictions: chi2(32)=34.33 Prob >chi2=0.356
Arellano-Bond test for AR(1) in first differences: z = -3.49 pr>z =0.000
Arellano-Bond test for AR(2) in first differences: z = -0.93 pr>z =0.354

Source: Own Estimations

Note that this estimation also includes the Czech Republic and Slovakia into the panel, since RCAs and FDI are available for them as well. Therefore the number of observations is rather high with 1127, although the maximum number of possible observations amounts to 1936 including all eight Eastern European new EU member states. This hints toward considerable gaps in the FDI data, since the RCA data is complete for the total sample. Still, the impact of the simultaneous FDI variable on comparative advantage in exports is not significant. This result does not change if we simply consider the impact in the subsample of high technology goods as seen in table 4.43.

However, the results for the subsample of labor intensive goods is at first sight rather surprising according to table 4.44. With a significant level of 99 percent, it is empirically shown that an increase in the FDI/GDP ratio in

Table 4.43. Dynamic Panel Regression Results for RCAs and FDI for High Technology Manufacturing Industries

Arellano-Bond Dynamic Panel-Data Estimation, Two-Step System GMM Results

Group variable: cross		Number of obs = 275				
Time variable: time		Number of groups = 36				
Number of instruments: 28		Obs per group: min = 4				
F(2,35) = 792.69		avg = 7.64				
Prob > F = 0.000		max = 10				
Dep.var: $lnrcamod_t$	Coef.	Corr. Std.Error	t	P>|t|	95 % Conf.Intervall	
$lnrcamod_{t-1}$	0.919	0.065	13.99	0.000	0.786	1.053
$lnfdigdp_t$	0.028	0.025	1.12	0.269	-0.023	0.080
constant	0.197	0.151	1.31	0.199	-0.109	0.505

Hansen test of overid. restrictions: chi2(25)=22.80 Prob >chi2=0.589
Arellano-Bond test for AR(1) in first differences: z = -2.29 pr>z =0.022
Arellano-Bond test for AR(2) in first differences: z = 1.29 pr>z =0.198

Source: Own Estimations

Table 4.44. Dynamic Panel Regression Results for RCAs and FDI for Labor Intensive Manufacturing Industries

Arellano-Bond Dynamic Panel-Data Estimation, Two-Step System GMM Results

Group variable: cross		Number of obs = 251				
Time variable: time		Number of groups = 33				
Number of instruments: 28		Obs per group: min = 3				
F(2,32) = 80.92		avg = 7.61				
Prob > F = 0.000		max = 10				
Dep.var: $lnrcamod_t$	Coef.	Corr. Std.Error	t	P>|t|	95 % Conf.Intervall	
$lnrcamod_{t-1}$	0.953	0.095	10.02	0.000	0.759	1.146
$lnfdigdp_t$	0.024	0.006	3.65	0.001	0.109	0.038
constant	0.192	0.086	2.22	0.034	0.158	0.368

Hansen test of overid. restrictions: chi2(25)=26.94 Prob >chi2=0.359
Arellano-Bond test for AR(1) in first differences: z = -2.52 pr>z =0.012
Arellano-Bond test for AR(2) in first differences: z = -1.50 pr>z =0.134

Source: Own Estimations

labor intensive industries by one percent leads to a rise in RCAs by 0.024 percent. The coefficient is very small, however, the significance is stunning. One explanation for this result could be the fact that a great part of FDIs in Eastern European countries were directed at labor intensive industries for which investors expect the comparative advantages most readily to pay off. At the same time one must realize that for both subsamples the number of observations is very low. From a maximum number of observations for each subsample of 440 (eight countries, five industries and eleven years), only 250-

270 are realized. Therefore the incompleteness of the data set might cause some distortion in the results.

Table 4.45. Dynamic Panel Regression Results for RCAs and Lagged FDI for Total Manufacturing

Arellano-Bond Dynamic Panel-Data Estimation, Two-Step System GMM Results						
Group variable: cross			Number of obs = 983			
Time variable: time			Number of groups = 153			
Number of instruments: 35			Obs per group: min = 2			
F(2,152) = 186.59			avg = 6.42			
Prob > F = 0.000			max = 9			
Dep.var:	Coef.	Corr.	t	P>|t|	95 % Conf.Intervall	
$lnrcamod_t$		Std.Error				
$lnrcamod_{t-1}$	0.880	0.056	15.46	0.000	0.768	0.993
$lnfdigdp_{t-1}$	0.013	0.010	1.27	0.207	-0.007	0.033
$constant$	0.065	0.066	0.98	0.329	-0.066	0.197
Hansen test of overid. restrictions: chi2(32)=35.11 Prob >chi2=0.323						
Arellano-Bond test for AR(1) in first differences: z = -3.18 pr>z =0.001						
Arellano-Bond test for AR(2) in first differences: z = -0.51 pr>z =0.610						

Source: Own Estimations

Moreover, one might also argue that it is questionable whether FDI can have a simultaneous positive effect on export shares, since foreign investment only pays off with some time delay. Therefore we use one and two years lagged FDI values as the explanatory variable in the next regressions. Table 4.45 shows the results for total manufacturing. The one period lagged FDI/GDP ratio shows a positive impact on RCAs only if one allows for an error probability of 20 percent. This is, however, not acceptable for most econometric analysis. Again, the results look different for the subsamples according to tables 4.46 and 4.47.

There seems to be empirical evidence for the hypothesis that FDI pays off with some time delay, since for both subsamples the one year lagged FDI/GDP ratio is significant. For high technology industries, a one percent increase in the FDI/GDP ratio results in an increase of modified RCAs by 0.057 percent with a significance level of 95 percent. For labor intensive industries such a rise results in an increase of the endogenous variable by 0.026 percent with a significance level of 99 percent. Finally, assuming that FDI expenditure pays off with a time lag of two years, no significant influence for the total sample or for the high technology industries' subsample can be found. For the labor intensive industries the impact of FDI with a time lag of two years, however, is significant (see table 4.48). The coefficient amounts to 0.019 with a significance level of 95 percent. Thus the first lag seems to have the strongest impact on comparative advantages. All in all it seems that the impact of FDI on modified RCAs is exposed to volatility, which indeed reflects volatility in

Table 4.46. Dynamic Panel Regression Results for RCAs and Lagged FDI for High Technology Manufacturing Industries

Arellano-Bond Dynamic Panel-Data Estimation, Two-Step System GMM Results

Group variable: cross			Number of obs = 240			
Time variable: time			Number of groups = 36			
Number of instruments: 27			Obs per group: min = 3			
F(2,35) = 477.67			avg = 6.67			
Prob > F = 0.000			max = 9			

Dep.var: $lnrcamod_t$	Coef.	Corr. Std.Error	t	P>|t|	95 % Conf.Intervall	
$lnrcamod_{t-1}$	0.847	0.054	15.58	0.000	0.737	0.958
$lnfdigdp_{t-1}$	0.057	0.025	2.26	0.030	0.005	0.108
constant	0.364	0.149	2.45	0.020	0.062	0.667

Hansen test of overid. restrictions: chi2(24)=23.25 Prob >chi2=0.505
Arellano-Bond test for AR(1) in first differences: z = -2.11 pr>z =0.035
Arellano-Bond test for AR(2) in first differences: z = 1.60 pr>z =0.109

Source: Own Estimations

Table 4.47. Dynamic Panel Regression Results for RCAs and Lagged FDI for Labor Intensive Manufacturing Industries

Arellano-Bond Dynamic Panel-Data Estimation, Two-Step System GMM Results

Group variable: cross			Number of obs = 218			
Time variable: time			Number of groups = 33			
Number of instruments: 27			Obs per group: min = 2			
F(2,32) = 246.16			avg = 6.61			
Prob > F = 0.000			max = 9			

Dep.var: $lnrcamod_t$	Coef.	Corr. Std.Error	t	P>|t|	95 % Conf.Intervall	
$lnrcamod_{t-1}$	1.026	0.061	16.68	0.000	0.900	1.151
$lnfdigdp_{t-1}$	0.026	0.009	2.85	0.008	0.007	0.045
constant	0.166	0.088	1.88	0.069	-0.013	0.346

Hansen test of overid. restrictions: chi2(24)=25.63 Prob >chi2=0.372
Arellano-Bond test for AR(1) in first differences: z = -2.38 pr>z =0.017
Arellano-Bond test for AR(2) in first differences: z = -0.94 pr>z =0.350

Source: Own Estimations

the FDI variable itself. In most cases there is no continuous development of sectoral FDI. On the contrary, it is rather volatile. This could explain the different impacts of the contemporary and the lagged FDI variables.

However, we now come back to the question of whether FDI follows comparative advantages or if comparative advantages are (partially) a result of FDI. We have shown so far that FDI has a positive impact on RCAs, mainly in the labor intensive industries. Since Eastern European countries do have extinct comparative advantages in labor intensive industries to which a great

Table 4.48. Dynamic Panel Regression Results for RCAs and by Two Periods Lagged FDI for Labor Intensive Manufacturing Industries

Arellano-Bond Dynamic Panel-Data Estimation, Two-Step System GMM Results

Group variable: cross			Number of obs = 185			
Time variable: time			Number of groups = 33			
Number of instruments: 24			Obs per group: min = 1			
F(2,32) = 143.48			avg = 5.61			
Prob > F = 0.000			max = 8			
Dep.var: $lnrcamod_t$	Coef.	Corr. Std.Error	t	P>|t|	95 % Conf.Intervall	
$lnrcamod_{t-1}$	1.005	0.066	12.22	0.000	0.871	1.140
$lnfdigdp_{t-2}$	0.019	0.009	2.11	0.043	0.000	0.037
constant	0.111	0.079	1.39	0.173	-0.051	0.273

Hansen test of overid. restrictions: chi2(21)=21.53 Prob >chi2=0.427
Arellano-Bond test for AR(1) in first differences: z = -2.10 pr>z =0.035
Arellano-Bond test for AR(2) in first differences: z = -0.77 pr>z =0.442

Source: Own Estimations

part of FDIs were allocated during the 1990s, this is evidence for the hypothesis that RCAs are (at least partially) a result of FDI. Foreign companies invest in industries for which they expect high returns, thus RCAs follow FDI. But does it also work the other way around? We analyze whether a high RCA attracts FDI, measured as a flow variable. If this were the case, FDIs would gradually reallocate towards higher technology industries in Eastern European countries, because many of these countries increasingly gain comparative advantages in these industries. We apply the same dynamic panel setting for the bivariate estimation of modified RCAs on FDI flows.[20] The results fulfill to a great extent the expectations. RCAs never have a significant impact on FDI flows for total manufacturing, neither for the labor intensive industries. This is the case for the contemporary relationship as well as for the impact of the lagged RCA by one or two years. On the contrary, the positive impact of RCA for the high technology industries is extraordinary. Tables 4.49, 4.50, and 4.51 show the results.

Both the contemporary and the lagged RCAs have a strong and significant positive impact on FDI flows, but only in high-tech industries. The one year lagged RCA has the strongest influence. An increase of the modified RCA by 1 % raises FDI flows one year later by 0.9 %. This correlation is significant with an error probability of less then 1 %. The same is true in terms of significance for the two year lagged, and the contemporary impact. Their magnitude is roughly a 0.8 % increase in FDI flows triggered by a 1 % increase of RCAs. Both the Hansen test and the AR tests indicate no problem within the estimation, however, the already-mentioned bias of GMM estima-

---

[20] Due to data unavailability of FDI flows at the industry level, they are calculated by the author using first differences of FDI stocks.

Table 4.49. Dynamic Panel Regression Results for FDI Flows and RCAs for High Technology Manufacturing Industries

Arellano-Bond Dynamic Panel-Data Estimation, Two-Step System GMM Results

Group variable: cross		Number of obs = 121				
Time variable: time		Number of groups = 29				
Number of instruments: 22		Obs per group: min = 2				
F(2,28) = 12.46		avg = 4.17				
Prob > F = 0.000		max = 8				

Dep.var: $lnfdiflow_t$	Coef.	Corr. Std.Error	t	P>|t|	95 % Conf.Intervall	
$lnfdiflow_{t-1}$	0.219	0.132	1.65	0.110	-0.052	0.491
$lnrcamod$	0.821	0.227	2.96	0.006	0.253	1.390
$constant$	1.549	0.374	4.13	0.000	0.781	2.317

Hansen test of overid. restrictions: chi2(19)=19.07 Prob >chi2=0.452
Arellano-Bond test for AR(1) in first differences: z = -2.29 pr>z =0.022
Arellano-Bond test for AR(2) in first differences: z = 0.75 pr>z =0.453

Source: Own Estimations

Table 4.50. Dynamic Panel Regression Results for FDI Flows and Lagged RCAs for High Technology Manufacturing Industries

Arellano-Bond Dynamic Panel-Data Estimation, Two-Step System GMM Results

Group variable: cross		Number of obs = 121				
Time variable: time		Number of groups = 29				
Number of instruments: 22		Obs per group: min = 2				
F(2,28) = 17.65		avg = 4.17				
Prob > F = 0.000		max = 8				

Dep.var: $lnfdiflow_t$	Coef.	Corr. Std.Error	t	P>|t|	95 % Conf.Intervall	
$lnfdiflow_{t-1}$	0.248	0.120	2.06	0.048	0.001	0.495
$lnrcamod_{t-1}$	0.900	0.237	3.79	0.001	0.413	1.386
$constant$	1.650	0.362	4.55	0.000	0.908	2.393

Hansen test of overid. restrictions: chi2(19)=16.56 Prob >chi2=0.620
Arellano-Bond test for AR(1) in first differences: z = -2.22 pr>z =0.026
Arellano-Bond test for AR(2) in first differences: z = 0.59 pr>z =0.553

Source: Own Estimations

tors due to the short time dimension is also valid here. Nevertheless, this is impressive empirical evidence for the hypothesis that FDI attracts RCAs to a great extent, or put it differently, FDI follows RCAs in high technology industries. Investors are influenced by industries' success and try to be part of this success by investing in this industry. Since RCAs strongly rise in many high-technology industries in Eastern European countries, one can expect a further reallocation of FDI toward these industries. Comparing the significant coefficients of the two bivariate estimations (RCA on FDI: 0.8-0.9, and FDI

Table 4.51. Dynamic Panel Regression Results for FDI Flows and by Two Periods Lagged RCAs for High Technology Manufacturing Industries

Arellano-Bond Dynamic Panel-Data Estimation, Two-Step System GMM Results						
Group variable: cross			Number of obs = 121			
Time variable: time			Number of groups = 29			
Number of instruments: 22			Obs per group: min = 2			
F(2,28) = 14.98			avg = 4.17			
Prob > F = 0.000			max = 8			
Dep.var: $lnfdiflow_t$	Coef.	Corr. Std.Error	t	P>|t|	95 % Conf.Intervall	
$lnfdiflow_{t-1}$	0.216	0.126	1.71	0.098	-0.042	0.474
$lnrcamod_{t-2}$	0.807	0.229	3.51	0.002	0.336	1.278
$constant$	1.656	0.372	4.45	0.000	0.894	2.418

Hansen test of overid. restrictions: chi2(19)=17.96 Prob >chi2=0.525
Arellano-Bond test for AR(1) in first differences: z = -2.32 pr>z =0.020
Arellano-Bond test for AR(2) in first differences: z = 0.75 pr>z =0.456

Source: Own Estimations

on RCA: 0.01-0.05) implies the following answer to the question stated above: FDI flow follows RCA to a much greater extent than RCA follows FDI stock.

Now we move on and control for the influence of one more technology and science-related variable, namely expenditure on research and development. R&D expenditure aggregated at the firm level for NACE 2-digit level industries is available for the Eastern European countries from Eurostat. The data is given in million Euro. The explanatory variable in our model additionally controls for the size of the sector by relating R&D expenditures to GDP. In that sense the method of calculating this variable is similar to the FDI stock variable. The FDI and the R&D variables also both show a strong and significant correlation with industrial production, which is also calculated as % of GDP. Leaving industrial output in the regression causes both R&D and production to become insignificant. We therefore drop industrial production as an explanatory variable. But before continuing, please note that we also controlled for the impact of R&D expenditure alone on modified RCAs. The estimations show that a simultaneous significant positive correlation is found for total manufacturing, but not for the subsamples. The impact of the one year lagged R&D expenditure is never significant, however, the two periods lagged variable has a significant impact in the total sample and in the labor intensive subsample.

Accordingly, the dynamic panel estimation with the R&D-extended basic specification reveals a small, but significant influence of the simultaneous R&D variable only for total manufacturing and only if imports remain in the specification, although their influence is insignificant. At the same time we find no significant correlation between R&D expenditure and import shares. Moreover, the low number of observations for the total sample size of only

Table 4.52. Dynamic Panel Regression Results for RCAs - Specification II (Lagged) for High Technology Industries

Arellano-Bond Dynamic Panel-Data Estimation, Two-Step System GMM Results

Group variable: cross		Number of obs = 142				
Time variable: time		Number of groups = 29				
Number of instruments: 28		Obs per group: min = 1				
$F(5,28) = 88.02$		avg = 4.90				
Prob > F = 0.000		max = 9				

Dep.var: $lnrcamod_t$	Coef.	Corr. Std.Error	t	P>|t|	95 % Conf.Intervall	
$lnrcamod_{t-1}$	0.827	0.052	15.72	0.000	0.719	0.935
$lnrdgdp_{t-1}$	0.035	0.023	1.54	0.134	-0.011	0.083
$lneuv$	0.034	0.030	1.13	0.268	-0.028	0.097
$lnwagerel$	-0.120	0.086	-1.39	0.176	-0.298	0.057
$lnimportrca$	0.185	0.061	3.01	0.005	0.059	0.311
$constant$	0.029	0.175	0.17	0.865	-0.328	0.388

Hansen test of overid. restrictions: chi2(22)=23.59 Prob >chi2=0.369
Arellano-Bond test for AR(1) in first differences: z = -1.72 pr>z =0.086
Arellano-Bond test for AR(2) in first differences: z = -0.23 pr>z =0.819

Source: Own Estimations

Table 4.53. Dynamic Panel Regression Results for RCAs - Specification II (Lagged by Two Periods) for High Technology Industries

Arellano-Bond Dynamic Panel-Data Estimation, Two-Step System GMM Results

Group variable: cross		Number of obs = 120				
Time variable: time		Number of groups = 21				
Number of instruments: 8		Obs per group: min = 2				
$F(5,20) = 50.98$		avg = 5.71				
Prob > F = 0.000		max = 8				

Dep.var: $lnrcamod_t$	Coef.	Corr. Std.Error	t	P>|t|	95 % Conf.Intervall	
$lnrcamod_{t-1}$	0.570	0.142	4.02	0.001	0.274	0.867
$lnrdgdp_{t-2}$	0.133	0.058	2.26	0.035	0.010	0.256
$lneuv$	0.057	0.062	0.91	0.372	-0.073	0.188
$lnwagerel$	-0.309	0.160	-1.93	0.068	-0.644	0.024
$lnimportrca$	0.365	0.123	2.96	0.008	0.107	0.623
$constant$	0.482	0.390	1.23	0.231	-0.332	1.297

Hansen test of overid. restrictions: chi2(2) = 0.66 Prob >chi2=0.720
Arellano-Bond test for AR(1) in first differences: z = -2.00 pr>z =0.046
Arellano-Bond test for AR(2) in first differences: z = -0.71 pr>z =0.476

Source: Own Estimations

538 instead of 1452 indicates that data on R&D expenditure is unfortunately rather fragmentary, which might be part of the explanation.

According to the bivariate estimation, we do not expect a significant impact including the first lag of R&D expenditure in the dynamic panel specification. This turns out to be true for total manufacturing and for the labor intensive industries. We do, however, find a significant coefficient for the high technology industries if we allow for an error probability of 13 percent (see table 4.52). A one percent increase in the R&D to GDP ratio results in a 0.035 percent higher RCA one year later. This seems to underline the importance of research and development for higher technology industries, which one would expect from theoretical and practical considerations. It also seems reasonable that research and development expenditure materializes with some time lag. Even a two year lag appears reasonable and is reinforced by the estimations, at least for the high technology subsample (see table 4.53).

However, due to the small number of observation left, one must also limit the number of instruments. Therefore instead of using one instrument for each time period, each variable and each lag distance as we did in all estimations before, we now only use one instrument for each variable and each lag distance. Therefore the number of instruments is reduced from 28 to 8. The results indicate that a one percent increase in the R&D/GDP ratio leads to an increase in modified RCAs by 0.13 percent two years later with a significance level of 95 percent. As compared to the one year lagged impact, this is a much stronger influence. Finally, one should not overlook the fact that the impact of export unit values is not robust for the R&D augmented specification, which might be due to the very small sample size that is merely available when including expenditure on research and development.

4.6.4 Summary of the Results

The very last estimation is an especially nice demonstration of the shortcomings of this dynamic panel regression. Due to the small data sample and especially due to the short period of observations, a completely unbiased estimation of the determinants of Eastern European countries' export specialization is not possible for the time being. Both the LSDV and the GMM estimators are biased, whereas it can be shown that the bias of the GMM estimator is smaller. Therefore the choice of estimation method fell in favor of the "system GMM", which seems to be the most appropriate estimation method for the underlying data.

Despite the problems with the econometric methods, one might argue that - when bearing in mind the shortcomings of the estimation techniques -, the results give important new insight into the dynamics of foreign trade specialization in new EU member states. The following bullet points sum up the results:

- Firstly, we find that adjustment dynamics in export specialization patterns are the fastest in high technology industries, as compared to labor intensive industries and total manufacturing.
- We put to record that the industrial production as a percentage of GDP indicating the size of an industry plays a very important role in explaining comparative advantages, especially with a time lag of one year. This is valid across all the 22 considered manufacturing industries.
- Eastern European countries are still specialized to a significantly stronger degree in labor intensive industries as compared to all other manufacturing industries, thus revealing a considerably higher comparative advantage in these areas.
- Export unit values as an indicator of product quality play an important role in explaining comparative advantages. This is valid in a cross-sectoral perspective, but especially for science-based industries and differentiated goods, which are situated at the upper end of the technology ladder. Furthermore export unit values seem to play hardly any role for labor intensive industries.
- Import shares and export shares are strongly and positively correlated especially for high-technology industries. This is evidence for knowledge and technology spill over that comes along with imports, in particular with intermediate imports. At the same time, gaining export shares in labor intensive industries does not depend on imports.
- Relative labor productivity and relative wages are highly correlated, showing that gains in labor productivity are to a great extent reflected in wage increases.
- Relative wages determine comparative advantages strongly, not only for labor intensive industries, but even at a cross-industrial basis. For high technology industries, however, relative wages hardly turn out to of significance.
- A contemporary positive impact of research and development expenditure is found for total manufacturing. For high technology industries the export enhancing effects seem to unfold only after one or two years. For labor intensive industries, no significant impact is found.
- Finally, foreign direct investment is strongly correlated both with labor productivity and industrial production. A contemporary impact on comparative advantages is found only for labor intensive industries. With a time lag of one year FDI stock has a positive impact both on labor intensive and on high tech industries. For labor intensive industries FDI even displays export enhancing effects after two years. A reversed influence can also be found with the development of RCAs strongly influencing FDI flows, but only for high-technology industries. All in all, RCA follows FDI to some extent mainly in labor intensive industries, where investors expect in Eastern Europe more profitability than in high technology industries. To a much greater extent FDI follows RCA in high-technology industries, where some of the Eastern European countries have begun to strongly in-

crease their competitiveness. Therefore one can expect a shift of FDI flows away from labor intensive industries towards high-technology industries for the upcoming years.

The results of the dynamic panel analysis are relevant, although at some points deficiencies due to data unavailability or methodological problems are visible. Missing values reduce the number of the observations dramatically at some point; including a lag structure into the analysis even further reduces the already short time dimension. The latter is most certainly highly problematic. However, despite the momentous outcome of the model, further research with longer and more extensive data sets will be needed to completely disclose the mechanisms behind these issues.

5

Policy Implications

Sustained growth is a major aim of national economic policy in EU countries. The framework for it is set by supranational policy, which should focus on the interaction of different national policies in order to create an efficient and competitive European economic area.

Being competitive is one of the most important goals set for the European Union in the 2000 Lisbon Strategy (EC, 2002). Competitiveness is defined as the ability of the economy to provide its population with high and rising standards of living and high rates of employment on a sustainable basis. For achieving this goal, competitiveness of the manufacturing industries is crucial. The EC (2002) sees three factors as key to industrial competitiveness:

- Firstly, being at the edge of knowledge is crucial. This implies more and effective efforts in education, vocational training and research.
- Innovation in every industrial sector is needed to stimulate the creation of novel products and more efficient processes.
- European industry should develop entrepreneurial capacity, which is able to take risks and grow newer and bigger businesses.

This implies that strong emphasis on competition and rather limited government intervention are adequate. At the same time one should consider the fact that countries eager to catch up, such as the new EU member states, can particularly benefit from FDI flows. One of the main policy conclusions relevant for raising foreign trade competitiveness, which can directly be derived from the econometric analysis in the previous chapter, is to highlight the importance of an investor friendly economic environment. The positive impact of FDI on the development of comparative advantages in foreign trade has clearly been empirically corroborated. Policy makers should focus on attracting FDI in diversified industries. Host countries of FDI may benefit through direct transfer of investment, know-how, management skills and technology. FDI can also enhance macro- and microeconomic restructuring. The positive effects of FDI depend on the size, the resource endowments and the state of development of the host country. At the same time FDI flows are determined by different incentives; four of them are prominent in the literature: resource seeking, market seeking, efficiency seeking and strategic asset seeking FDI (Zielinska-Glebocka, 2005). Depending on the driving forces of FDI, its contribution to enhancing competitiveness may be different. In any case a host country can attract FDI by offering political and legal security. Also creating a business environment, which allows for efficient operations of economic agents is crucial. Governments can offer fiscal incentives through tax rebates, or financial incentives through subsidized loans and credits, or non-financial incentives such as an adequate infrastructure system (Zielinska-Glebocka, 2005). Although new EU member states have been very successful in attracting FDI since the beginning of the 1990s, a great part of FDI was connected to privatization activities. Therefore new EU member states will have to develop strategies in order to maintain high FDI flows.

Being attractive for FDI is also crucial in terms of labor market developments. Although, the Eastern European new EU member states witnessed high FDI inflows and relatively favorable economic development in the past decade, among others Poland, Hungary, the Czech Republic still show rather high - partially stubborn - unemployment rates. At first it seems that labor markets in the new EU member states will benefit from outsourcing and off-shoring from Western European companies, which is for sure not deniable. However, as European integration proceeds, firms in new EU member states themselves face considerable competitive pressure for outsourcing internationally, e.g. from Asian countries such as China. Given high sustained unemployment rates in many new EU member states, one must be worried about unemployment problems. Jobless growth could be one of the new problems in the new EU member states. To the extent that the mass unemployment problem contributes to social and political conflicts as well as political radicalization, high long term unemployment could contribute to political destabilization which in turn would raise the political risk premium and weaken growth in the long run. When dealing with competitiveness, one has to distinguish between

1. competitiveness of firms, which is displayed for example by comparative advantages on export markets, and
2. competitiveness of an economy, which is displayed by the reaction of factor markets to intensified economic integration and globalization.

Only if factor markets, especially labor markets, are able to adjust themselves in such a way that massive unemployment can be avoided, can one state that an economy is being competitive. Since the share of industry in gross value added has been declining in European countries, the ability of the services sector, which gains more and more grounds in gross value added, to create new jobs is crucial for economy-wide competitiveness. Moreover, policy makers have to put emphasis on upgrading human capital formation by fostering training, education and skill developing job placements, which will be important for enhancing productivity and encouraging the creation of new firms, which often not only create new jobs but contribute to overall flexibility and innovativeness.

It is inevitable that policymakers stimulate innovations and thus enhance the quality of products to gain competitiveness on international markets. Underlying econometric analysis shows the positive influence of export unit values on revealed comparative advantage especially for higher technology products, thus stating that a higher quality product can better be placed on international markets than a low quality product. Therefore quality upgrading by enforcing innovativeness is one of the main ingredients of a successful economic policy not only in Eastern European countries. This implies a continuous process of restructuring towards more advanced sectors of production with medium or high technology intensity, which is on a European scale particularly crucial for the new EU member states. However, on a global scale of competitiveness, support for innovation, knowledge and technological progress is important especially for the Western European countries if they aim at being competitive against the world technology leaders such as the United States of America. The Lisbon Strategy provides a good plan in this direction, however, its implementation requires active measures by the EU countries.

One area of active measures concerns expenditure on research and development (R&D). The positive impacts of R&D expenditure on comparative advantages of foreign trade were shown empirically in the previous chapter. Yet also from a theoretical and a political perspective it is clear that national R&D programs are likely to generate a positive effect on economic development and on competitiveness of countries and industries. However, due to cross-border benefits through international technology spillovers there is some risk that national policymakers will cut incentives for R&D expenditures, causing them to decline, since it can be expected that positive external effects of innovation would not be fully internalized in the EU. However, the EU institutions could be quite useful in innovation policy, particularly by regularly analyzing innovation dynamics in EU countries and regions. More transparency could generate stronger incentives towards adequate national policy reforms.

Infrastructure is also an important issue when dealing with competitiveness, because it reduces transaction costs for doing business. Distance effects of trade are strongly negative for peripheries such as Eastern or Southern European countries. This might be a consequence of poor infrastructures, which underlines the importance of policies fostering infrastructure improvement, which should decrease the market access gap between the EU's center and its peripheries. Integration of poorer and less-developed regions into regional trading blocks must be accompanied by income redistribution mechanisms which should be linked (among others) to investment in infrastructure. Yet the quality of infrastructure also matters. Badly planned infrastructure might result in the ineffectiveness of large investments on competitiveness of industries or on long run growth of the economy (Nunez, 2005).

More generally, governance matters for competitiveness. Issues such as rule of law, institutional burdens or high bureaucracy can prevent investment and reduce competitiveness. A solid and functioning legal system and an adequate and efficient bureaucracy are crucial prerequisites for investment and sustainable growth. Trade issues, in particular, as discussed in detail in the previous chapters can be influenced by different strands of economic policy. Below we will briefly deal with the impact of competition, trade, industrial and structural policy in the enlarged European Union.

5.1 Competition Policy

The legal basis for the application of the competition policy in the EC is in its Treaty, Articles 81 to 90. The EU member states are required to adopt an economic policy *"conducted in accordance with the principle of an open market economy with free competition"* (WTO, 2004). Four main objectives pursued by competition policy may be identified as (Neumann, 2001, p: 1):

- Establishing a competitive order as an end in itself to safeguard economic freedom;
- Maintaining a competitive order to foster economic efficiency and technological and economic progress;
- Providing fair competition, which implies prohibition of deceptive practices, threat, extortion, and unfair advantages through government subsidies;
- Maintaining a decentralized structure of supply, because small and medium size enterprises are considered the backbone of a demoratic society.

The main competition policy tools of the EU are: antitrust rules, merger regulations, liberalization of monopolistic economic sectors, and the control of state aid (WTO, 2004). In terms of antitrust rules, the Treaty outlaws anti-competitive agreements such as price-fixing or market-share cartels between economic actors that may affect trade between the member states. Only those agreements which are beneficial on balance to economic efficiency and consumers' interests serve as an exception. However, the Commission must grant exceptions on an individual basis. Regulations of the EU on mergers tries to avoid a situation in which competition is impeded, especially through a dominant position created by mergers or acquisitions. State aid in the EU must not distort competition in the EU. However, exceptions may be granted under certain circumstances, such as supporting small and medium-sized enterprizes, research and development, environmental protection or boosting employment and training, or specific sectors. The main focus of policy is the redirection of state aid toward horizontal objectives (WTO, 2004).

The new EU member states have to implement the EC's acquis in competition policy with a few transitional arrangements. These concern the phasing-out of fiscal aid to small and medium-sized enterprises, which is not compatible to EC rules as well as incompatible fiscal aid to large companies in regional investment aid. Also, the provision of state aid for the restructuring of ship-building and steel industries will have to be phased-out. The expiry dates lie between 2005 and 2011 (WTO, 2004).

All in all, successful competition policy encourages adjustment, allocative efficiency, and innovation in the enlarged EU, thus maintaining a competitive European economic environment.

5.2 Trade Policy

Through economic integration in the EU trade integration has also proceeded at a rapid pace. As a result some sectors in the former EU 15 countries face increased competition, as we have seen in the previous chapter. This is especially the case for some scale intensive and resource intensive industries as well as increasingly for some differentiated goods. In these industries possible negative trade effects exist through the crowding out of domestic producers by competitors from the new EU member states which are attractive as production sites due to the combination of well educated human capital and relatively low unit labor costs. Thus production is to some extent reallocated from the old to the new EU member states. Trade vulnerability analysis shows that the implications are heterogenous for the old EU member states (Nunez, 2005). At the same time it is questionable whether the advantages for the new EU member states are long-lasting. It is economically reasonable to assume that through the process of convergence within the enlarged EU, wage differentials will fall reducing these advantages in new EU member states, making them of temporary character. Still, in the EU 15 countries there is need for restructuring in a number of industries, which are either sensitive to trade vulnerability or of strategic importance. In Eastern European countries there is need for restructuring towards more advanced and more technology intensive industries.

As already described in chapter 2, trade policy in terms of trade liberalization through reducing tariffs is almost completely implemented within the European Union, at least as far as trade in goods is concerned. Therefore not much needs to be done here. Manufacturing especially enjoys rather free trade conditions; the remaining trade barriers mostly concern agricultural products. However, reducing non-tariff barriers to trade is also crucial, which still exist within the EU and which constitute a major obstacle to the completion of the internal market in the European Community. Non-tariff barriers are restrictions to imports, which can take the form of state subsidies or national regulations on such areas as health, environment or safety, quotas, intellectual property laws or curruption.

On the contrary, trade in services needs further liberalization. As indicated previously, the development of the services sector and its factor markets are crucial for the competitiveness of the EU and its member states, because a great part of domestic value added is generated in the services sector. Free trade in services is a prerequisite for the EU's beneficial development, and improving service sectors can boost overall competitiveness. Trade barriers in services must be removed - as has been proposed by the EC (2002a)-, because future growth and employment creation in the EU and especially in the new member states will depend to a great extent on the development of services.

5.3 Industrial Policy

According to the 2004 European Competitiveness Report, manufacturing competitiveness as an important part of industrial competitiveness is crucial, although the reallocation of resources from industry to services has been taking place in the old EU member states since the beginning of the 1990s and in the new EU member states since the mid 1990s. Preventing de-industrialization is an aim which has been uttered by several European political leaders and has also been dealt with by the EC. In its publication "Fostering Structural Change: an Industrial Policy for an Enlarged Europe" (EC, 2004a), the EC stated that de-industrialization is not inevitable, and mobilizing resources to avoid de-industrialization is desirable.

At the same time it seems that neither de-industrialization nor structural change in the new EU member states per se are main barriers for competitiveness in Europe. Therefore policies, which subsidize specific sectors should be carefully monitored and controlled in line with EU competition policy (Zielinska-Glebocka, 2005). Nevertheless, industrial policy should be tailored to the needs of particular sectors, which means that the EU should develop a sectoral dimension of industrial policy. This implies that effectiveness should be analyzed at the sectoral level, but policy instruments should be of a horizontal nature. Thus interventionism as implemented in the past must not come back in practice. There is no need or justification that European integration and changes in competitiveness calls for the implementation of targeting-related industrial policy, rather industrial policy shall use horizontal measures. Moreover, industrial policy should be designed in such a way as to foster innovation, investment and human capital as well as enterprize spending on research and development. Besides, both the EC and the member states' national governments should continue their effort in improving the quality of the regulatory framework, because industrial competitiveness and thus industrial policy rest on the pillars of regulation and institutions. Improving the regulatory framework may include the use of regulatory quality indicators or the exchange of good practice.

Finally, one should bear in mind that manufacturing is a main recipient of state aid. There seem to be general agreement upon the fact that policies subsidizing sectors in decline do not generally improve their prospects but rather delay their restructuring. The period of decline is made longer, and adjustment will be even harder at the end. This can be seen in some resource intensive industries such as mining and quarrying, which have been heavily subsidized for decades in several old and new EU countries without being able to raise productivity or stop the decline of these sectors. Therefore the main objective of state aid should be to contribute to improving the business environment in the EU and improving the regulatory framework. To summarize, instead of a sectoral nature, state aid should be of horizontal type. This helps to promote entrepreneurship and might create a friendly environment for small and medium size enterprizes.

5.4 Structural and Cohesion Policy

The aim of the EU structural policy, which consists of four different funds, is to resolve structural, economic and social problems in the EU (EC, 2005d). The four funds available are:

1. European Regional Development Funds
2. European Social Fund
3. European Agricultural Guidance and Guarantee Fund
4. Financial Instrument for Fisheries Guidance.

The main priority of all four funds is the Objective 1 regions which are regarded as being in need of promoting, because their GDP per capita does not exceed 75 % of the EU average, or population density is very low, or they are extremely peripheral. Structural funds imply European co-financing on development projects that respond to national priorities agreed upon between the Member State and the EC.

The aim of the cohesion policy which was established in 1994 is to reduce economic and social disparities. The cohesion funds finance major infrastructure and environmental projects (EC, 2005d). The least prosperous member states of the Union whose gross national product per capita is below 90 % of the EU average are eligible. Between 1993 and 1999, the fund included ECU 15.150 million at 1992 prices, for the time period 2000-2006 it includes EUR 28.212 million at 2004 prices (EC, 2005d). Since EU Eastern enlargement the eligible countries are Greece, Portugal, Spain, and all the 10 new EU member states: Cyprus, Czech Republic, Estonia, Hungary, Latvia, Lithuania, Malta, Poland, Slovakia and Slovenia. Between January 2000 and 2004 the four cohesion countries, Greece, Portugal, Spain and Ireland, were eligible. Ireland was deemed ineligible already before EU eastern enlargement, while the other three cohesion countries remained eligible; therefore changes in the cohesion funds are not too dramatical for the old EU member states. In terms of the quantitative volume of support the eligible old EU member states receive roughly 70 % of the cohesion funds between 2000 and 2006 (EC, 2005d).

Structural and cohesion funds comprise up to one-third of total EU budget, and the right measures to these policies depend on the outcome of many problems and dilemmas which the EU currently faces.[1] One concerns the interrelationship between the evaluation of integration and the spatial concentration of production. Does an increase in liberalization lead to industrial concentration? Previous analysis does not confirm this, at least at the country level. Another dilemma concerns the rationale of structural policy. Given that structrual funds often fail to boost economic growth, would it not be more productive to invest in regions with the greatest growth potential rather than in the less promising regions? Structural funds rather have social transfer connected backgrounds (Zielinska-Glebocka, 2005).

In line with the predictions of the New Economic Geography, problems with regional dimensions have arisen in the EU such as strong geographic agglomeration at the regional level or the development of core versus periphery regions. As shown by Cappelen et al. (1999), European countries converge in terms of growth rates, but this is not the case for European regions. On the contrary, there is empirical evidence for a rising gap in economic terms between several European regions. The so-called "European Growth Club" regions keep on departing from the lesser developed European regions, which is one of the key challenges for European regional and cohesion policy. European regional policy should be in best case a mixture of income, education and infrastructure policy in order to reduce regional disparities. A balanced mix of policies, fostering income, skill levels and infrastructure should ensure the optimal development of the European Union and its regions.

The new EU member states have a special need for infrastructure investment, which can be channelled to them through structural funds. However, they must be co-financed by the national governments. This can, on the one hand, create budgetary problems by engaging public financing. On the other hand, it might be the right measure to prevent the wrong allocation of structural funds. It is crucial that the new EU member states ensure the efficient allocation of resources as the driving force behind structural funds rather then ensuring the prompt absorption of EU funds (Zielinska-Glebocka, 2005). It would be wise to shift structural funds away from mere cohesion and convergence related aims towards innovation and R&D enhancing interests. Community funds should support knowledge, technological process and innovation instead of purely supporting convergence and cohesion. To some extent, this has also been laid down in the Lisbon strategy.

To conclude, for policy makers in new EU member states it is essential to foster training & education, investment activities as well as to enforce the creation and maintenance of an investor friendly economic and political environment. EU 15 countries need to boost innovation, technological development, and R&D activities. Enabling labor markets to adjust to changes in the course of European integration is a major challenge for all EU 25 countries.

---

[1] For a detailed analysis of structural and policy issues in connection with the EU-Eastern enlargement, see Welfens and Wziatek-Kubiak (eds.), 2005.

6

Conclusions

The integration of goods has progressed rather far within the enlarged European Union. Moreover, business cycle correlation is rather strong between the old and the new EU member states, which is a sign that the two regions undergo similar boom and recession times and tend to be exposed to similar shocks. Still, there are strong adjustment processes underway in the course of European integration, especially in the new EU member states.

In a dynamic open economy one may anticipate structural changes over time and changes in trade specialization. This book deals with analyzing foreign trade specialization patterns within the enlarged EU with a special focus laid on the new EU member states. From a theoretical point of view Traditional Trade Theories such as Ricardo or Heckscher-Ohlin predict that factor endowments and technological differences play a major role when explaining trade specialization patterns. Accordingly, the new EU member states are expected to specialize in labor and resource intensive industries, which can actually be seen during the early 1990s. Furthermore, they tend to be competitors in these industries of the less developed old EU countries such as the cohesion countries. However, the share of intra-industry trade is increasing in intra-EU trade, which cannot be explained by the Traditional Trade Theories, rather by the New Trade Theory. Different demand characteristics, the so called "Love of Variety", and scale economies determine trade patterns to a large extent according to the New Trade Theory. In empirical studies these effects seem to play a significant role in explaining specialization patterns in the enlarged EU. On the contrary, backward and forward linkages and spatial characteristics as described by the New Economic Geography are not yet found to play a significant role in empirical studies for the enlarged EU. In our view, this is however rather due to data availability problems especially for the new EU member states and not to the unimportance of the predictions of the New Economic Geography models. Improving data availability and quality might show more meaningful results for the direct empirical applications of trade theory models in future research. Moreover, developing a generalized and empirically applicable trade theory model as a combination of the so far rather different strands of theories should be one of the main challenges for future theoretical research.

Applying simple analytical tools to identify intra-EU trade specialization in the three largest new EU member states and the cohesion countries shows - in the spirit of Traditional Trade Theory models - that Poland exports to the EU 15 rather low and some medium technology (or labor intensive) products just like Greece and Portugal, and to a lesser extent Spain. The Czech Republic, however, shows clear specialization patterns also in the field of medium and even high technology products, while Hungary and Ireland mainly specialize in the export of high technology. Yet in Hungary, we also find export specialization in some very low technology products in the 1990s. This might bring about considerable intersectoral wage differentials. Weighted measures of sectoral comparative advantages underline these findings for the new EU members states and for Greece and Portugal. For Ireland and Spain, however, we find strong dependencies on just one or two industries such as motor vehicles for Spain and chemicals and office machinery and computers for Ireland. Countries should always try to foster development in diversified industries in order to avoid strong economic vulnerability and in order to maintain sustainable economic development. A natural caveat, however, is the size of the respective country.

The ability of some new EU member states such as Hungary or the Czech Republic to display distinct comparative advantages in high technology industries just a decade and a half after the beginning of system transformation shows that catching-up economies have good opportunities partially thanks to integration and globalization. Most of these comparative advantages emerge from outsourcing and offshoring, creating typical bazaar-type economies within which sectoral industrial production consists to a large extent of foreign intermediates (and only to a small extent of domestic intermediates and value added). However, as we see from their dynamic economic development, these type of activities do not harm but rather boost their growth perspectives. From this point of view, being a bazaar is not disadvantageous, but is rather a merit for Eastern European countries.

Industrial competition has increased in some industries in the enlarged EU. New EU member states have been gaining competitive power and improving the quality of supplied goods in scale intensive industries and in some differentiated goods since the middle of the 1990s. At the same time, most new EU member states and cohesion countries still have a strong comparative disadvantage in science-based industries, which underlines the importance of fostering R&D expenditure. All in all, one can see that - disregarding some exceptions - high quality manufacturing goods tend not to be supplied by cohesion and new EU countries on the EU 15 market, which raises the importance of economic policy in order to increase the competitiveness of European countries and industries, especially in light of the goals of the Lisbon Strategy for the EU over the next decade.

Achieving the Lisbon goal of being the most dynamic and innovative economic area in the world requires avoiding massive national or regional disparities in the enlarged EU in the spirit of the NEG. Therefore the question of economic convergence of EU member states and their specialization patterns is crucial. Convergence is especially important for countries aiming to have a common monetary policy as in the EMU. Concerning trade specialization patterns and applying the well know concepts of β- and σ-convergence, we find that at the intra-country cross sectoral level there is a strong tendency to de-specialization, thus to convergence. On the other side of the coin, we find a strong tendency towards de-concentration of industries at the inter-sectoral cross country level. These findings are not surprising, but rather soothing when thinking about the future development of the enlarged EU.

In order to positively influence the future economic development of the enlarged EU, one must be aware of the factors driving successful specialization patterns. Within the framework of a dynamic panel analysis for the new EU member states we find that sectoral industrial production as a percentage of GDP indicating the size of an industry is with a time lag of one year important in fostering comparative advantages in terms of exports. Also export unit values as an indicator for product quality are able to enhance comparative advantages especially in high-technology industries. This might be due to a positive link between profitability and export unit value on the one hand, and between product upgrading and profitability on the other. Moreover, import and export shares are strongly correlated, which shows that imports are a main source of technology and know-how spillovers. For labor intensive industries within which revealed comparative advantages are - though declining - still significantly higher than in all other manufacturing industries, relative wages to the old EU member states strongly determine comparative advantages. At the same time, relative wages and productivity are strongly correlated; thus a rise in labor productivity is directly reflected by a rise in wages, which is shown empirically for the new EU member states. This indicates that the new EU countries cannot in the long run rely on their comparative advantages in terms of a wage gap towards the old EU member states, since these effects are temporary and will to a great extent run out in the near future. For this reason, being competitive in high-technology and differentiated goods will be crucial and can be enhanced by fostering expenditure on R&D, which pays off with some time lag. Last but not least, we should stress the importance of FDI, which fosters comparative advantages in labor intensive industries and to a lesser extent also in higher-technology industries. Interestingly, in high-technology industries a rise in comparative advantages also brings about a rise in FDI flows. Thus, comparative advantages follow FDI in labor intensive industries for which investors obviously expect higher profitability than in high technology industries in Eastern European countries. To an even larger extent, however, FDI follows comparative advantages in high-technology industries, where some of the Eastern European countries have begun to increase competitiveness. Therefore one can expect and should foster a shift of FDI flows away from labor intensive towards high-technology industries in the medium term. Moreover, this brings some relief to the above-mentioned fear of not being able to hold relative wage related economic advantages in the new EU member states.

Finally, what are the implications for economic policy? In terms of competitiveness, creating broader potentials for production and exports of knowledge-based and differentiated products is important. Also fostering innovation and entrepreneurial capacity should help enhance competitiveness. Furthermore, creating an investor friendly economic environment attracts domestic and foreign investment, which has a clear positive effect on the development of trade specialization patterns and on competitiveness of firms. Enabling competitiveness of the whole economy, however, implies that factor markets can adjust to the challenges of international integration in order to avoid massive unemployment. This also is an argument for developing human capital on the one hand, but for flexible and not over-regulated labor markets on the other hand, which are able to absorb unemployment across sectors due to intensified structural change by creating new jobs in dynamic economic sectors such as services. In terms of competition policy, maintaining open markets is crucial. Trade policy needs to continue to ensure free trade of goods, but also create free trade in services. Liberalization has to include removing non-tariff trade barriers, which are still a main obstacle to the completion of the free internal market in the enlarged EU and is often neglected when dealing with trade policy issues. Industrial policy should aim at preventing de-industrialization, which is a common long term threat for the EU. Furthermore, industrial policy needs to be tailored to the needs of particular sectors, so that industrial policy does have a sectoral dimension, but without subsidizing sectors in decline. Such subsidies generally do not improve these declining sectors' prospects, but rather delay their restructuring. Structural and cohesion policies have to deal with the challenge of reducing economic and social disparities within EU regions and economies. At the same time community funds should support knowledge, technological process and innovation, instead of purely supporting convergence and cohesion. Most importantly in the new EU countries, it is essential to foster education as well as investment and to enforce the maintenance of an investor friendly environment. EU 15 countries should put the emphasis on boosting innovation, technological development, and R&D activities. Enabling labor markets to adjust to changes in the course of European integration is a major challenge for all EU 25 countries.

There has always been and will always be diverging views within and on the European Union in terms of integration, trade and economic development. Especially the role of economic policy is often rather controversial. Nevertheless, there should be no doubt about the necessity of taking into account - besides the economic issues dealt with in this book - social and environmental issues when dealing with deep integration at the edge of globalization, as we do when we deal with the European Union. It seems that European integration can help us understand the challenges that lie ahead.

A

NACE Rev. 1.1 Classification

D   Manufacturing
15 Manufacture of food products and beverages
    151 Production, processing and preserving of meat and meat products
    152 Processing and preserving of fish and fish products
    153 Processing and preserving of fruit and vegetables
    154 Manufacture of vegetable and animal oils and fats
    155 Manufacture of dairy products
    156 Manufacture of grain mill products, starches and starch products
    157 Manufacture of prepared animal feeds
    158 Manufacture of other food products
    159 Manufacture of beverages
16 Manufacture of tobacco products
    160 Manufacture of tobacco products
17 Manufacture of textiles
    171 Preparation of spinning of textile fibres
    172 Textile weaving
    173 Finishing of textiles
    174 Manufacture of made-up textile articles, except apparel
    175 Manufacture of carpets and rugs
    176 Manufacture of knitted and crocheted fabrics
    177 Manufacture of knitted and crocheted articles
18 Manufacture of wearing apparel; dressing and dyeing of fur
    181 Manufacture of leather clothes
    182 Manufacture of other wearing apparel and accessories
    183 Dressing and dyeing of fur; manufacture of articles of fur
19 Tanning and dressing of leather, manufacture of luggage, handbags,
    saddlery, harness and footwear
    191 Tanning and dressing of leather
    192 Manufacture of luggage, handbags and the like, saddlery and
        harness
    193 Manufacture of footwear

20 Manufacture of wood and of products of wood and cork, except
    furniture; manufacture of articles of straw and plaiting materials
    201 Sawmilling and planing of wood, impregnation of wood
    202 Manufacture of veneer sheets; manufacture of plywood, lamin-
        board, particle board, fibre board and other panels and boards
    203 Manufacture of builders carpentry and joinery
    204 Manufacture of wooden containers
    205 Manufacture of other products of wood; manufacture of articles
        of cork, straw and plaiting materials
21 Manufacture of pulp, paper and paper products
    211 Manufacture of pulp, paper and paperboard
    212 Manufacture of articles of paper and paperboard
22 Publishing, printing and reproduction of recorded media
    221 Publishing
    222 Printing and service activities related to printing
    223 Reproduction of recorded media
23 Manufacture of coke, refined petroleum products and nuclear fuel
    231 Manufacture of coke oven products
    232 Manufacture of refined petroleum products
    233 Processing of nuclear fuel
24 Manufacture of chemicals and chemical products
    241 Manufacture of basic chemicals
    242 Manufacture of pesticides and other agro-chemical products
    243 Manufacture of paints, varnishes and similar coatings, printing ink
    244 Manufacture of pharmaceutical, medicinal chemicals and botanical
        products
    245 Manufacture of soap and detergents, cleaning and polishing
        preparations, perfumes and toilet preparations
    246 Manufacture of other chemical products
    247 Manufacture of man-made fibres
25 Manufacture of rubber and plastic products
    251 Manufacture of rubber products
    252 Manufacture of plastic products
26 Manufacture of other non-metallic mineral products
    261 Manufacture of glass and glass products
    262 Manufacture of non-refractory ceramic goods other than for con-
        struction purposes; manufacture of refractory ceramic products
    263 Manufacture of ceramic tiles and flags
    264 Manufacture of bricks, tiles and construction products, in baked
        clay
    265 Manufacture of cement, lime and plaster
    266 Manufacture of articles of concrete, plaster and cement
    267 Cutting, shaping and finishing of ornamental and building stone
    268 Manufacture of other non-metallic mineral products
27 Manufacture of basic metals

271 Manufacture of basic iron and steel and of ferro-alloys
272 Manufacture of tubes
273 Other first processing of iron and steel
274 Manufacture of basic precious and non-ferrous metals
275 Casting of metals
28 Manufacture of fabricated metal products, except machinery and equipment
281 Manufacture of structural metal products
282 Manufacture of tanks, reservoirs and containers of metal; manufacture of central heating radiators and boilers
283 Manufacture of steam generators, except central heating water boilers
284 Forging, pressing, stamping and roll forming of metal; powder metallurgy
285 Treatment and coating of metals; general mechanical engineering
286 Manufacture of cutlery, tools and general hardware
287 Manufacture of other fabricated metal products
29 Manufacture of machinery and equipment n.e.c.
291 Manufacture of machinery for the production and use of mechanical power, Except aircraft, vehicle and cycle engines
292 Manufacture of other general purpose machinery
293 Manufacture of agriculture and forestry machinery
294 Manufacture of machinetools
295 Manufacture of other special purpose machinery
296 Manufacture of weapons and ammunition
297 Manufacture of domestic appliances n.e.c.
30 Manufacture of office machinery and computers
300 Manufacture of office machinery and computers
31 Manufacture of electrical machinery and apparatus n.e.c.
311 Manufacture of electric motors, generators and transformers
312 Manufacture of electricity distribution and control apparatus
313 Manufacture of insulated wire and cable
314 Manufacture of accumulators, primary cells and primary batteries
315 Manufacture of lighting equipment and electric lamps
316 Manufacture of electrical equipment n.e.c.
32 Manufacture of radio, television and communication equipment and apparatus
321 Manufacture of electronic valves and tubes and other electronic components
322 Manufacture of television and radio transmitters and apparatus for line telephony and line telegraphy
323 Manufacture of television and radio receivers, sound or video recording or reproducing apparatus and associated goods
33 Manufacture of medical, precision and optical instruments, watches and clocks

331 Manufacture of medical and surgical equipment and orthopaedic appliances

332 Manufacture of instruments and appliances for measuring, checking, testing, navigating and other purposes, except industrial process control equipment

333 Manufacture of industrial process control equipment

334 Manufacture of optical instruments and photographic equipment

335 Manufacture of watches and clocks

34 Manufacture of motor vehicles, trailers and semi-trailers

341 Manufacture of motor vehicles

342 Manufacture of bodies (coachwork) for motor vehicles; manufacture of trailers and semi-trailers

343 Manufactures of parts and accessories for motor vehicles and their engines

35 Manufacture of other transport equipment

351 Building and repairing of ships and boats

352 Manufacture of railway and tramway locomotives and rolling stock

353 Manufacture of aircraft and spacecraft

354 Manufacture of motorcycles and bicycles

355 Manufacture of other transport equipment n.e.c.

36 Manufacture of furniture, manufacturing n.e.c.

361 Manufacture of furniture

362 Manufacture of jewellery and related articles

363 Manufacture of musical instruments

364 Manufacture of sports goods

365 Manufacture of games and toys

366 Miscellaneous manufacturing n.e.c.

37 Recycling

371 Recycling of metal waste and scrap

372 Recycling of non-metal waste and scrap

List of Figures

List of Tables

References

1. Ahn. S.C. and P. Schmidt (1995). Efficient Estimation of Models for Dynamic Panel Data. Journal of Econometrics, Vol. 68: 5-27.
2. Amiti, M. (1999). Specialization Patterns in Europe. Weltwirtschaftliches Archiv, Vol. 135: 1-21.
3. Anderson, T.W. and Cheng Hsiao (1981). Estimation of Dynamic Models with Error Components. Journal of the American Statistical Association, Vol. 76: 598-606.
4. Anderson, T.W. and Cheng Hsiao (1982). Formulation and Estimation of Dynamic Models Using Panel Data. Journal of Econometrics, Vol. 18.
5. Arellano, M. and S. Bond (1991). Some Tests of the Specification for Panel Data: Monte Carlo Evidence and an Application to Employment Equations. The Review of Economic Studies, Vol. 58(2):277-297.
6. Arellano, M. and O. Bover (1995). Another Look at the Instrumental Varaible Estimation of Error-Components Models. Journal of Econometrics, Vol. 68: 29-51.
7. Baldwin, R.E. (1971). Determinants of the Connodity Structure of U.S. Trade. American Economic Review, Vol. 61: 126-146.
8. Balassa, B. (1965). Trade Liberalization and Revealed Comparative Advantage. Manchester School, Vol. 33: 99-123.
9. Baldwin, R.E. and G.G. Cain (2000). Shifts in Relative U.S. Wages: The Role of Trade, Technology and Factor Endowments. Review of Economics and Statistics, Vol. 82: 580-595.
10. Baldwin, R., R. Forslid, Ph. Martin, G.I.P. Ottaviano, and F. Robert-Nicoud (2003). Economic Geography and Public Policy, Princeton University Press.
11. Baltagi, B.H. (2001). Econometric Analysis of Panel Data. Second Edition. John Wiley & Sons, LTD. Chichester.
12. Bartelsman, E.J. and W. Gray (1996). The NBER Manufacturing Productivity Database. NBER Technical Working Paper No. 205.
13. Barro, Robert and Sala-i-Martin (1991). Convergence Across States and Regions. Brookings Papers on Economic Activity, Vol. 1: 107-58.
14. Barro, Robert and Sala-i-Martin (1992). Convergence. Journal of Political Economy, Vol. 100(2): 223-251.
15. Barro, Robert and Sala-i-Martin (1995). Economic Growth. Mc GrawHill, New York.

16. Beelen, E. and B. Verspagen (1994). The Role of Convergence in Trae and Sectoral Growth. In: J.Fagerberg, B. Verspagen and N. von Tunzelmann (eds.) The Dynamics of Technology Trade and Growth. London: Edward Elgar.

17. Ben-David, D., Nordstrom, A. and A. Winters (1999). Trade, income disparity and poverty. WTO special studies 5, Geneva.

18. Berman, E., J. Bound and z. Griliches (1994). Changes in the Demand for Skilled Labor within U.S. Manufacturing: Evidence from the Annual Survey of Manufactures. Quarterly Journal of Economics, Vol. 104: 367-398.

19. Bernard, Andrew B. and Steven Durlauf (1995). Convergence in International Output. Journal of Applied Econometrics, Vol. 10: 97-108.

20. Blundell, R.W. and S. Bond (1998). Initial Conditions and Moment Restrictions in Dynamic Panel Data Models. Journal of Econometrics, Vol. 87(1): 115-143.

21. Borbély, D. (2004). Competition Among Accession and Cohesion Countries: Comparative Analysis of Specialization within the EU Market. EIIW Working Paper No. 122, Wuppertal.

22. Borbély, D. and K.-J. Gern (2003). Die EU-Osterweiterung - Makro-ökonomische Aspekte aus der Sicht der Beitrittsländer. Die Weltwirtschaft, No. 4 - 2003, Springer.

23. Borbély, D. and C.-P. Meier (2003). Zum Konjunkturverbund zwischen der EU und den Beitrittsländern. Vierteljahreshefte zur Wirtschaftsforschung 72(2): 492-509, Berlin.

24. Bowen, H.P., Leamer, E.E. and Sveikauskas, L. (1987). Multicountry, Multifactor Tests of the Factor Abundance Theory. American Economic Review, Vol. 77: 791-809.

25. Brakman, S., Garretsen, H., and Schramm, M. (2004). Putting New Economic Geography to the Test: Free-ness of Trade and Agglomeration in the EU Regions. Paper presented at the HWWA conference on "New Economic Geography - Closing the Gap between Theory and Empirics, October 14-15 2004, Hamburg.

26. Bruelhart, M. (1998). Trading Places: Industrial Specialization in the European Union. Journal of Common Market Studies, Vol. 36(3): 319-346.

27. Bruelhart, M., M. Crozet, and P. Koenig (2004). Enlargement and the EU Periphery: The Impact of Changing Market Potential. HWWA Discussion Paper No. 270, HWWA, Hamburg.

28. Buch, C., F. Toubal, and J. Kleinert (2004). The Distance Puzzle: On the Interpretation of the Distance Coefficient in Gravity Equations. Economic Letters, Vol. 83(3): 293-298.

29. Cantwell, J. (1989). Technological Innovation and Multinational Corporations. Oxford: Blackwell.

30. Cappelen, A., J. Fagerberg and B. Verspagen (1999). Lack of Regional Convergence. In: Fagerberg, J. Guerrieri, P., and Verspagen, B. (eds.) The Economic Challenge for Europe. Adapting to Innovation Based Growth. Edward Elgar, Cheltenham. pp: 130-148.

31. Carstensen, K. and F. Toubal (2004). Foreign Direct Investment in Central and Eastern European Countries: a Dynamic Panel Analysis. Journal of Comparative Economics, Vol. 32: 3-22.

32. Central Statistical Bureau of Latvia (2005). http://www.csb.lv/avidus.cfm (last access 23 September 2005).

33. Crozet, M. (2004). Do Migrants Follow Market Potentials? An Estimation of a New Economic Geography Model. Journal of Economic Geography, Vol. 4: 439-458.
34. Dalum, B., Laursen, K. and Villumens, G. (1996). The Long Term Developement of OECD Export Specialisation Patterns: De-specialisation and Stickiness. DRUID Working Paper No. 96-14.
35. Dalum, B., Laursen, K., Villumsen, G. (1998). Structural Change in OECD export specialisation patterns: De-specialisation and "Stickiness". DRUID & IKE Group, Department of Business Studies, Aalborg University.
36. Davis, D. (2000). Understanding International Trade Patterns: Advances of the 1990s. Integration & Trade, Vol. 4: 61-79.
37. Davis, D. R., D. E. Weinstein, S. C. Bradford, and K. Shimpo (1997). Using international and Japanese regional data to determine when factor abundance theory of trade works. American Economic Review, Vol. 87: 421-446.
38. Davis, D.R. and D. E. Weinstein (2001). An Account of Global Factor Trade. American Economic Review, Vol. 91: 1423-1453.
39. Dixit, A. K., and J. E. Stiglitz (1977). Monopolistic competition and optimum product diversity. American Economic Review, Vol. 67: 297-308.
40. DIW (2005). Erste Bilanz der EU-Osterweiterung: Importe der neuen Mitgliedsländer aus der Eurozone gewinnen an Bedeutung. Deutsches Institut fr Wirtschaftsforschung, Wochenbericht Nr. 20/2005, Berlin.
41. Djankov, S. and B. Hoeckman (1997). Determinants of the Export Structure of Countries in Central and Eastern Europe. World Bank Economic Review, Vol. 11(3): 471,487.
42. Dornbusch, R., S. Fischer, and P.A. Samuelson (1980). Heckscher-Ohlin Trade Theory with a Continuum of Goods. Quarterly Journal of Economics, Vol. 95: 203-224.
43. Dyker, A.E. and S. Kubielas (2000). Technology and Structure in the Polish Economy under Transition and Globalization. Economic Systems 24(1): 1-24.
44. Ethier, W. J.(1982). National and International Returns to Scale in the Modern Theory of International Trade. American Economic Review, Vol. 72: 950-959.
45. EBRD (2004). Transitition Report, European Bank for Reconstruction and Development, London.
46. European Central Bank (2005). http://www.ecb.int/ecb/enlargement/html/index.en.html (last access 18 November, 2005).
47. European Central Bank (2005a). http://www.ecb.int/ecb/history/ec/html/index.en.html (last access 17 November, 2005).
48. European Commission (2001). Einheit Europas - Solidarität der Völker - Vielfalt der Regionen. Zweiter Bericht ber den wirtschaftlichen und sozialen Zusammenhalt. Luxemburg.
49. European Commission (2002). Communication from the Commission to the Council, the European Parliament, the Economic and Social Committee and the Committee of the Regions - Industrial Policy in an Enlarged Europe. http://europa.eu.int/comm/enterprise/enterprise_policy/industry/communication_structural_change.htm (last access 18 November, 2005).
50. European Commission (2002a). Proposal for a Directive of the European Parliamant and of the Council on services in internal market. COM(2004)2(03)final, Brussels.

51. European Commission (2004). Intra- and Extra-EU trade. COMEXT Annual Database. CD-Rom Supplement 2.
52. European Commission (2004a). Fostering Structural Change: an Industrial Policy for an Enlarged Europe. COM(2004)274 final, Brussels.
53. European Commission (2005). AMECO Database - Economic and Financial Affairs - Indicators.
    http://europa.eu.int/comm/economyfinance/indicators.html (last access on 12 November, 2005).
54. European Commission (2005a). Free Movement of Goods.
    http://www.europa.eu.int/comm/enterprise/regulation/goods/intro_en.html (last access on 18 November, 2005).
55. European Commission (2005b). The Europe Agreements.
    http://europa.eu.int/comm/enlargement/pas/europe_agr.htm (last access on 23 November, 2005).
56. European Commission (2005c). Industrial Policy in an Enlarged Europe.
    http://europa.eu.int/comm/enterprise/enterprise_policy/industry/communication_policy.htm (last access on 24 November, 2005).
57. European Commission (2005d). The Structural Funds.
    http://europa.eu.int/comm/regional_policy/funds/prord/sf_en.htm (Last access on December 10, 2005).
58. European Parliament (2003). Task Force Enlargement. Basic Statistics and Trade. June 2003.
    http://www.europarl.eu.int/enlargement_new/statistics/pdf/22a1_06_03_en.pdf (last access on 17 November, 2005).
59. Eurostat (2005). http://epp.eurostat.cec.eu.int (last acces on 14 November, 2005).
60. Eurostat (2005a). Input-Output Tables, Brussels.
61. Evans, Paul (1998). Using Panel Data to Evaluate Growth Theories. International Economic Review, Vol. 39: 295-306.
62. Feenstra, R.C. (2004). Advanced International Trade: Theory and Evidence. Princeton University Press.
63. Feenstra, R.C. and G.H. Hanson (1996). Foreign Investment, Outsourcing, and Relative Wages. In: Feenstra, C.R., G.M. Grossman and D.A. Irwin (eds.) The Political Economy of Trade Policy: Papers in Honor of Jagdish Bhagwati. Cambridge, MIT Press.
64. Feenstra, R.C. and G.H. Hanson (1997). Foreign Direct Investment and Relative Wages: Evidence form Mexico's Maquiladoras. Journal of International Economics, Vol. 42: 371-393.
65. Feenstra, R.C. and G.H. Hanson (1999). The Impact of Outsourcing and High-Technology Capital on Wages: Estimates for the U.S. 1979-1990. Quarterly Journal of Economics, Vol. 114: 907-940.
66. Feenstra, R.C. and G.H. Hanson (2003). Global Production Sharing and Rising Inequality: A Survey of Trade and Wages. In E.K. Choi and J. Harrigan (eds.), Handbook of International Trade. Oxford, Blackwell.
67. Fidrmuc, J. (1998). Application of Gravity Models to Commodity Groups and Trade Projections between the EU and the CEECs. Manuscript: Institute for Advanced Studies, Vienna.
68. Fontegné L., M. Freudenberg and D. Uenal-Kesenci (1999). Haute Technologie et Échelles de Qualité: de Fortes Asymmtries en Europe. CEPII, Paris.

69. Forslid, R., Haaland, J.I., Midelfart-Knarvik, K.H. und O. Mestad (2002). Integration and Transititon: Scenarios for the Location of Production and Trade in Europe. Economics of Transition, Vol. 10(1): 93-117.
70. Fourastié, J. (1954). Die grosse Hoffnung des 20. Jahrhunderts. Köln-Deutz.
71. Fujita, M. und Krugman, P. und Venables A.J. (1999). The Spatial Economy: Cities, Regions and International Trade. MIT Press, Cambridge, MA.
72. Fujita, M. und Krugman, P. (2004). The New Economic Geography: Past, Present and the Future. Papers in Regional Science, Vol. 83: 139-164.
73. Gaulier, G. (2003). Trade and Convergence: Revising Ben-David. CEPII, Working Paper No. 2003-06.
74. Geishecker, I. (2002). Outsourcing and the Relative Demand for Low-Skilled Labour in German Manufacturing. New Evidence. German Institute for Economic Research, DIW-Berlin, Discussion Paper No. 313.
75. German Council of Economic Advisors (2005). Sachverständigenrat zur Begutachtung der Gesamtwirtschaftlichen Entwicklung.
http://www.sachverstaendigenrat-wirtschaft.de (last access 17 November, 2005).
76. Görg, H., Hijzen, A. and R.C. Hine (2001). International Fragmentation and Relative Wages in the U.K. Leverhulme Centre for Research on Globalization and Economic Policy, University of Nottingham, Research Paper 2001/33.
77. Greenaway, D., Hine, R. C. and Milner, Ch.(1995). Vertical and horizontal intra-industry trade: a cross industry analysis for the United Kingdom. The Economic Journal, Vol. 105: 1505-1518.
78. Harrigan, J. (2000). International Trade and American Wages in General Equilibrium, 1967-1995. In Robert C. Feenstra, ed., The Impact of International Trade on Wages. Chicago: University of Chicago Press.
79. Harrigan, J. and R.A. Balaban (1999). U.S. Wage Effects in General Equilibrium: The Effects of Prices, Technology, and Factor Supplies, 1963-1991. NBER Working Paper No. 6981.
80. Hart, P. (1974). The Dynamics of Earnings. Economic Journal, Vol. 86(3): 541-565.
81. Hart, P.E. (1994). Galtonian Regression Across Countries and the Convergence of Productivity. Discussion Papers in Quantitative Economics and Computing, Series E.II.
82. Haskel, J.E. and M.J. Slaughter, (2001). Trade, Technology and U.K. Wage Inequality. Economic Journal, Vol. 110: 1-27.
83. Head, K. and T. Mayer (2003). The Empirics of Agglomeration and Trade. CEPR Discussion paper No. 3985. Also in: V. Henderson and J-F. Thisse (eds.) The Handbook of Regional and Urban Economics, Vol. IV, North Holland.
84. Heckscher, E. (1949). The Effect of Foreign trade on Distribution of Income. Ekonomisk Tidskrift, pp: 497-512, 1919; reprinted in H.S. Ellis and L.A. Metzler (eds.), A. E. A. Readings in the Theory of International Trade, Philadelphia: Blakiston, pp: 272-300.
85. Helpman, E. and P.R. Krugman (1985). Market Structure and Foreign Trade. Cambridge: MIT Press.
86. Hildebrandt, A. und J. Wörz (2005). Patterns of Industrial Specialization and Concentration in CEECs: Theoretical Explanations and their Empirical Relevance. In: Welfens P.J.J. und A. Wziatek-Kubiak (eds.): Structural Change and Exchange Rate Dynamics: The Economics of the EU-Enlargement. Springer, Heidelberg.

87. Hoekman, B., and Djankov, S. (1997). Determinants of the Export Structure of Countries in Central and Eastern Europe. The World Bank Economic Review, Vol. 11(3): 471-487.

88. Hsiao, Cheng (1986). Analysing Panel Data. Cambridge University Press, Cambridge, UK.

89. Im, K.S., Pesaran, M.H., and Shin, Y. (1995). Testing for Unit Roots in Heterogenous Panels. DAE, Working Paper No. 9526. University of Cambridge.

90. IMF (2005). International Financial Statistics, International Monetary Fund, Washinton, D.C.

91. Islam, Nazrul (1995). Growth Empirics: A Panel Data Approach. Quarterly Journal of Economics, Vol. 110: 1127-70.

92. Jakab, Z., Kovcs, M.A. and A. Oszlay (2001). How far has Trade Integration Advanced? An Analysis of the Actual and Potential Trade of Three Central and Eastern European Countries. Journal of Comparative Economics, Vol. 29(2): 276-292.

93. Jones, R.W. (1965). The Structure of Simple General Equilibrium Models. Jounral of Political Economy, Vol. 73: 557-72.

94. Judson, R.A. and A.L. Owen (1999). Estimating Dynamic Panel Data Models: A Guide for Macroeconomist. Economic Letters, Vol. 65: 9-15.

95. Kaminski, B., (1999). Hungary's Integration into EU Markets: Production and Trade Restructuring. Washington DC, mimeo.

96. Kiel Institute for World Economics (2005). Joint Economic Forecast of the Leading German Economic Research Institutes, Fall 2005. http://www.uni-kiel.de/ifw/pub/konjunkt.htm (last access 17 November, 2005).

97. Kiviet, J.F. (1995). On Bias, Inconsistency and Efficiency of Various Estimators in Dynamic Panel Models. Jounral of Econometrics, Vol. 68: 53-78.

98. Klodt, H. (1993). Technology-Based Trade and Multinationals' Investment in Europe: Structural Change and Competition in Schumpeterian Goods. In: Klein, M.W. and P.J.J. Welfens (eds.) Multinationals in the New Europe and Global Trade. Springer Berlin Heidelberg.

99. Krugman, P. R.(1979). Increasing Returns, Monopolistic Competition, and International Trade. Journal of International Economics, Vol. 9: 469-479.

100. Krugman, P.(1991). Geography and Trade. The MIT Press.

101. Krugman, P.(1991a). Increasing Returns and Economic Geography. Journal of Political Economy, Vol. 99: 483-499.

102. Krugman, P. und Venables, A. (1995). Globalization and the Inequality of Nations. Quarterly Journal of Economics, Vol. 60: 857-880.

103. Kumar, P. (2000). Wage Inequality in the US: What Do Aggregate Prices and Factor Supplies Tell? World Bank, Manuscript.

104. Lancester, K. (1975). Socially Optimal Product Differentiation. American Economic Review, Vol. 65: 567-85.

105. Lancester, K. (1979). Variety, Equity, and Efficiency. New York: Columbia University Press.

106. Lancester, T. (2000). The Incidental Parameter Problem since 1948. Journal of Econometrics, Vol. 95: 391-413.

107. Laursen, K. and I. Drejer (1997). Do Inter-sectoral Linkages Matter for International Export Specialisation? Danish Reasearch Unit for Industrial Dynamics, DRUID Working Paper No. 97-15.

108. Leamer, E. (1980). The Leontief Paradoxon, Reconsidered. Journal of Political Economy, Vol. 88: 495-503.

109. Leamer, E. (1984). Source of International Comparative Advantage: Theory and Evidence. Cambridge, MIT Press.

110. Leontief, W.W. (1953). Domestic Production and Foreign Trade: The American Capital Position Re-examined. Proceedings of the American Philosophical Society, Vol. 97: 332-349.

111. Linder, S. (1961). An Essay on Trade and Transformation. New York: Wiley.

112. Markusen, J. R. (1995). The Boundaries of Multinational Enterprises and the Theory of International Trade. Journal of Economic Perspectives, Vol. 9: 169-189.

113. Markusen, J. R. (1998). Multinational Firms, Location and Trade. The World Economy, Vol. 21: 735-756.

114. Markusen, J. R. and J. R. Melvin (1981). Trade, factor prices and gains from trade with increasing returns to scal. Canadian Journal of Economics, Vol. 14: 450-469.

115. Markusen, J. R., and A. J. Venables (1996). The Theory of endowment, intra-industry and multinational trade. CEPR Discussion Paper, No. 1341.

116. Markusen, J. R., and A. J. Venables (1998). Multinational firms and the new trade theory. Journal of International Economics, Vol. 46: 183-203.

117. Marques, H., and H. Metcalf (2005). What Determines Sectoral Trade in the Enlarged EU? Review of Development Economics, Vol. 9(2): 197-231.

118. Micco, A., Stein, E. and G. Ordonez (2003). The Currency Union Effect on Trade: Early Evidence from EMU. Economic Policy, Vol. 18(37): 315-356.

119. Midelfart, K.H., Overman, H., Redding, S. and Venables, A.J. (2000). The Location of European Industry. European Commission, DG Economic and Social Affairs. Economic Paper No. 142. Brussels.

120. Midelfart, K-H., H.G. Overman, and A.J. Venables (2003). Monetary Union and the Economic Geography of Europe. Jounral of Commom Market Studies, 41(5): 847-868.

121. Neumann, M. (2001). Competition Policy. Edward Elgar, Cheltenham, UK.

122. Nickell, Stephen (1981). Biases in Dynamic Models with Fixed Effects. Econometrica, Vol. 49(6).

123. Nunez J. (2005). Policy Implications of Changes in Competitiveness Patterns of the Member States and the EU. Paper presented at the Final Conference of the EU Project HPSE-CT-2002-00148, Brussels.

124. OECD (2005). STAN Industrial Database, Organisation for Economic Cooperation and Development, Paris.

125. OECD (2005a). Main Economic Indicators, Organisation for Economic Cooperation and Development, Paris.

126. OECD (2004). Anbert Database, Organisation for Economic Cooperation and Development, Paris.

127. OECD (1987). Structural Adjustment and Economic Performance. Organisation for Economic Cooperation and Development, Paris.

128. Ohlin, B. (1933). Interregional and International Trade. Campbridge, MA: Harvard University Press.

129. Pavitt, K. (1984). Sectoral Patterns of Technical Change: towards a Taxonomy and a Theory. Research Policy, Vol. 13: 353-369.

130. Pavitt, K. (1989). International Patterns of Technological Accumulation. In: N. Hood and J.E. Vahlne (eds.) Strategies in Global Competition. London: Croom Helm.

131. Polish Official Statistics (2005). http://www.stat.gov.pl/english/index.htm (last access on 24 September 2005).

132. Puga, D.(1998). Urbanisation patterns: Europe versus Less Developed Countries. Journal of Regional Science, Vol. 38: 231-252.

133. Puga, D. (1999). The rise and fall or regional inequalities. European Economic Review, Vol. 43: 303-334.

134. Quah, Danny (1995). Galton's Fallacy and Tests of Convergence Hypothesis. Scandinavian Journal of Economics, Vol. 95: 427-443.

135. Redding, S. and A.J. Venables (2003). Economic Geography and International Inequality. Journal of International Economics, Vol. 62: 53-82.

136. Ricardo, D.(1817). On the Principles of Political Economy and Taxation, London.

137. Roodman, D. (2005). xtabond2: Stata module to extend xtabond dynamic panel data estimator. Center for Global Development, Washington. http://econpapers.recep.org/software/bocbocode/s435901.htm (Last access on 17 September, 2005).

138. Rybczynski, T.N. (1955). Factor Endowments and Relative Commodity Prices. Economica, Vol. 22: 336-341.

139. Samuelson, P. (1952). Spatial Price Equilibrium and Linear Programming. American Economic Review, Vol. XLII: 283-303.

140. Serlenga, L. and Y. Shin (2004). Gravity Models of the Intra-EU Trade: Application of the Hausman-Taylor Estimation in Heterogenous Panels with Common Time-specific Factors. University of Edinburgh, mimeo.

141. Sinn, H-W. (2005). Basar-Ökonomie Deutschland. Ifo Schnelldienst 6. Munich.

142. Soete, L. and B. Verspagen (1994). Compeing for Growth: The Dymanics of Technology Gaps. In. L. Painetti and R. Solow (eds.) Economic Growth and the Structure of Long-term Development. London: Macmillan.

143. Soós K. A. (2002). Upgrading on the Periphery: Accession Countries' Exports to the EU in International Comparison, 1993-2000. Revue Elargissement, No. 22.

144. Slaughter, M. (2000). What Are the Results of Product-Price Studies and Whan Can We Learn from Their Differences? In: R.C. Feenstra, ed., The Effects of International Trade on Wages. Chicago: University of Chicago Press.

145. Statistical Office of Slovenia (2005). http://www.stat.se/default.asp (last access on 23 September, 2005).

146. Stolper, W.F. and P.A. Samuelson (1941). Protection and Real Wages. Review of Economic Studies, Vol. 9: 58-73.

147. Tinbergen, J. (1962). Shaping the World Economy. New York: Twentieth Century Fund.

148. Tondl, G. (1999). The changing pattern of regional convergence in Europe. Review of Regional Research, Vol. 19: 1-33.

149. Tondl, G. (2001). Convergence after Divergence? Regional Growth in Europe. Wien, New York.

150. Trefler, D. (1993). International Factor Price Differences: Leontief Was Right! Journal of Political Economy, Vol. 101: 961-987.

151. Trefler, D. (1995). The Case of Missing Trade and Other Mysteries. American Economic Review, Vol. 85: 1029-1046.

152. Vanek, J. (1968). The Factor Proportions Theory: The N-Factor Case. Kyklos, Vol. 21: 749-754.

153. Venables, A. J.(1998). The international division of industries: clustering and comparative advantage in a multi-industry model. CEPR Discussion Paper No. 1961.

154. Venables, A. J. (2001). Geography and International Inequalities: The Impact of New Technologies. CEPR Discussion paper No. 507.

155. Venables, A. J., Rice, P. G., and Stewart M.(2003). The Geography of Intra-Industry Trade: empirics. in: Topics in economic analysis & policy. - Berkeley, California: bepress.com, Vol. 3.

156. Welfens, P.J.J. (1995). Grundlagen der Wirtschaftspolitik, Springer, Heidelberg Berlin.

157. Welfens, P.J.J. and Wziatek-Kubiak, A. (2005). Structural Change and Exchange Rate Dynamics - The Economics of the EU Eastern Enlargement. Springer, Berlin Heidelberg.

158. WIIW (2004). Industrial Database Eastern Europe, CD-ROM, June 2004, The Vienna Institute for International Economic Studies, Vienna.

159. WIIW (2005). Database on Foreign Direct Investment in Central, East and Southeast Europe, CD-ROM, May 2005, The Vienna Institute for International Economic Studies, Vienna.

160. WIIW (2005a). http://www.wiiw.at/e/statistics.html (last access on 23 September 2005), The Vienna Institute for International Economic Studies, Vienna.

161. Windmeijer, F.A.G. (2000). A Finite Sample Correction for the Variance of Linear Two-Step GMM Estimator. Institute for Fiscal Studies, Working Paper Series 00/19. London.

162. WTO (2004). Trade Policy Review, European Communities, 23 June, World Trade Organisation, Geneva.

163. Zielinsa-Glebocka A. (2005). Policy Implications of Changes in Competitiveness Patterns of the Candidate Countries for the EU. Directions of Policy Modification in Reactions. Paper presented at the Final Conference of the EU Project HPSE-CT-2002-00148, Brussels.

Index